# Breaking Free
# of the
# Co-dependency Trap

# Breaking Free
# of the
# Co-dependency Trap

## REVISED EDITION

**Barry K. Weinhold, PhD & Janae B. Weinhold, PhD**

**Foreword by John Bradshaw**

New World Library
Novato, California

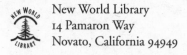

New World Library
14 Pamaron Way
Novato, California 94949

Text design by Tona Pearce Myers

Library of Congress Cataloging-in-Publication Data
Weinhold, Barry K.
Breaking free of the co-dependency trap / Barry K. Weinhold, Janae B. Weinhold ; foreword by John Bradshaw.
    p.    cm.
Includes bibliographical references (p. 255) and index.
ISBN 978-1-57731-614-5 (pbk. : alk. paper)
    1. Codependency. 2. Codependents—Rehabilitation.  I. Weinhold, Janae B. II. Title.
RC569.5.C63W345 2008
362.29—dc22                                        2007045536

First New World Library printing, February 2008
ISBN: 978-1-57731-614-5
Printed in Canada on 100% postconsumer-waste recycled paper

g  New World Library is a proud member of the Green Press Initiative.

10  9  8  7  6  5  4  3  2

*To all the individuals, couples, and partners
who are serving as pioneers in creating new forms of relationships*

# Contents

# Foreword

**B**reaking Free of the Co-dependency Trap is a welcome addition to the literature on co-dependency. The Weinholds are expert clinicians. Their offering is crucial for establishing the legitimacy of co-dependency as a true, life-threatening clinical entity.

Using their knowledge of developmental psychology, Barry and Janae have identified co-dependency as the failure to complete one or more of the important developmental tasks of early childhood. They see the problem as especially focused on a failure to complete the early task of separation, sometimes called the second birth or psychological birth. This fits well with my own definition of co-dependency as a dis-ease of lost selfhood.

The Weinholds' developmental approach differs radically from the medical approach, which sees co-dependency as permanent, progressive, and incurable. Developmental stuckness can be remedied. There is hope and promise for all of us.

The greatest sense of hope in this book results from the precise and practical tools for recovery that the Weinholds present us. These are proven methods used by the authors both to help their clients and to work on their own co-dependency issues. Janae and Barry *walk the walk* as they *talk the talk*. This is crucial. I demand it of my treatment people at the Life Plus Co-dependency Treatment Unit.

I believe with the authors that the most crucial issue in recovery is the creation of a new relationship committed to working out interdependent intimacy. The core of co-dependency is the shame-based ruptured self. This self-rupture results from a broken relationship (see chapter 8). Therefore a new relationship committed to this work is necessary to heal it.

This book is far too rich to highlight in a foreword. I am amazed at the thoroughness of this treatment. Part 1 is a true summary of the state of our knowledge about co-dependency. Part 2 covers all the major tools for recovery.

My heartfelt advice is for you to read and study this book carefully and then read it again. Bravo, Barry and Janae! This book is a gift!

— John Bradshaw, *New York Times* bestselling author,
voted one of the 100 most influential writers on emotional health
in the 20th century, and senior fellow
at the Meadows Treatment Center, Wickenburg, Arizona

# Introduction

In this book we examine both the causes of co-dependency and how to recover from it. Co-dependency is present in an estimated 98 percent of the adult population and is responsible for most human misery. It is caused by early developmental trauma during the first six months of life, which interferes with secure bonding. The other side of the coin is counter-dependency, which is caused by developmental trauma between the ages of six months and thirty-six months, and which interferes with the separation process and the psychological birth. This book focuses on the co-dependency side of the coin, and our companion book, *The Flight from Intimacy: Healing Your Relationship of Counter-dependency — the Other Side of Co-dependency*,[1] focuses on the other side. Many people have unidentified and unhealed traumas from both stages of development and need help recognizing and healing both.

## CAUSES OF ADULT CO-DEPENDENCY

Between birth and three years of age, children complete a series of essential developmental processes. The two most important involve secure bonding between mother and child and the child's psychological separation from its parents. If the bonding process is successfully completed in the first year, children feel safe enough to explore the world around them. Then between ages two and three, they are able to complete the "psychological birth." This occurs when children separate psychologically from their mothers and fathers and are able to function on internal power rather than relying on others to direct their lives. These children develop a sense of Self that enables them to accept responsibility for their actions and behavior, to share, to cooperate, to manage their aggressive impulses, to respond appropriately to the authority of others, to verbalize feelings, and to cope with feelings of fear and anxiety. If children do not successfully complete these developmental processes, they become psychologically dependent on others. Rather than living with a strong sense of Self that is emotionally separate from others, they seek out co-dependent relationships. The unconscious purpose of these relationships is to help them experience secure bonding.

Co-dependency in adults exists when two psychologically dependent people form a relationship with each other for the unconscious purpose of completing their early bonding processes. In such a relationship, the two partners re-create a symbiotic connection much like ones they had with their mothers. Their co-dependent relationship appears to be made up of two half-persons attempting to create one whole person. Because both partners lacked secure bonding in early childhood, neither is free to feel or act independently of the other, so they stick together like glue. The focus is always on the other person, not on oneself. Each hopes the other person will provide what he or she never got in early childhood: intimacy and secure bonding. Their relationship *cannot* grow, because this goal is never conscious or spoken. As a result, each looks to the other to make the necessary growth happen. When it doesn't, the partners try to control each other, blame their problems on each other, and expect the other person to always behave in certain ways to bring them closer together and meet their needs for unconditional love, affection, and nurturing. Because each one is focused on the other person, both are able to avoid looking at themselves and focusing on their self-development. In co-dependent relationships, the focus is always outward, not inward.

In this book, we present a radically different framework for understanding co-dependency. We use a *developmental* perspective that focuses on growth, rather than a medical approach that often regards co-dependency as a primary illness. A primary illness is defined as permanent, pervasive, progressive, and terminal. However, co-dependency, caused by the developmental trauma of incomplete bonding during the first six months of life, leaves a residue of relationship issues that are possible to remedy. From a developmental perspective, the process of recovering from co-dependency involves

- identifying the developmental traumas that caused your co-dependency issues;
- identifying and completing the incomplete developmental processes that are keeping you developmentally stuck;
- becoming more fully aware of yourself and how you respond to situations so you can feel freer and make better choices;
- exercising more control over your own life; and
- evolving to a higher level of human consciousness.

## THE MEDICAL MODEL:
## FULL RECOVERY IS NOT POSSIBLE

The medical model defines co-dependency as either a genetically inherited illness with unknown causes or a disease associated with alcoholism and dysfunctional families. In either case it is considered incurable. According to the medical model's prognosis, the best you, as a co-dependent person, can hope for is long-term treatment and a support system that will help you avoid the addictive agent (other dependent people) and, therefore, keep you from forming destructive co-dependent relationships. The medical model assumes that support groups and psychotherapy are essential to keep you on a nonaddictive path, because, without this support, you will likely remain an addict. Your fate is outside your conscious control, caused by internal and subconscious addictive reactions that can easily overpower you. In other words, you cannot hope to be free of the disease.

## A NEW DEFINITION OF FREEDOM

Our developmental approach to co-dependency redefines freedom. Whether an individual's behavior is the result of free will or of conditioned responses is an issue that has been discussed for centuries. But the human will is neither absolutely free nor absolutely governed by conditioned responses. What is truly important is whether or not you *feel* free. Do you feel relatively free to direct your own life, or do you feel that others control it to a large extent?

The two prevailing definitions of freedom are: (1) freedom from some kind of bondage, and (2) freedom from freedom itself — that is, recognition that freedom is an illusion, something that doesn't exist. The medical approach offers a deterministic view that claims it's impossible to use your free will to change your co-dependent behaviors.

Our developmental definition of freedom stresses self-awareness. True freedom comes from within, and not from without. True freedom cannot be achieved by focusing on the social ills outside you. To be free you must first focus on the psychological ills that exist inside you. By becoming more aware of your inner life and identifying why you act and react the way you do in certain situations, you can begin to master the forces that control you and keep you from feeling free. The more aware you become of early trauma in your childhood, and the more you recognize how it controls your life, the more freedom you will experience in your life.

## TWO TYPES OF RECOVERY PROGRAMS

There are two traditional approaches to recovering from co-dependency. In the first approach, we include most of the twelve-step programs, such as Alcoholics Anonymous, Overeaters Anonymous, and Co-Dependents Anonymous. These recovery programs promise only limited recovery for those who successfully complete their steps, because they place too much emphasis on the disease model. Members of twelve-step groups learn that they are sick and powerless over substances, activities, or people. While this helps ease some of people's guilt about the pain and suffering they might have caused their family or friends, it can prevent them from looking at the psychological issues involved in their addictions. Because of this emphasis on external causes, a "Higher Power" is frequently viewed as an external parental force that controls and rewards sobriety. Bill Wilson, the founder of Alcoholics Anonymous, intended for the "Higher Power" to facilitate a deep spiritual awakening that he believed was necessary for full recovery.[2] Despite its limitations, however, this is an important first step to recovery. This type of recovery program has helped millions of people move away from devastating problems with addictions. If people do not stay away from the things over which they have no control, they cannot benefit from more extensive recovery programs.

In the second type of recovery program, advocated by Earnie Larsen, Robert Subby, and Anne Wilson Schaef, the focus shifts to helping people rebuild their lives and create more effective relationships.[3] However, this type of program, too, maintains that the *disease* of co-dependency can only be arrested, not cured. But such programs do suggest that some of the problems of co-dependency in relationships can be repaired. Some people involved in these programs do eventually see that co-dependency may be not a primary illness but the result of "self-defeating learned behaviors, that are greatly exaggerated and complicated by a pathological relationship to a chemically dependent [or co-dependent] person."[4]

## A NEW APPROACH TO FULL RECOVERY

Our developmental approach is a third kind of recovery program, and it goes much farther than the other two approaches. It is based on the belief that co-dependency is not a primary illness but is caused by early trauma that can be overcome with the proper information, tools, and support. It focuses on full recovery and the fullest possible development of human potential, and it provides more hope and a more positive attitude toward recovery.

Our approach is based on the Developmental Systems Theory, a theory we created that permits us to look at the evolution of all human systems through a developmental lens. We found in our research that all human systems go through four successive stages of development: co-dependent, counter-dependent, independent, and interdependent stages. Each stage entails the successful completion of essential developmental processes. What prevents the completion of these developmental processes and disrupts human development are unidentified and unhealed developmental traumas, particularly ones sustained during the co-dependent and counter-dependent stages.[5]

We believe in our approach because we have successfully used it on ourselves and with our clients. We've seen people fully recover from the crippling effects of co-dependency. The process is not an easy one to use, nor is it necessarily a quick one. We spent a number of years and put in a lot of work to get where we are today in our relationship. But by using the tools presented in this book, you will see an immediate improvement in your relationships with others.

As more and more people successfully break free of their co-dependency traps and refuse to accept limited views of human behavior, it becomes easier and quicker for others to do the same. Part of the reason it has been so difficult for people to change is that many of our society's cultural beliefs and practices encourage co-dependent behavior. As people change themselves, cultural attitudes and beliefs change too.

Another unique feature of this book is that it focuses heavily on the tools for recovery rather than merely describes the problem of co-dependency. The most powerful form of recovery comes not from therapy but from committed relationships. These are relationships in which people are committed to seeing the relationship itself as a tool for healing, and they supplement it with individual or couples therapy, support groups, or self-reflective work to support the therapeutic process occurring in the relationship.

The quantum physicist and futurist Peter Russell predicts in his book *The Global Brain* that the consciousness age will follow the information age. He predicted that the consciousness age would begin around the year 2000. "This represents a time when the needs for food, material goods and information are adequately satisfied and the major thrust of human activity is moving on to exploring our inner frontiers. Self-development would become our prime goal."[6]

We agree with Russell that we are moving in this direction, and we based the first edition of this book partly on his prediction. We now see, in retrospect, that his prediction was fairly accurate and that we are in a new age of consciousness. Our goal is to help people see who they really are and to provide them with tools to realize their fullest possible potential evolution of consciousness.

# Part 1
# CO-DEPENDENCY REVISITED

# 1. Co-dependency
## Getting Stuck in Infancy

We estimate that approximately 98 percent of all Americans suffer from symptoms of co-dependency. We believe that fewer than 1 percent of these people are fully aware of the impact of co-dependency on their lives, and even fewer are taking steps to change themselves.

### SYMPTOMS OF CO-DEPENDENCY

The following is a list of some of the major symptoms of co-dependency:

- being "addicted" to people
- feeling trapped in abusive, controlling relationships
- having low self-esteem
- needing constant approval and support from others in order to feel good about yourself
- feeling powerless to change destructive relationships
- needing alcohol, food, work, sex, or some other outside stimulation to distract you from your feelings
- having undefined psychological boundaries
- feeling like a martyr
- being a people-pleaser
- being unable to experience true intimacy and love

To make matters worse — if that's possible — co-dependency is perceived by the medical community and many medically oriented therapists as a disease. If you are diagnosed as having "caught" co-dependency, like one catches a cold, your doctor or therapist likely sees co-dependency as similar to other illnesses — as permanent, pervasive, progressive, and even terminal.

According to much of the literature on co-dependency, you will never recover from it. The best you can hope for is to "hang out" with others who are recovering from co-dependency. If you attend support meetings regularly and work on yourself, you will not get worse *and* you might not be as bad off as you were before you started treatment.

This sounds depressing, doesn't it? Well, this book will not depress you. It can help you lift your heavy burden. It presents a positive developmental approach to the treatment and healing of co-dependency that is based on more than thirty years of research and experience in successfully helping people heal their co-dependency.

## ASSUMPTIONS OF THE NEW APPROACH

Our approach assumes the following about the cause and treatment of co-dependency:

- It is not a primary illness. It's a disorder caused by unidentified developmental trauma during the first six months of life. Developmental trauma involves energetic disconnections between children and their mothers that are either too long or too frequent. Adult caregivers who are unaware of children's social and emotional needs cause this trauma in infants and children unconsciously and without malicious intent. Developmental trauma prevents the completion of secure bonding and other essential developmental processes during infancy. The lack of secure bonding delays another major developmental process of early childhood, one often referred to as the psychological birth, which, ideally, should be completed between ages two and three. Because it is not possible to become psychologically separate unless secure bonding occurs first, we believe that at least 98 percent of the population is still struggling with both co-dependency and counter-dependency issues. And because parents typically haven't completed their own bonding and separation processes, they can't help their children complete them. They may even subconsciously resist their children's attempts to become securely bonded and psychologically separate.

- It is a cultural phenomenon. Because of the pervasive nature of the problem, our whole culture might be described as co-dependent. Our American social structure may actually depend on the perpetuation of this behavior. Seen from a cultural perspective, major institutions in our society inadvertently support co-dependent behavior. In fact, throughout history, most societies have been structured so that some groups rank above others, such as men over women and management over labor. With one group more powerful and in control of the resources, it is easy to create and sustain co-dependent relationships. Today, as people change their co-dependent behaviors, they are changing the larger social structure.

- Co-dependent patterns continue to recycle. When a person doesn't complete a developmental process, such as secure bonding, within the first six months of life, the need for completing it is carried along as excess baggage into the next stage of development. As a result, it's almost impossible for this person to successfully separate from his or her parents during the next stage of development. If bonding and separation are not completed during the developmental replay that occurs between ages twelve and sixteen, these uncompleted processes are carried on into adulthood and continue to disrupt the person's relationships and families. Co-dependent patterns repeat because they contain early developmental trauma that is unidentified and unhealed.

- It is a healing in progress. Adult co-dependency, with all its painful symptoms, is, in reality, an attempt to heal. There is a natural drive in all of us to heal and experience wholeness. We simply need to cooperate in this healing process to make it work. By forming co-dependent relationships, we are attempting to complete the secure bonding process we were unable to complete in early childhood.

- Recovery requires specific tools and understanding. When people understand the causes of co-dependency and are given the tools and support they need, they can and will heal themselves and eliminate the disruptive effects of co-dependency from their lives.

- Recovery requires a systematic approach. Because all parts of our culture support co-dependency, it's necessary to use a systemic approach as well as an individual approach to healing co-dependency. Therapy for couples, families, and groups is an effective way to help individuals break their habits of co-dependency and to consciously work to heal their co-dependency with their partners in committed relationships.
- There is no blame. It takes two or more people to create co-dependent relationships. Therefore, one person cannot be blamed for causing co-dependency in a relationship. Once you understand why you acquired co-dependent behaviors, you will have more compassion for yourself and your partner.

## A NEW DEFINITION OF CO-DEPENDENCY

Drawing on the above assumptions, we define co-dependency as a failure to complete the essential developmental process of secure bonding and the developmental tasks associated with it. Developmental psychologist Margaret Mahler and her associates did extensive research to help identify the process of moving from psychological oneness with the mother at birth to psychological autonomy at about age two or three.[1]

Mahler found that people who have successfully completed the essential developmental processes of the co-dependent and counter-dependent stages of development are no longer dependent on people or things outside themselves. They have a solid inner sense of uniqueness and of who they are. They can get close to others without fearing they will lose themselves. They can effectively meet their needs by asking others directly when they need help. And finally, they can maintain positive self-esteem even when criticized by others. Mahler also discovered that a failure to complete this vital developmental process can rob people of their full humanness and force them to live severely limited lives dominated by fears, compulsive behaviors, and addictions.

The successful development of psychological autonomy during the counter-dependent stage, according to Mahler, requires having two conscious parents who have dealt with enough of their own psychological hang-ups to be able to help their child. The following list tells you what you, as a parent, can do to assist your children in successfully completing this process of developing autonomy, or the psychological birth:

- Meet your children's needs for nurturing, protection, and emotional attunement in order to securely bond with them.
- Help your children learn how to reregulate their emotions when they've become dysregulated.
- Accept your children as they are, not as you would like them to be.
- Allow for the full expression of emotions, and accept and respond to your children's needs for eye-to-eye, ear-to-ear, skin-to-skin, and brain-to-brain contact.
- Support and encourage your children in the healthy exploration of their world by saying yes to them twice as often as you say no to them.
- "Kid proof" the immediate environment so your children can safely explore their world.
- Encourage the expression of independent thoughts, feelings, and actions appropriate for your children's ages.
- Provide understanding, support, and nurturing when your children need it.
- Model effective psychological independence by directly asking for what you want, expressing your own feelings effectively, setting appropriate limits, and negotiating directly to meet your needs, rather than using power plays and games. Research indicates that young children learn appropriate behaviors by modeling the behaviors of others around them.

## CHARACTERISTICS OF CO-DEPENDENCY

When you look closely at the characteristics of people with co-dependent behaviors, you usually find behavior patterns more typical of infants than of fully functioning adults. This is because they are still trying to complete what they failed to complete as infants. We've listed the common characteristics of co-dependency. As you read the following list, place a check mark next to those you recognize in yourself:

_____ You're unable to distinguish your own thoughts and feelings from those of others (you think about and feel responsible for other people and their problems).

_____ You seek the approval and attention of others in order to feel good.

_____ You feel anxious or guilty when others have a problem.

_____ You do things to please others even when you don't want to.

_____ You don't know what you want or need.

_____ You rely on others to define and take care of your wants or needs.

_____ You believe that others better understand what is best for you.

_____ You collapse when things don't work out the way you expect them to.

_____ You focus all your energy on other people and on their happiness.

_____ You try to prove to others that you are good enough to be loved.

_____ You don't believe you can take care of yourself.

_____ You believe that everyone else is trustworthy.

_____ You idealize others and are disappointed when they don't live up to your expectations.

_____ You whine or pout to get what you want.

_____ You feel unappreciated and unseen by others.

_____ You blame yourself when things go wrong.

_____ You think you are not good enough.

_____ You fear rejection by others.

_____ You live your life as if you are a victim of circumstances.

_____ You're afraid to make mistakes.

_____ You wish others would like or love you more.

_____ You don't make demands on others.

_____ You're afraid to express your true feelings for fear that people will reject you.

_____ You let others hurt you without trying to protect yourself.

_____ You don't trust yourself and your own decisions.

_____ You find it hard to be alone with yourself.

_____ You pretend that bad things are not happening to you, even when they are.

_____ You keep busy so you don't have to think about things.

_____ You act as though you don't need anything from anyone.

_____ You experience people and life as either all good or all bad.

_____ You lie to protect and cover up for people you love.

_____ You feel scared, hurt, and angry but try not to let it show.

_____ You find it difficult to sustain intimacy with others.

_____ You find it difficult to have fun and be spontaneous.

_____ You feel anxious most of the time and don't know why.

_____ You feel compelled to work, eat, drink, or have sex even when you don't seem to get much enjoyment from the activity.

_____ You worry that other people will leave you.

_____ You feel trapped in relationships.

_____ You feel you have to coerce, manipulate, beg, or bribe others to get what you want.

_____ You cry to get what you want.

_____ You feel controlled by the feelings of others.

_____ You're afraid of your own anger.

_____ You feel helpless and powerless to change yourself or your situation.

_____ You feel like someone else ought to change in order for you to feel better.

If you checked more than half the items above, you know you have co-dependency issues to resolve. Someone once joked, "You know you are co-dependent if you are dying and someone else's life flashes in front of you." The characteristics of co-dependency reflect an outer-directed focus in life — you expect others to direct your life in some important area. Co-dependency in a relationship occurs when two people, both seeking from the other the symbiosis they experienced during their unfinished, early-childhood bonding process with their mothers, come together to form one complete person. Each feels he or she cannot function well without the help of the other person. This prevents personal growth and the maturation of the relationship until it is made conscious and worked on cooperatively. Eventually one of the two partners grows tired of the unholy alliance and strives to change things. This person may even end the relationship and start another, blaming his or her co-dependency problems on the partner in the earlier relationship. Lacking information about the causes of co-dependency, and lacking the tools and support necessary to break the pattern, this person will likely fail to change and will soon be embroiled in yet another co-dependent relationship.

*A Comparison of Co-dependent and Counter-dependent Behaviors*

By looking at a brief comparison between co-dependent and counter-dependent behaviors, you can see that they are truly opposite sides of the same coin. In relationships, one person typically shows more co-dependent behaviors and the other exhibits counter-dependent behaviors. However, it's not unusual to see the two reverse their roles. We've seen this happen many times while counseling couples. When this flip happens, couples often believe they have experienced some great healing. Not so!

Behavioral differences between co-dependency and counter-dependency include the following:

| Behaviors of a Co-dependent Person | Behaviors of a Counter-dependent Person |
|---|---|
| • clings to others | • pushes others away |
| • acts weak and vulnerable | • acts strong and invulnerable |
| • is overwhelmed by his or her feelings | • is cut off from his or her feelings |
| • is other-centered | • acts self-centered |
| • is addicted to people | • is addicted to activities or substances |
| • is easily invaded by others | • is "armored" against others' attempts to get close |
| • has low self-esteem | • has falsely inflated self-esteem |
| • acts incompetent | • tries to "look good" |
| • has depressed energy | • has manic energy |
| • is insecure | • acts secure |
| • feels guilty | • blames others |
| • craves intimacy and closeness | • avoids intimacy and closeness |
| • acts self-effacing | • acts grandiose |
| • displays victim behaviors | • tries to victimize others before they can victimize him or her |
| • is a people-pleaser | • is a people-controller |
| • was neglected as a child | • was abused as a child |

*A New Twelve-Step Program for Recovering from Co-dependency*

The following list briefly describes our self-directed method of recovery from co-dependency, which expands the traditional twelve-step process:

1. *Recognize co-dependent patterns.* Admit there is a problem you cannot solve with your current information and resources.

2. *Understand the causes of the problem.* Learn how to identify the effects of unhealed developmental traumas in your relationships.

3. *Unravel co-dependent relationships.* Learn to identify the symptoms of the problem as they exist in your current relationships and take steps to heal them.

4. *Reclaim your projections.* Stop blaming your problems on others.

5. *Eliminate self-hate.* Stop blaming and criticizing yourself for your mistakes and imperfections.

6. *Eliminate power plays and manipulation.* Stop manipulating others to get what you want.

7. *Ask for what you want.* Be willing to ask for what you want all the time, rather than expecting others to know what you want.

8. *Learn to feel again.* Learn to fully feel and express all your feelings.

9. *Heal your inner child.* Begin developing a stronger inner awareness of your thoughts, feelings, values, needs, wants, and desires.

10. *Define your own boundaries.* Learn to define the psychological boundaries between yourself and others.

11. *Learn to be intimate.* Healing yourself involves learning how to be close to others so that you can get the necessary information, nurturing, mirroring, and secure bonding you need. Mirroring is especially important. It involves others seeing you at a "being," or soul, level and appreciating your inner qualities, such as compassion and empathy, rather than praising you for what you do or possess.

12. *Learn new forms of relationship.* Learn to live in a fluid state of relationship with your True Self and with others, which will allow the development of your fullest potential.

This recovery process takes time and effort. We generally recommend that people plan to spend about one month in recovery for every year that they have lived. Thus, a thirty-six-year-old person can expect to spend three years working on recovery while breaking free of his or her co-dependent patterns. However, you can and will see immediate, significant progress toward your goal.

## Resources for Recovery

Couples in a committed relationship can experience an accelerated process of recovery if they use all the resources we describe here. We urge you to use as many of the following recovery resources as possible:

- Maintain a conscious, committed relationship with another person who is also willing to break his or her co-dependency patterns.
- Seek couples therapy or family therapy with someone who uses a systemic approach to treating co-dependency.
- Take part in a support group in which other people are working on similar issues. Some Co-Dependents Anonymous and Adult Children of Alcoholics groups might provide you with this support. Be careful to find the right support group for you.
- Read other developmental books and articles about recovery from co-dependency, such as those by John Bradshaw.[2]
- Take courses and workshops that provide information on the causes of co-dependency and tools for treating it.
- Use tools to help you explore your inner realms, such as trauma reduction techniques, meditation, breath work, journal keeping, yoga, dream analysis, art work, inner child work, feeling work, and some of the martial arts, such as tai chi and aikido. We discuss these in part 2 of this book.

## CASE EXAMPLE

I (Barry) received a call from Mary, a former student of mine, who seemed worried about her thirty-one-year-old daughter, Sara. Mary thought Sara was seriously depressed and suicidal, and she asked me if I would have time to see Sara soon. I found a space in my schedule, and Mary said, "I'll call her and find out if she'll come to see you, and then I'll call you back and let you know." This was my first clue that co-dependency might be behind this problem. I said, "Mary, I'd prefer that Sara call me directly to set up the appointment, if that's all right with you." There was a brief silence on the phone as

Mary pondered my request. Finally, as if she hadn't thought of that option, she said, "Well, I guess that's okay. I'll tell her to call you."

In my first session with Sara, after taking a brief history, I asked her to rate her depression on a scale of one to ten, with ten being the most depressed she could imagine. Sara replied, "About nine." I asked her about her relationships and about growing up in her family. Her answers confirmed my initial suspicion that she was hooked into co-dependent relationships. Her parents had overprotected and controlled her as a child. Her mother was highly critical of her, always demanding perfection. Her father was distant, and her parents fought constantly.

She had very low self-esteem and trouble with people invading her psychological space. She had trouble saying no to co-workers and bosses who often asked her to do extra work. In her relationships with men, she always tried to please her partner but never felt successful, and she often felt unloved. She tended to see people as all good or all bad, and was frequently disappointed that people didn't pay attention to her or take care of her needs. She had tried to live an independent life, hoping to convince herself and others that she didn't need to be close to anyone. The truth was that she was desperately lonely and had built a thick wall around herself. Now the wall was starting to crack, and she didn't know what to do.

She seemed shocked when I asked her if she thought her mother and father might come to therapy with her. She thought she could get her mother there, but not her father, who didn't believe in therapy ("That's for crazy people," he'd told Sara). I explained that I believed she had never become psychologically autonomous from her mother, and that she would probably continue to have unsatisfying relationships until she broke free of the patterns that kept her from using her own internal power.

As homework, I asked her to make two lists of the unfinished business she still had with her mother. On the first list she was to write down all the things she wished her mother had said or done to her when she was a child that she now thought, had she gotten them, would have made her life easier. On the second list she was to write down all the things she remembered her mother saying and doing to her when she was a child that she now saw as harmful to her as an adult.

Her mother came with her to the next session, and Sara began with her lists. I explained that the first list represented events related to her co-dependency. She probably dreamed that her mother and others in her life would know what she needed without her asking. The second list, I explained, represented traumas related to her counter-dependency issues that kept her feeling angry and resentful.[3] She decided to start with the second list, and I explained that she first needed to express her anger and resentment directly to her mother before she would be able to actually receive the love and affection she wished for.

Sara started with, "Mother, you were always criticizing me, and I could never do anything right for you. I felt awful." Mary replied, "Yes, I did criticize you, and that was my own need for perfection that I put on you. I know I shouldn't have done that. I was so ill-prepared to be a parent and felt overwhelmed most of the time." The pattern was much the same with the other items on Sara's list. Mary would acknowledge the truth in Sara's complaint and express her guilt at not doing better. When the session ended, I felt that the process was not complete, so I asked Mary if she would return with her daughter the following week. She agreed.

At the beginning of the next session, I found out that neither woman had liked what had happened at the previous week's session, and that they almost hadn't come back. Sara said, "I feel bad telling my mother these things. All she does is feel more guilt." Mary said, "I had trouble sleeping several nights this week. I was really upset." I decided to focus on Mary's guilt.

I asked her what it would take for her to forgive herself for not doing a better job of raising her daughter. She said she didn't know. Then I said, "Could you ask your daughter to forgive you?" Mary looked scared, like she wanted to leave. Finally, she said, "Yes, I think I might be able to do that sometime." Obviously she wanted to put it off. I said, "Your daughter is sitting right here, and this is an excellent opportunity for you to get this resolved." After some more thought she turned to her daughter and said, "Sara, will you forgive me for what I did to you when you were a child?" Sara replied immediately, "Of course, I forgive you, Mother." Mary flinched as if to discount what Sara had said. When I saw Mary do this, I asked her to go inside and feel the forgiveness in her body. She closed her eyes and said she felt a black shaft going down to the pit of her stomach. Suddenly it was filled with light, and her stomach stopped hurting.

Then I asked Mary to look inside and see if she needed any more for-giveness. She said she felt a sick place even deeper inside of her that needed to be healed, so she asked again, "Sara, will you forgive me?" This time Sara reached over and hugged her mother, and again said, "Yes, Mother, I forgive you." The two embraced and cried. After they separated, I asked Mary to look inside again to see if that had gotten down to the sick place deep inside of her. Again she closed her eyes and, as she sat there, two buttons of her dress, which was buttoned down the front, popped open. Sara, seeing this, exclaimed, "Mother, the guilt is popping out of you." We all laughed, and then they embraced again.

Suddenly I understood the dynamic that had created their turbulent relationship. I said, "Mary, you've been relating to Sara with your guilt and not your love, and Sara feels that discomfort. She may believe that you really don't want to do things with her, and that the only reason you are doing things with her is because you feel guilty or feel sorry for her. This probably contributes to her low self-esteem. She doesn't want to ask you for anything, fearing that you will say yes from your guilt. She needs to know that you really want to be with her and want to do things with her, and that you will say no if you don't want to be with her." Sara confirmed my statement and added, "I want a relationship as an equal friend with you, not with you as my guilty mother. I, too, feel guilty sometimes when I ask you to do things with me, but I don't tell you. Will you agree to a new relationship with me based on love and not on guilt?" Mary said, "Yes, I want that very much."

As the session came to a close, I said to Sara, "Do you want to continue in therapy to work further on your depression and low self-esteem?" Sara looked straight at me and said, "No, I don't think I want any more therapy at this time. I want to work on this by myself for a while. I feel stronger and more confident that I can take care of myself better now. This work with Mom has really helped me. I have lots of questions to ask her about things that happened when I was a child, and I think she can give me the answers I need." Then she added, "When I'm ready to deal with my dad, I'll probably be back and drag him along. I think I can convince him to come with me."

This case illustrates how *quickly* major, lifelong co-dependencies can begin to change. Obviously, it's not always possible to get parents and/or children together in therapy to resolve these issues, and it isn't necessary. If

Sara's mother had not cooperated and come to therapy with her, I would have asked Sara to imagine her mother sitting in an empty chair in my office and talk to her about her feelings and their unresolved issues. I believe we would have achieved similar results. What was necessary for Sara was to get a clear picture of the co-dependent and counter-dependent patterns so that she could discover what held her co-dependency together. Guilt and shame are common emotions that keep the co-dependent/counter-dependent dynamic active.

### Awareness Activity

### How Co-dependent Are You?

This self-quiz, which illustrates the typical characteristics of co-dependent people, may help you determine the degree to which co-dependency is present in your life. Please answer these questions honestly. Usually the first answer that comes to you is the most honest and most accurate.

DIRECTIONS: Place a number in the blank before each statement to indicate the degree to which the statement is true.

1 = Never   2 = Occasionally   3 = Frequently   4 = Almost always

\_\_\_\_\_ I tend to assume responsibility for others' feelings and/or behavior.

\_\_\_\_\_ I have difficulty identifying my feelings, whether happy, angry, scared, sad, or excited.

\_\_\_\_\_ I have difficulty expressing my feelings.

\_\_\_\_\_ I am afraid of, or worry about, how others may respond to my feelings or behavior.

\_\_\_\_\_ I minimize problems and deny or alter the truth about the feelings or behavior of others.

\_\_\_\_\_ I have difficulty forming or maintaining close relationships.

\_\_\_\_\_ I am afraid of rejection.

\_\_\_\_\_ I am a perfectionist and judge myself harshly.

\_\_\_\_\_ I have difficulty making decisions.

\_\_\_\_\_ I tend to be reactive to others, rather than act on my own.

\_\_\_\_\_ I tend to put other people's wants and needs first.

_____ I tend to value the opinion of others more than my own.

_____ My feelings of worth come from outside myself, through the opinions of other people or from activities that validate my worth.

_____ I find it difficult to be vulnerable and ask for help.

_____ I try to always be in control, or, to the contrary, I avoid being in a position of responsibility.

_____ I am extremely loyal to others, even when that loyalty is unjustified.

_____ I tend to adopt "all or none" thinking.

_____ I have a high tolerance for inconsistency and mixed messages.

_____ I have emotional crises and chaos in my life.

_____ I seek out relationships in which I feel needed, and I attempt to keep them that way.

_____ Total score

SCORING: Add the column of numbers to find your score. Use the following guidelines to interpret your level of co-dependency.

60–80 A very high degree of co-dependent behavior patterns

40–59 A high degree of co-dependent behavior patterns

30–39 Some co-dependent and/or counter-dependent behavior patterns

20–29 A few co-dependent and/or a high degree of counter-dependent behavior patterns

## SUMMARY

Co-dependency is a cultural and evolutionary problem that almost everyone struggles with at some point, so there is no stigma or shame about having co-dependency issues. When viewed from a developmental perspective, there is no need to feel you have some dreaded disease or to feel hopeless or helpless. Recognizing co-dependency issues as an opportunity for personal growth and discovery can help you break free of cultural and family patterns that prevent you from evolving into who you really are at a soul level.

# 2. The Medical Model
## Stuck in Hopelessness

Co-dependency was once defined by most members of the medical and therapeutic communities as a primary *disease* that had an onset, a definable course, and a predictable outcome, and it was considered by many to be incurable. People were diagnosed as co-dependent and told they could only hope to advance to a "recovering" stage, that they would never reach full recovery. This attitude permeated the addictions treatment field because the study of co-dependency, once called "co-alcoholism," had its roots in the study of alcoholism.

Since the introduction of managed care in the mental health field in the mid-1990s, the perspective on co-dependency has shifted. It's now treated in six therapy sessions augmented by prescription medications. We consider this approach to be almost as hopeless as the co-alcoholism and disease models.

## AN OVERVIEW OF TRADITIONAL APPROACHES

Alcoholics Anonymous, which began in the late 1930s, developed a set of key assumptions about alcoholism that initially promised full recovery as an attainable outcome. Originally, the various forms of medical treatment of alcoholism were intended to serve as an adjunct to the grassroots treatment approach of Alcoholics Anonymous. However, the idea that alcoholics are victims of an incurable disease gradually permeated the therapeutic models for treating not only alcoholism but also eating disorders, compulsive gambling, and co-dependency.

## Key Assumptions of the Medical Model

The medically influenced mental health model for treating addictions operates on a set of assumptions used to both diagnose illnesses and prescribe treatment for them. Here are some of the commonly accepted assumptions about co-dependency:

- Addictions are genetically inherited.
- Once you have the addiction, you will always have it.
- You will probably marry someone who will help you maintain your addiction. Your only hope for moving toward recovery is to trust something or someone outside of yourself — a Higher Power, a twelve-step program or group, a sponsor, or a therapist.
- Prescription drugs can treat co-dependent behavior.
- Alcoholic family systems, often with multiple patterns of addictions, are the chief source of co-dependency.
- Behavioral patterns learned in an alcoholic or otherwise dysfunctional family can be changed or modified in six therapy sessions.
- You will *always* be considered a victim of your addiction.
- Being co-dependent is an identity. It is like being an alcoholic: it's who you are.

## Traditional Definitions of Co-dependency

Based on these assumptions, most approaches to co-dependency define the problem in rather limited ways. To begin with, co-dependency is usually defined as a primary illness, linking it with alcoholism and drug addiction. As a result, much of the early literature focused on the negative aspects of co-dependency, reinforcing the deep sense of shame often associated with addictions that one might also associate with having the "co-dependency illness."

Mental health practitioners in the addictions field believed that identifying alcoholism and eating disorders, and now co-dependency, as illnesses would reduce the shame associated with being addicted. While it's true that this eliminated some of the social stigma connected with alcoholism and other addictions, it introduced limited thinking — the belief that you can never recover from your "illness." Shame can prevent you from seeking treatment until you reach a crisis point. By that time you may be in a deep state of hopelessness and despair, which you must overcome before you can address the real problem. But calling co-dependency an illness can just trap you in the world of prescription drugs and the disease-based medical model that perpetuates hopelessness. Even cancer patients receive more hope and encouragement than this!

What those involved in the diagnosis and treatment of co-dependency seem to have missed is the role that trauma plays. Prenatal trauma, birth trauma, and bonding trauma experienced during the co-dependent stage of development are the major causes of co-dependent behaviors in adults. All these very early developmental traumas involve disruptions in the relationship between the child and the mother, and these traumas anchor patterns of dependency, neediness, and low self-esteem. Ultimately, they delay normal development and interfere with children's attempts to become separate and individuated. For this reason, we refer to them as "developmental traumas."

Developmental traumas occurring during the co-dependent stage of development leave a set of subtle and virtually invisible psychological and biological symptoms in children whose trusted adult caregivers are not emotionally attuned to them and who do not respond to their needs for nurturing, protection, safety, and guidance in timely and appropriate ways. Infants and young children experience this loss of emotional attunement as an overwhelming state of emotional distress that can create long-term changes in their bodies and psyches and leave symptoms of post-traumatic stress. The following inventory can help you determine if you experienced trauma during the co-dependent stage of development.

## SELF-QUIZ

### *Identifying Developmental Trauma*

DIRECTIONS: Evaluate the presence and/or severity of each issue presented in the following statements. Place a number in the blank before each statement to indicate the degree to which the statement is true.

1 = Never    2 = Occasionally    3 = Frequently    4 = Almost always

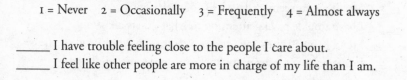

_____ I have trouble feeling close to the people I care about.

_____ I feel like other people are more in charge of my life than I am.

_____ I seem reluctant to try new things.

_____ I have trouble keeping my weight down.

_____ I'm easily bored with what I'm doing.

_____ I have trouble accepting help from others even when I need it.

_____ I work best when I'm under a lot of pressure.

_____ I have trouble admitting my mistakes.

_____ I tend to forget or not keep agreements I make.

_____ I have trouble handling my time and money effectively.

_____ I use intimidation or manipulation to settle my conflicts.

_____ I feel personally attacked when someone quarrels with me.

_____ I have difficulty giving and receiving compliments.

_____ I have a short fuse when I feel frustrated with myself or others.

_____ I tend to blame others for causing the problems I have.

_____ I feel like I have a huge empty place inside me.

_____ It's hard for me to have positive thoughts about my future.

_____ Inside I feel like a tightly coiled spring.

_____ When I get anxious, I tend to eat or drink too much.

_____ I feel empty and alone.

_____ I tend to question the motives of others.

_____ I feel unloved by others.

_____ I have a hard time defining what I want or need.

_____ When I get into a conflict, the other person gets his or her way.

_____ I tend to overreact to certain people and/or situations that bug me.

_____ I feel like I'm on an emotional roller coaster.

_____ I have trouble sticking with any spiritual practices I start.

_____ Important people in my life have abandoned me emotionally or physically.

_____ I have trouble concentrating on what I'm doing.

_____ When I think about my childhood, I draw a big blank.

_____ I have trouble experiencing the intimacy I want in my relationships.

_____ I have trouble falling asleep and staying asleep.

_____ I tend to "walk on eggs" around certain people or situations.

_____ I avoid places or situations that remind me of experiences from my past.

_____ I have recurring bad dreams about what happened to me in the past.

_____ My thoughts seem to have a life of their own.

_____ I have trouble paying attention to what others are saying.

_____ I tend to avoid situations and people that could cause me distress.

_____ I experience big gaps in my memory about my childhood.

_____ I have a hard time knowing what I feel inside.

_____ Total score

SCORING: Add up the column of numbers to find your score. Use the following guidelines to interpret it.

40–82 Some evidence of developmental trauma
83–120 Moderate evidence of developmental trauma
121–160 Strong evidence of developmental trauma

FURTHER ANALYSIS: Look at the content of the items on which you scored 3 or 4. These items might provide clues to possible developmental traumas.

## CASE EXAMPLE

Elaine's struggle with the eating disorder anorexia illustrates the recurrence of developmental trauma. As a child she experienced several traumatic shocks. Her mother was hospitalized (without Elaine) for postpartum bleeding for several days when Elaine was just a week old. This was followed by her mother's undiagnosed period of postpartum depression. Then Elaine's brother was born when she was twenty months old, and her mother again struggled with postpartum depression.

Elaine tried harder and harder to be the perfect daughter, hoping that somehow, through her own "perfection," she could get her mother's love and attention. By the end of her junior year in high school, she was so thin that her mother feared for her health. She sought treatment for Elaine with several therapists, who focused on Elaine's symptoms. After several months of no success with therapy and a decrease in Elaine's weight, her mother finally sought help from a physician.

The physician immediately persuaded her mother that hospitalization was necessary. A hospital in a large city several hundred miles away had just recently created a live-in clinic that kept patients for several months while putting them through an expensive, insurance-subsidized recovery program. The program emphasized the medical aspects of the disease, with its extensive medical and psychological tests and prescription drugs. The clinic itself, built especially for the treatment of eating disorders, was designed to simulate a comfortable homelike environment.

Elaine's mother, convinced by the physician's authoritarian manner and Elaine's previous lack of success in counseling, consented to a six-week period of hospitalization. This necessitated Elaine's withdrawal from high school classes in her senior year and separated her from her family. Her mother was required to make long drives to visit her during the treatment and was expected to pay large sums for the fees that her insurance company did not cover.

As a result of this treatment, Elaine became more compliant with her doctor's and mother's wishes and ate more regularly. She continued to take medication and undergo therapy to help her maintain her ability — though still severely limited — to cope with her eating issues. In the long run, Elaine's fate is still uncertain because only the *symptoms* were treated. One could assume that she remained a co-dependent, recovering anorexic and continued to live a limited life at home, where her mother and her doctors could monitor her health and her life.

## Another Approach

We found this case particularly interesting because Elaine's struggle included hospitalizations that separated her from her mother and replayed the developmental traumas she experienced after her birth and her brother's birth. Recognizing and treating the developmental traumas that caused her eating disorder might have been much more effective.

Rather than seeing Elaine as the "identified patient" in the family and treating her individual symptoms, it would have been more useful to look at the trauma in her history. By looking at Elaine's relationship with her mother and working directly with the whole family to discover the family's disturbances, a family systems therapist might have revealed the core cause of her anorexia. Employing a therapist to explore the family traumas of which Elaine was a part might have made it possible for Elaine to express her stored-up feelings about her childhood traumas. Furthermore, a therapist could have provided Elaine with the support she needed to complete her psychological birth so that she didn't need to use rebellious, dysfunctional behaviors as a way of separating from her family.

Because of the systemic nature of trauma patterns, particularly those anchoring co-dependency, people who try to change themselves often meet with massive resistance from parents, spouses, and children. In Elaine's family, for example, it was easier for her mother and father to see her as the "identified patient" and get expensive treatment for her than to look at the trauma that caused her behavior. Families stuck in co-dependency don't want things to change. They're afraid they will be forced to take care of themselves and to look more deeply at their behavior. This is a risk that people with co-dependency issues usually do not want to take.

### Recognizing Co-dependent and Healthy Messages

Because co-dependency permeates our culture, recognizing how our communication and language structures reinforce it can be difficult. The following two lists show how one set of messages encourages co-dependency and the other encourages healthy independent and interdependent behavior:

| Co-dependent Messages | Healthy Messages |
| --- | --- |
| You're stubborn. | You can ask for what you need. |
| You should be perfect. | You can make mistakes. |
| Hurry up. | You can take your time. |
| Overadapt to others. | You can think about what you want. |
| Try hard. | You can do it. |
| You must be strong. | You can feel and have needs. |
| You're special. | You can be yourself. |
| Work hard. | You can play and have fun. |
| You're confused. | You can think and feel at the same time. |
| You're stupid. | You can think and be effective. |
| Don't be so selfish. | You can be spontaneous. |
| You're dull. | You can be creative. |
| You're sick or crazy. | You can stay well. |
| Always be right. | You can admit you're wrong. |
| You must distrust others. | You can trust others. |
| Be careful. | You can relax and let go. |
| You have to be dependent to be loved. | You can be independent and be loved. |

## THE STAGES OF RECOVERY

We recognize three stages of recovery. In the first one, an individual focuses on breaking free of addictions to substances — alcohol, food, or drugs. In this approach you can be a "dry drunk" — that is, sober or free from your addictions, while still ignoring your underlying childhood traumas and dysfunctional relational patterns. Your dysfunctional relationships may continue, but you may replace one addiction with another, such as work, shopping, or exercise. This stage requires participation in Alcoholics Anonymous or another, similar support group network to treat the substance addiction.

The second stage of recovery involves rebuilding your life and relationships. If your substance abuse damaged your relationships, this stage is extremely important. During this time, you learn more about the traumas of your childhood and replace dysfunctional attitudes and behaviors with more functional ways of living and thinking. While your goal at this stage is to heal your wounds, you must still recognize that addiction to substances must end before you can heal.

This book is about the third stage of recovery. In it we identify addictions as the result of trauma during the co-dependent stage of development. Our approach focuses on helping people to complete the essential developmental processes left over from childhood and reach full recovery. We use a systemic approach and avoid labeling the person with co-dependency issues as sick. Our approach is a hopeful one, and it offers the possibility of reaching your full potential as a human being.

In our model, co-dependency is *not* an identity — it is a *behavior*. It does not define who you are, and there is no shame associated with it. Co-dependent behavior is simply leftover stuff from your childhood. If you know that you lacked nurturing and unconditional care as a child, and you can find people who can give it to you, then your co-dependency can be changed!

This approach differs radically from the disease-oriented model that has been sold to the American public. Our developmental model looks at the scientific research about human development and concludes that human beings are wonderfully self-correcting creatures. When people are given accurate information and effective tools, they can heal their developmental traumas and complete the process of secure bonding that they failed to complete on schedule in childhood. In doing so, they can free themselves of co-dependent behaviors.

## SUMMARY

Disease-focused treatments, which do not take a systemic view of co-dependency and offer little or no hope of full recovery, are typically used by practitioners entrenched in the medically influenced model of mental health. Rather than searching for the traumatic roots of addiction in a family system, these folks frequently zero in on the most obvious symptoms and attempt to modulate them with drugs and cognitive or behavioral therapy tools. When therapists using the medical model continue to focus on finding a "cure" for an addiction, as if it were an "illness," there can be no progress or healing.

The medical model of mental health is particularly unhelpful for a pervasive problem such as co-dependency. It's time to look at co-dependency in a broader context, one that doesn't judge individuals but recognizes co-dependency as a fixable developmental behavior that is part of the human race's evolution. We, as a species, are richly endowed and capable of living up to our fullest potential. By breaking our individual co-dependent patterns, and by initiating social change that supports our individual work, we become part of the greatest personal and social transformation in all of recorded history.

# 3. The Co-dependent Culture

Most people still see co-dependency as an individual or family problem. In contrast, we see it as a "systems" problem: we focus on systemic causes that go far beyond the individual and family. Our Developmental Systems Theory maps the evolution of all human systems and shows the essential developmental processes for each stage of development at each level of human systems: the individual, the couple, the family, the organization, the culture, the nation-state, and the evolution of the human race.[1]

The two following charts illustrate and summarize our evolutionary model of human development. They show that each human system must complete the same four stages of development and similar essential developmental processes. Individuals who do not complete these stages and processes become developmentally delayed at a personal level. This prevents them from creating not only healthy couple and family relationships but also healthy organizations, cultures, and nation-states. Ultimately, this blocks the evolution of the human species.

# THE DEVELOPMENTAL STAGES AND ESSENTIAL DEVELOPMENTAL PROCESSES: MICROSYSTEMS

| Stage of Development Primary Process | Essential Developmental Processes of Individual Evolution | Essential Developmental Processes of Couple Evolution | Essential Developmental Processes of Family Evolution |
|---|---|---|---|
| Co-dependency<br><br>Bonding | • The Mother has good prenatal care<br><br>The child:<br>• experiences nonviolent birth and interventions to heal birth trauma<br>• experiences consistent, secure bonding with parents<br>• experiences secure bonding with immediate family<br>• builds a secure internal working model of self/others<br>• develops primal trust through consistent, resonant connections with parents<br>• develops emotional resiliency skills<br>• builds healthy emotional communication and social engagement skills with parents and others | The couple:<br>• creates secure and consistent bonding experiences with each other<br>• establishes deep primal trust in each other<br>• develops ways to quickly repair any disruptions to couple resonance<br>• establishes good communication and social engagement skills with each other<br>• establishes an identity as a couple | The family:<br>• creates secure bonding experiences between parents and children<br>• establishes primal trust between family members<br>• establishes healthy emotional communication and social engagement skills among family members<br>• establishes an identity as a family |

| | The child | Members of the partnership | Parents and children / The family |
|---|---|---|---|
| *Counter-dependency* / Separation | **The child:**<br>• completes psychological separation from parents<br>• bonds with extended family<br>• resolves internal conflicts between oneness and separateness<br>• develops healthy narcissism<br>• learns to trust and regulate thoughts, feelings, and behaviors in socially appropriate ways<br>• completes the psychological birth to become an individual | **Members of the partnership:**<br>• become functionally separate individuals in the relationship<br>• identify and accept individual differences in thoughts, feelings, and behaviors in each other<br>• resolve internal conflicts between needs of self<br>• develop effective win-win ways to resolve conflicts between wants, needs, values, and beliefs | **Parents and children** learn to assert their individual needs and have them supported by other family members<br>**The family:**<br>• uses fair, equitable, and nonshaming methods of limit-setting and discipline<br>• resolves conflicts effectively between needs of parents and needs of children |
| *Independence* / Mastery | **The child or individual:**<br>• masters self-care<br>• masters functional autonomy from parents<br>• masters object constancy<br>• masters effective social engagement skills<br>• develops core personal values and beliefs<br>• bonds with peers<br>• bonds with nature | **Members of the partnership:**<br>• master self-sufficiency within the relationship<br>• develop autonomy within the couple relationship<br>**The couple:**<br>• develops core values and beliefs as a couple<br>• achieves object constancy as a couple<br>• bonds with nature as a couple | **The family:**<br>• develops individual and couple autonomy within the family structure<br>• develops core values and beliefs as a family<br>• achieves object constancy as a family<br>• bonds with nature as a family |

# THE DEVELOPMENTAL STAGES AND ESSENTIAL DEVELOPMENTAL PROCESSES: MICROSYSTEMS (*continued*)

| *Stage of Development/ Primary Process* | *Essential Developmental Processes of Individual Evolution* | *Essential Developmental Processes of Couple Evolution* | *Essential Developmental Processes of Family Evolution* |
|---|---|---|---|
| **Inter-dependence**<br><br>**Cooperation** | **The child or individual:**<br>• learns to cooperate with others<br>• learns to negotiate to meet needs<br>• learns to accept responsibility for personal behavior and life experiences<br>• develops a social conscience<br>• bonds securely with peers and other adults<br>• bonds securely with own children<br>• understands the influence of incomplete developmental processes on one's life and how to heal developmental traumas<br>• bonds securely with the culture | **Members of the partnership:**<br>• learn to cooperate with each other in getting important needs met in the relationship<br>• experience the deepest human connection possible with each other<br>• develop equality in the relationship<br>• cooperate to help each other heal developmental traumas<br>• cooperate to develop each member's fullest human potential | **The family:**<br>• builds consensus among family members<br>• learns to cooperate so all important needs are met<br>• creates rituals that sustain a spiritual dimension in the family<br>• creates divisions of labor based on individual interests and abilities<br>• cooperates to help each other heal developmental traumas<br>• cooperates to develop each member's fullest potential as a human being |

# THE DEVELOPMENTAL STAGES AND ESSENTIAL DEVELOPMENTAL PROCESSES: MACROSYSTEMS

| Stage of Development/ Primary Process | Essential Developmental Processes of an Organization | Essential Developmental Processes of a Culture or a Nation-State | Essential Developmental Processes of the Human Race |
|---|---|---|---|
| Co-dependency<br><br>Bonding | • Creates bonding experiences for employees<br>• Builds trust between employers and employees<br>• Creates an organizational identity<br>• Provides for the basic needs of employees and managers<br>• Fosters healthy emotional communication and social engagement skills between employees and employers<br>• Builds an organizational esprit de corps | • Creates bonding experiences that unify all subcultures around common values and practices<br>• Builds trust between the leaders and the citizens<br>• Creates a national identity<br>• Establishes healthy emotional communication and social engagement skills for all citizens<br>• Provides opportunities for all citizens to meet their basic needs<br>• Builds a national esprit de corps | • Bonds securely with the world of nature<br>• Creates a connection with the supernatural<br>• Establishes an identity as a species<br>• Develops right-brain functions within the individual |

THE DEVELOPMENTAL STAGES AND ESSENTIAL DEVELOPMENTAL PROCESSES: MACROSYSTEMS

*(continued)*

| Stage of Development/ Primary Process | Essential Developmental Processes of an Organization | Essential Developmental Processes of a Culture or a Nation-State | Essential Developmental Processes of the Human Race |
|---|---|---|---|
| Counter-dependency Separation | • Supports employees as they assert their needs; takes them seriously<br>• Identifies and promotes the unique contributions of each employee to the organization<br>• Uses fair, equitable, and nonshaming methods of limit-setting with employees<br>• Establishes rules and policies in equitable ways<br>• Resolves internal conflicts between the needs of employees and the needs of employers<br>• Understands the influence of incomplete developmental processes on work performance and provides ways to heal developmental traumas at work | • Supports all citizens as they assert their needs; takes them seriously<br>• Guarantees freedom of expression and protects minority and cultural rights<br>• Identifies and promotes the unique contributions of every citizen to the nation<br>• Establishes fair, equitable, and nondiscriminating laws and national policies<br>• Uses the rule of law to provide equal justice for all citizens<br>• Identifies the unique strengths of cultures and the nation<br>• Develops effective ways to resolve conflicts between the needs of cultural groups and between nations<br>• Understands the influence of incomplete developmental processes on national health and provides ways to heal developmental traumas of all citizens | • Explores ways to become functionally separate from nature<br>• Establishes diversity in the species<br>• Develops left-brain functions within the individual<br>• Creates separate nation-states<br>• Creates religions that are based on the supernatural and separate from nature<br>• Resolves conflicts between nations and religions |

| | | | |
|---|---|---|---|
| *Independence* / Mastery | • Creates an organizational culture with mutually determined values and beliefs<br>• Supports individual autonomy within the organizational structure<br>• Gives employees responsibility for self-regulation of emotion and self-care<br>• Fosters employees' true pride in their work<br>• Provides specialized training and development for each employee to enhance individual contributions to the organization | • Creates a national culture that honors and protects diversity of all cultures<br>• Creates an economic and social safety net for those in need<br>• Guarantees the voting rights of all citizens<br>• Gives citizens responsibility for self-regulation of emotion and self-care<br>• Fosters true cultural and national pride among citizens | • Reunites with the world of nature as partners<br>• Develops whole-brain thinking functions and "both/and" thinking<br>• Creates individual cultures<br>• Celebrates the diversity between cultures<br>• Resolves conflicts of need between cultures<br>• Provides for the basic needs of all citizens<br>• Develops systemic thinking |
| *Inter-dependence* / Cooperation | • Creates organizations run cooperatively by employees and employers<br>• Utilizes team-building activities<br>• Promotes cooperation-building between teams<br>• Creates rituals that build and sustain employee morale<br>• Creates divisions of labor based on individual interests and abilities<br>• Fosters cooperation among employees to develop each person's fullest potential as a human being | • Cooperates to create three interdependent and balancing branches of government with equal power to govern<br>• Cooperates to build consensus between cultural groups and between nations<br>• Cooperates to create meaningful national rituals that build and sustain citizen morale<br>• Creates equal opportunities for all citizens to develop their fullest potential | • Establishes a planetary partnership culture based on cooperation and respect for differences<br>• Develops the global brain<br>• Develops transsystemic thinking |

## DOMINATOR VERSUS PARTNERSHIP MODELS

Riane Eisler's *The Chalice and the Blade* provides a more in-depth historical review of culture on our planet and gives an evolutionary look at two basic forms of relationship that she calls the "dominator" and "partnership" models.[2] She provides a detailed analysis of the challenges and problems that each model has created. Eisler's study looks at the whole of human history, including prehistory, and the whole of humanity — both its male and female halves. She weaves together evidence from art, archeology, religion, social science, history, and numerous other fields to help create a new story about our cultural origins. Eisler's *The Power of Partnership* applies the partnership paradigm to contemporary social systems.[3] Both books provide a comprehensive perspective that can help us transcend the "battle of the sexes" for control and domination, where many contemporary feminists have gotten stuck. Eisler's view is much longer and deeper.

## THE PARTNERSHIP SOCIETY

When Eisler delved into prehistory, she found numerous legends and archeological records that described a prehistoric civilization whose culture was organized quite differently from what we know today. According to these records, large areas in Europe and the Middle East enjoyed a long period of peace and prosperity. The social, technological, and cultural development of the civilization that existed in these areas followed a steady evolutionary path toward higher consciousness.

This civilization, which she identifies as a "partnership" society, was based on unity, cooperation, and mutual need. The society valued the life-giving and nurturing qualities that we might identify as feminine. Burial tombs of this era reveal a wealth of statues and artifacts devoted to the worship of a female deity, the Great Mother. These artifacts, along with ancient art, myth, and historical writings, indicate a deep reverence for life, caring, compassion, and nonviolence.

The archeological evidence also reveals that this early social structure was based on equality. Power, risk taking, and rewards were shared without regard to gender. This cooperative approach helped create unity and harmonious relationships among people and between the people and the planet. Eisler contends that at some point in prehistory, perhaps about 3500 BCE, this thirty-thousand- to forty-thousand-year era began to wane, and the qualities of the feminine were gradually replaced with more masculine values that created a completely different kind of civilization, which she identifies as a dominator society.

## THE DOMINATOR SOCIETY

Dominator societies, according to Eisler, exalt the qualities we stereotypically associate with masculinity, and they value life-taking and destructive activities, such as conquest and warfare. This social structure, which is based on inequality, generally ranks one part of society over the other. Even though the cultural values are what we today think of as "hard," or more "masculine," dominator societies can be either matriarchal or patriarchal. The higher ranked group holds the power, takes the risks, and reaps the rewards, leaving the lower ranked group powerless and, often, in poverty. Rather than linking people cooperatively, this model ranks them competitively, creating a hierarchy supported by force or the threat of force. This creates an atmosphere of distrust, separation, and intimidation.

In studying Eisler's model of social structures, it becomes clear that the dominator model creates a co-dependent society, and the partnership model creates an interdependent society in which people work cooperatively to support each other. Extending her model, a comparison of the two might look like the table on page 38.

As we look at co-dependency through a larger lens, we can see that it permeates the very fabric of our dominator model of society. It's in every institution, including our religious ones. Christianity, the prevailing Western religion, is especially embedded in the dominator model. It uses hierarchy in its management system and also operates as a cultural police force for advancing and maintaining the dominator model.

## THE INFLUENCE OF CHRISTIANITY

Christianity was introduced to the world at a time when the worship of feminine values had already been pushed underground. Jesus's message reflected reverence for partnership models of relationship, rather than dominator models. For many of the people enslaved by Roman legions during that era, partnership was difficult to understand. This made it difficult for Jesus's

| Co-dependent Society | Interdependent Society |
|---|---|
| • creates hierarchies ultimately backed by force or the threat of force | • creates heterarchies in which people are linked together by common need |
| • the group higher in the hierarchy holds the power of decision making; the lower-ranked group is powerless | • the heterarchical group shares equally in decision making |
| • the higher ranked group assumes responsibility, risk taking, and the means of production, and it reaps large rewards, while the lower ranked group provides support and labor and reaps minimal rewards | • the heterarchical group shares equally in risk taking, responsibility, capital investment, means of production, rewards, labor, and support |
| • uses comparative "you or me" thinking | • uses cooperative "you and me" thinking |
| • uses a co-dependent form of relationship between the two to hold the system together | • uses an interdependent form of relationship within one large group to hold the system together |
| • values life-taking and other destructive activities such as war and exploitation | • values life-generating and nurturing qualities such as compassion and nonviolence |
| • utilizes rigid sex roles | • utilizes fluid sex roles |
| • treats diversity judgmentally | • treats diversity nonjudgmentally |
| • uses fear to create separation | • uses hope to create unity |

contemporaries to recognize his true message, as noted in Matthew 20:25–28: "You know that the rulers of the gentiles dominate them, and their great men exercise authority over them. It shall not be so among you [Christians]: But whoever would be great among you must be your servant, and whoever would be first among you must be your slave. Even as the son of man came not to be served but to serve, and to give his life as a ransom for many."

Jesus's point was that authentic leadership is a form of service to the whole. He understood that when the lord adopts the role of the servant, both ranks or categories perish and a new order is instituted. Jesus demonstrated this point graphically when he washed the feet of his disciples during the Last Supper. With this act he symbolized the demolition of a whole pattern of domination and submission, creating a partnership model for the world.

Jesus also violated the rigid, male-dominated, sexually segregated social and political norms of his times by associating freely with women, many of whom played major roles in early Christianity. At the same time, he preached what Eisler calls a "partnership spirituality," elevating the feminine values of compassion and nonviolence, which previously existed mainly among the subservient.[4]

This partnership model of religion was not only preached but also practiced by many early Christians, some of whom were known as Gnostics. These early Christians formed communities that were radically different from the rigid, male-dominated households, villages, and cities of their times. In Gnostic communities, women and men worked and lived together in equal partnership. As Eisler notes, the important part played by women is perhaps reflected most dramatically in the Gnostic Gospels, later banned as heretical by the orthodox church. These show that Mary Magdalene was probably the most important of the disciples responsible for helping Jesus spread his teachings.

These early Christians also permitted equal access to information, equal participation in the church's rites and rituals, and equal claims to spiritual knowledge. They believed that each individual could make direct contact with the spiritual realms, and that intermediaries such as priests, bishops, and other hierarchical figures were unnecessary intrusions. At each worship service, they drew lots to determine who would perform the ministerial roles. They did not confuse roles with the people who performed them.

Various early sects of Christians eventually divided into two camps. The Orthodox Christians created a system based on hierarchy, in contrast to the nonhierarchical structure of the Gnostics. These two groups came into conflict, with the Orthodox group eventually gaining power. Starting about 200 CE, all references to the deity as both Mother and Father were labeled heresy, and women were again officially excluded from the priesthood. Early in the third century, the Orthodox group also ordered all Gnostic writings to be destroyed, beginning a long and vengeful campaign to wipe out Gnosticism's partnership values and its challenge to the emerging male-dominated church and family.[5] This done, Christianity was well on its way to becoming precisely the kind of violent, hierarchical system against which Jesus had rebelled. Institutionalized Christianity, with its emphasis on male superiority, has helped to perpetuate a dominator model of society over the past two thousand years.[6]

Thus, one of the true messages of Christianity — partnership — was lost. The distorted teachings that remained were used to keep people powerless and hopeless. According to Christian dogma, the average human being would never reach heaven without the priests, bishops, and other intermediaries of the male-dominated church hierarchy. Those who intuitively sensed that these teachings were untrue and refused to follow the church's dogma were threatened with damnation to an eternal hell. Women and men who remembered the teachings of the Great Goddess and the partnership model of spirituality were methodically persecuted. This persecution reached epidemic proportions in the Middle Ages, when an estimated 100,000 people judged as witches or heretics were killed, many by being burned at the stake.[7]

Whole villages identified with this pagan religion were eradicated. This campaign was carried out with as much dedication and purposefulness as any war that the world has known. This inquisition against the feminine is still present today in some ultra-conservative religions.

Many contemporary cultural historians, such as José Argüelles, recognize that this religious war continues, and that now it has become a war against the earth itself.[8] Feminists such as Susan Griffin have examined the parallels between the treatment of women and the treatment of the planet.[9] The rise in domestic violence and rape parallels the rise in underground nuclear testing. The high incidence of hysterectomies among women parallels the increasing acceptance of the strip mining of coal and minerals. The attitude that women are objects to be used and then cast aside has supported the emergence of a disposable society that throws away the planet's resources in the form of plastic, cardboard, and other paper as containers for food in the fast-food chains and processed food in the grocery stores. It is necessary for us to recognize the real causes of our cultural dysfunction so that we know how to begin to change it.

## CO-DEPENDENT SYSTEMS

From this perspective we can see that the causes of co-dependency go right to the heart of our social structure. Any culture that ranks one gender over another, one religion over another, or one race over another has organized a society that can only be co-dependent. The dominator culture of the American South prior to the Civil War is another example of a co-dependent society. Wealthy landowners managed their lives of ease and luxury by using the labor of black slaves to fulfill their economic and personal needs. Most of the gentry were helpless in basic survival skills such as cooking, gardening, and caring for their animals. The black people, by contrast, had basic survival skills but often lacked the ability to plan and manage. When the Emancipation Proclamation ended slavery, both groups discovered their areas of helplessness and co-dependency, which contributed to the eventual collapse of the whole system.

While co-dependency itself did not cause the fall of the South, the fact that co-dependent values and beliefs underpinned its dominator structure was a major factor. Any system in which members are not encouraged to be self-reliant, self-directed, and individually responsible creates passive people who are apathetic, helpless, fearful, and unable to implement the changes that need to be made in the culture. This is evident in many authoritarian cultures, whether Eastern or Western, technologically developing or developed, ancient or modern. And it's still a major problem in our democratic society today. Our systemic orientation to the dominator model remains a basic obstacle to both personal and social health.

Using the dominator model versus partnership model as a framework, let's explore how the dominator model affects our culture's economic system. Most of the economic systems of the Western world are based on some form of capitalism with an owner/worker structure. The owner sector (which includes stockholders as well as those with investments who do the actual managing) provides the risk taking necessary to capitalize operations, assumes the responsibility of either success or failure, and reaps the majority of the rewards. The owner sector controls the entire venture, including decisions about hiring and firing.

The worker sector, on the other hand, usually has little or no investment, no responsibility, and very little financial risk. Workers provide the labor (negotiated at the lowest possible cost to the owners) so that the owner sector can make the highest profit possible. Workers, in return for their free-dom from financial risk and responsibility, have little or no job security. Workers, who are at the mercy of the owners, keep their jobs based on whether or not the owners are making a profit. The owners profit most when the workers will work at the lowest possible wage. This is a clear case of a co-dependent relationship.

Co-dependency permeates all other Western institutions too: medicine, education, religion, politics, and the military. In health services, physicians and therapists assume an authoritarian role as they seek to use their personal power to cure illness and disease by dispensing drugs. Patients are treated like some kind of a mechanical device with broken parts, with their bodies and minds addressed separately. In the traditional health care system, the power now lies with managed care corporations. Patients (not clients), who are powerless and considered ignorant about their needs for services, are treated by providers according to corporate directives.

A similar scenario exists in education. Those who rank highest in the hierarchy have the power. The student is the least consulted component of the system. The content of most education is established by the culture and transmitted by teachers, who direct and evaluate the performance of stu-dents. The educational hierarchy assumes that students know little or noth-ing and forces them into compulsory attendance. Students' self-development, interests, needs, and individual differences are the least considered factors in creating educational experiences. More and more, the system is designed to "program" individuals so they will be compliant cogs in a machine.

In religion, a hierarchy also maintains a system in which the laity need priests, bishops, ministers, and other clergy to structure and interpret their spiritual experiences. The Catholic Church, for example, ranks priests over nuns in order to maintain patriarchal values.

Political systems rank people hierarchically according to power, partic-ularly economic, racial, and gender power. Western politics supports those who are rich, white, and male, perpetuating a pervasive labor/management culture. The United States has essentially one political party, the capitalist or corporate party, which has liberal and conservative branches often called the Democratic and Republican parties. Both branches promote co-dependent structures and programs, because capitalism, as it is practiced in this coun-try, is formed on the dominator model.

Cultural hierarchies use military power to enforce dominator models. They all support the life-taking, destructive values designed to keep people mistrustful, fearful, and separate. Each of these cultural institutions, though different in function, supports the principles of the dominator model. If we examine the structural model of our most intimate relationships, we can see these same dominator behaviors and values. It becomes clear that the hierarchical structures at every level of our culture must change if we are to break free of the co-dependency trap. Such changes will cause a radical shift in the way we see ourselves and view our world. This is the kind of shift that Owen Waters and we have described as a "shift in consciousness."[10]

## COUNTER-DEPENDENT SYSTEMS

Counter-dependency is also an inherent component of dysfunctional social systems. While people with unresolved co-dependency issues often look to the government to function as their primary caretaker and expect to be taken care of through extensive social programs that address their dependency needs, those with unresolved counter-dependency issues tend to see the government as the primary source of economic oppression because of the high taxes it levies on its citizens. Rather than looking at the need for a social safety net to protect children, the disabled, and the elderly, who truly are dependent on others for their welfare, those with counter-dependency issues react against their own dependency issues by denying those with authentic needs support through government programs.

The struggle between those with unresolved co-dependency issues and those with counter-dependency issues is at the heart of much of our culture's political process. The Democratic Party is perceived as supporting co-dependent behaviors and the Republican Party is perceived as supporting counter-dependent behaviors. Neither co-dependency- nor counter-dependency-oriented social systems make us responsible for taking care of our own needs or for looking at how our personal behavior is part of a larger problem. In the charts presented earlier in this chapter, you can see the essential developmental processes that need to be completed in organizations, cultures, and nation-states stuck in the co-dependent and counter-dependent stages of development, before they can move out of those stages. The challenge for all of us is to individually complete the essential developmental processes that will support our evolution and help us create more functional organizations, cultures, and nation-states.

## THE CONSCIOUSNESS REVOLUTION:
## WHY BREAK FREE OF CO-DEPENDENCY?

Some people have asked us, "Why all the fuss over something that has worked for many generations?" Our response to this is: "Evolution." Since the 1960s, there has been a virtual explosion of information and knowledge about us as human beings — about our brains, our development, and about the universe in which we live. Much of this information is a result of the evolution of consciousness.

For the first time, we understand the astounding potential of human capacities. A few scientists and other researchers, working independently at first, eventually grew into a network of individuals from the fields of science, religion, philosophy, and education, all working to create a new picture of human possibilities. According to this picture, we human beings

- are able to learn and think in multiple ways (visually in symbols, kinesthetically with the body, proprioceptively with feelings, and auditorily with words);
- have two hundred or more senses that come from cross-sensing, such as tasting colors or smelling sound;[11]
- are able to shift into different brain-wave frequencies at will, consciously altering our states of awareness;
- are able to create and direct our own destinies by means of thoughts or images generated internally;
- are able to heal ourselves of what have been considered terminal illnesses, through the use of meditation, nutrition, affirmations, psychotherapy, and exercise; and
- are capable of being "self-aware," that is, aware of being aware and able to observe ourselves and our behavior — which allows us to make new choices and break patterns of co-dependency and counter-dependency.

This new view of human possibilities began in the 1960s, just as many people were recognizing the degree of their dependence on large social and governmental systems. People began to yearn for growth, greater opportunities, authenticity, and self-determination. A self-development movement arose, one that promoted the idea of adopting values that support the fullest unfolding of human potential. Embedded in this human potential movement was a growing awareness of how the traditional ways of childbirth, parenting, family life, and the educational system can interfere with the development of our full humanness.

Psychologists began to investigate the causes of emotional trauma in both adults and children and to explore new ideas about human possibility. In researching these two things simultaneously, psychologists began to see correlations between the quality of child-rearing practices and the level of potential that people were able to achieve. It became clear that the way the dominator culture raises its children has interfered with the development of their capacities. Most of us, it seems, are stuck at a certain level of development, unable to become psychologically interdependent. We are not generally aware that our culture's parenting practices make it difficult for children to complete the bonding and separation processes of the co-dependent and counter-dependent stages of development. Unfortunately, the inability to complete these stages obstructs the awakening of interdependent consciousness. We must understand the process of human development at a very personal level — its stages, challenges, and tasks, and the pitfalls. The next chapter takes a closer look at this process and describes our developmental approach to recovery in more detail.

## SUMMARY

The human race is evolving and moving away from dominator social structures and toward partnership models of relationship. This shift supports feminine, life-giving values such as nurturing, empathy, and planning for generations yet unborn that are at the core of our developmental approach to healing co-dependency. While this evolutionary shift is happening in all parts of our society, it is being experienced most intensely in couple and family structures and in small group situations such as work, schools, and churches. There are periods when this change process can feel intense and lonely.

So we want you to know that the work that you are doing on yourself, in your most intimate relationships, in both your family of origin and family of creation, and in your work and social relationships is very important. As you break free of the co-dependency trap, you inspire others to also become free. While this is a valuable social motivation, the most important outcome is that you learn to experience and express who you are at a soul level.

# 4. A Developmental Approach to Recovery

The developmental approach to recovery we present in this book identifies co-dependency as a developmental problem that involves the whole family system. Co-dependency is caused by developmental trauma during the first six months of life that interferes with the completion of the secure bonding process and the essential developmental tasks associated with it.

If some kind of trauma disrupts the completion of the secure bonding process and the developmental tasks associated with it, the unmet needs for unconditional love, nurturing, protection, and primal trust will continue to recycle during life, seeking completion. The result of incomplete or insecure bonding is co-dependent behavior. Adults with co-dependency issues often find themselves stuck while trying to complete this bonding process. They become very attached to or dependent on another person. If they were emotionally, physically, or sexually abused as small children, they may have prematurely separated from their parents by being counter-dependent, and may act like they don't need anything from others. Or they may cycle back and forth between co-dependency and counter-dependency.

Virtually all the research on early child development has been reassessed since the early 1980s, because it focused almost exclusively on the mother-child relationship. The role of the father is critical in the bonding and separation processes of child development.[1] This recent information supports partnership parenting and invalidates certain common practices of the dominator model, which leaves much of the care of children to women.

It's really important for fathers to bond with their children during the co-dependency stage. While bonding with the mother is critical, it's very difficult for children to separate from their mothers unless they are also bonded with their fathers. The job of fathers is to help children move beyond their mothers, and to help them master the larger world. In the beginning, this may involve holding babies, playing with them, taking them out for rides in the stroller, and exploring the park. If they become securely bonded with their fathers during the co-dependency stage, they will turn to their fathers when they grow older for help in mastering the practical matters of living independently and becoming self-sufficient. While mothers are also involved in this process, it's important for children to value and appreciate their fathers' special contributions to both their bonding and autonomy.

## PRINCIPLES OF OUR DEVELOPMENTAL APPROACH

In our developmental approach, we view painful and anxiety-producing life events as being related to developmental crises rather than to psychiatric breakdowns or mental illnesses. We've identified the following key developmental principles for understanding the causes of co-dependency:

- All development is a continuous process from conception until death. It is sequential, in that each task is the stepping-stone for the next one.
- Any essential developmental process that isn't mastered at the age-appropriate time is carried forward as excess baggage into subsequent developmental stages. If too many essential developmental processes are not completed successfully on schedule, development stalls.
- Incomplete developmental processes press for completion at every opportunity. Any situation that resembles a previous one involving an incomplete process will push that process to the forefront. People who experienced developmental trauma during the co-dependent stage of development often report being flooded by old feelings or old memories. They feel that they snap back in time and automatically find themselves reenacting a traumatic emotional experience.

- When people realize it's trauma that causes them to overreact to certain people or situations, they're able to learn new, more effective responses. Through increased awareness of the source of their trauma, and with the help of increased communication skills and trauma elimination tools, people can clear the trauma and move forward in their development.

## THE FOUR STAGES OF DEVELOPMENT

In our developmental model, co-dependency is the first of four stages to be completed by the age of twenty-nine. Ideally, the developmental process should occur in the following way.

When we are born, we are already in the first stage: co-dependency. Nature provides a symbiotic relationship between child and mother in which neither experiences separation between them. This is nature's way of insuring that the human infant will get the care it needs to survive. Mother and child live together enmeshed in an energetic field of unity, working on the essential processes of bonding and creating trust. This stage lasts about six months, until the child begins to crawl.

The second stage of the development process is the counter-dependent stage. During this period, which peaks between eighteen and thirty-six months of age, the essential developmental process is separation. By this time, both parents and child strongly need to become more independent from each other. The child has a strong drive to explore the world and be separate (and conveys the message "I want to do it myself"), while the parents yearn to spend more time on their long-term interests, such as their careers and their marital relationship. (The separation process, which occurs gradually over a period of two to three years, is discussed in detail in chapter 5.)

If the separation stage is completed without any problems, then, by about age three, the child is ready to move into the third stage: independence. During this stage, which usually lasts until about age six, the child is able to function autonomously much of the time and still feels and acts related to his or her parents and family.

Upon completion of this stage, the child is ready to move into the next stage of development: interdependence. In this fourth stage, which usually lasts from age six to age twenty-nine, the degree of relationship between the child and others fluctuates. At times the child may wish to be close, and at other times she or he may wish to be more separate. The child's primary task during this stage is to develop the ability to move back and forth comfortably between oneness and separateness.

## THE ESSENTIAL DEVELOPMENTAL PROCESSES
## OF EARLY CHILDHOOD

The two essential developmental processes to be completed during the period from birth to three years of age are bonding and separation. From ages three to six, the child masters everyday tasks and functional autonomy. Between six and twenty-nine years of age, the child's essential developmental tasks are learning cooperation and negotiation. We've summarized these stages of development and their essential developmental processes and tasks in the charts on pages 51–54.

## BONDING: THE ESSENTIAL DEVELOPMENTAL PROCESS
## OF THE CO-DEPENDENT STAGE

If anything interferes with the bonding process between the mother and child, the child not only gets stuck in co-dependency but also has difficulty trusting others. Newborn babies almost immediately bond with both the mother and the father. The sound of their voices, the sight of their faces while they hold or feed the child, the feel of their skin, and the smell of their bodies are constant anchors for the child indicating that there is order and consistency in a seemingly chaotic and confusing world.

Developmental researchers Marshall Klaus, Phyllis Klaus, and John Kennell have contributed much to our understanding of the bonding process.[2] We've summarized their findings here:

- The optimal period for bonding begins within the first few minutes after birth and ends after twelve to twenty-four hours. Klaus and Kennell suggest that, during this time, both parents spend a significant amount of time having skin-to-skin and other sensory contact with their newborn.

- The parents need to see that their child is responding to their

# THE DEVELOPMENTAL STAGES AND ESSENTIAL DEVELOPMENTAL PROCESSES OF INDIVIDUAL EVOLUTION

| Stage of Development and Primary Task | Essential Developmental Processes of Individual Evolution | Suggested Experiences for Completing the Essential Developmental Processes of Individual Evolution |
| --- | --- | --- |
| *Co-dependency*<br><br>(Conception to Six Months)<br><br>**Bonding and Attachment** | • **Mother** receives good prenatal care and support<br><br>**Child:**<br>• experiences a nonviolent birth with immediate interventions to heal any birth trauma<br>• achieves consistent, secure bonding and attachment with mother and/or other adult caregivers<br>• learns primal trust in parents through a consistent resonant connection<br>• learns emotional resiliency skills<br>• creates a secure internal working model of self/other<br>• learns healthy emotional communication and social engagement skills with parents and others<br>• bonds securely with siblings and extended family | **Mother:**<br>• maintains a high-quality diet and reduces environmental stressors to prevent the risk of cortisol production during pregnancy<br>• receives effective postnatal emotional and physical support<br>• provides nurturing, respectful touch and eye contact; she gazes at, sings to, and speaks to the child in loving ways<br><br>**Parents:**<br>• plan for and want the child<br>• build prenatal relationship with the child<br>• use nonviolent birthing practices<br>• nurse and room-in at the hospital and have prolonged skin-to-skin contact between child and each parent in the first 12–24 hours following birth<br><br>**Child:**<br>• gets timely emotional and tactile comforting to help heal developmental traumas caused by disruptions in resonant connection to parents<br>• receives unconditional love from parents<br>• receives authentic mirroring and validation of his or her essence from parents<br><br>**Immediate and extended family members:**<br>• provide consistent, nurturing, and empathic contact<br>• provide comfortable and protective environment to meet the child's needs for safety and survival |

## THE DEVELOPMENTAL STAGES AND ESSENTIAL DEVELOPMENTAL PROCESSES OF INDIVIDUAL EVOLUTION (*continued*)

| Stage of Development and Primary Task | Essential Developmental Processes of Individual Evolution | Suggested Experiences for Completing the Essential Developmental Processes of Individual Evolution |
|---|---|---|
| *Counter-dependency*<br><br>(Six to Thirty-six Months)<br><br>**Separation and Individuation** | **Child:**<br>• completes the psychological separation process with parents<br>• learns to safely explore his or her environment<br>• learns to trust and regulate his or her own thoughts, feelings, and behaviors in socially appropriate ways<br>• internalizes appropriate physical and social limits<br>• develops healthy narcissism<br>• resolves internal conflicts between oneness and separateness (I'm okay, you're okay)<br>• bonds with self<br>• continues to build secure internal working model<br>• completes his or her individuation or psychological birth process | **Parents:**<br>• offer timely help in healing any narcissistic wounds or developmental traumas that interfere with resonance<br>• give the child permission and support to safely explore his or her environment; they give the child twice as many yeses as nos during this time<br>• rearrange environment to provide safety<br>• understand and respect the child's need to develop internal regulation of emotions, especially shame<br>• help the child identify self-needs, as opposed to the needs of others<br>• model how to directly ask to have one's needs met<br>• use nonshaming responses in limit-setting and discipline<br>• give positive support for the child's efforts to develop an autonomous Self<br><br>**Adult caregivers:**<br>• help the child quickly reestablish the resonant connection with the mother when it's disrupted<br>• offer empathy and compassion as the child learns to regulate his or her conflicting emotions, thoughts, and behaviors<br>• offer authentic mirroring and validation of the child's essence<br>• offer permission for the child to be a separate individual and to trust his or her internal impulses |

## THE DEVELOPMENTAL STAGES AND ESSENTIAL DEVELOPMENTAL PROCESSES OF INDIVIDUAL EVOLUTION (*continued*)

| *Stage of Development and Primary Task* | *Essential Developmental Processes of Individual Evolution* | *Suggested Experiences for Completing the Essential Developmental Processes of Individual Evolution* |
|---|---|---|
| *Independence*<br><br>(Three to Six Years)<br><br>**Mastery of Self and Environment** | **Child:**<br>• masters self-care<br>• masters the process of becoming a functionally autonomous individual separate from parents<br>• masters object constancy<br>• develops and trusts his or her own core values and beliefs<br>• has secure bonding experiences with nature<br>• learns effective social engagement skills<br>• develops secure internal working model of self/other<br>• bonds securely with peers | **Parents:**<br>• rearrange home environment to support the child's mastery of self-care (eating, dressing, and toilet training)<br>• support the child's development of effective internal limits and consequences<br>• help the child learn appropriate deferred gratification of his or her wants and needs<br>• help the child learn effective emotional self-regulation and control<br>• help the child learn to trust his or her inner sense of wisdom and guidance<br>• provide the child with experiences for the safe exploration of nature<br>• help the child develop sensory relationships with nature<br>• provide for reciprocal social interactions with other children<br>• teach cross-relational thinking, including empathy and respect for others<br>• help the child develop cause/effect problem-solving skills<br><br>• **Immediate and extended family members** offer nurturing, supportive, and consistent contact<br><br>• **Adults** model win-win solutions to conflicts |

| THE DEVELOPMENTAL STAGES AND ESSENTIAL DEVELOPMENTAL PROCESSES OF INDIVIDUAL EVOLUTION (*continued*) | | |
|---|---|---|
| *Stage of Development and Primary Task* | *Essential Developmental Processes of Individual Evolution* | *Suggested Experiences for Completing the Essential Developmental Processes of Individual Evolution* |
| *Inter-dependence*<br><br>(Six to Twenty-nine Years)<br><br>**Cooperation and Negotiation Skills** | Child:<br>• learns to cooperate with others<br>• learns to negotiate with others to get his or her needs met<br>• learns to accept responsibility for his or her personal behaviors and life experiences<br>• experiences secure bonding with peers and other adults<br>• develops a social conscience<br>• bonds securely with his or her culture<br>• bonds securely with the planet<br>• lives his or her life as an authentic adult<br>• bonds securely with own children<br>• understands the influence of incomplete developmental processes on his or her life and how to successfully heal developmental traumas | • **Parents** model effective cooperative social engagement skills in couple, family, and peer relationships<br><br>Child:<br>• seeks to learn negotiation skills to get his or her needs met in healthy ways<br>• seeks solutions to his or her conflicts that honor the needs of all parties involved<br>• seeks adult validation of the importance of keeping his or her relationship agreements<br>• seeks an adult model that can teach him or her empathy and compassion for others<br>• seeks adults who can teach him or her intuitive language and thinking skills<br>• seeks nurturing, supportive, and consistent contact from immediate and extended family members<br>• seeks support from parents and other adults on how to build sustainable relationships with other adults and how to find a primary love partner<br>• seeks adult input on the values of his or her cultural group and how to overcome any limits imposed by family and culture<br>• seeks personal meaning and a personal mission within the context of the "global family"<br>• seeks information and skills for healing his or her developmental traumas<br>• seeks assistance in developing systemic and transsystemic thinking<br><br>• **Adults** encourage the development of an internalized "safety parent" allowing safe risk-taking behaviors |

attempts to bond. Otherwise they may get discouraged and withdraw from their baby, making bonding more difficult.

- Everyone present during the birth process will bond with the child. This suggests that immediate and extended family members should be present at the birth of the child.

- A newborn with a life-threatening illness will experience bonding issues. Parents often hold back their affection for fear of loss in case the child dies. Fathers have difficulty bonding with the child if the mother experiences life-threatening complications during the birth process. Fathers who are not present at their child's birth also may have more trouble bonding with him or her.

- Children are able to sense worry or tension between the parents during the first few hours after birth. This can imprint the child and have long-term effects on his or her development.

- Even if the optimal period of bonding is disrupted by illness, bonding can occur subsequently if the parents continue to establish sensory contact with the child whenever possible.

It appears from the research of Margaret Mahler and her colleagues that the child's ability to achieve autonomy or separateness at age two or three depends on whether the child has been able to complete the secure bonding process.[3] The more securely a child bonds with the mother and father during the first days and months of life, the easier it is for the child and the parents to successfully complete the separation process. Mothers and fathers who are not fully bonded with their child are more likely to be neglectful or abusive than are parents who have bonded with their child.

A child who doesn't fully bond with her or his parents will become disengaged instead. Disengaged children behave differently from bonded children. They are afraid of the world, and they fear change. They approach others with a timidity and caution that makes exploring the unknown a much more difficult task. These children have difficulty perceiving subtle or intuitive signals, so they tend to react to situations rather than anticipate them. They need concrete, overt, physical signals, such as touch or very specific sensory cues, to guide their actions. Disengaged people, in order to compensate for their lack of bonding, close off their feelings, become rigid in their thinking and eventually develop compulsive behaviors in order to numb or quiet their increasing sense of anxiety about the uncertainty of life.

By contrast, children who are fully bonded are not afraid to explore their world, and they delight in novelty and change. They are receptive to others and open to learning. They can pick up on subtle and intuitive signals that allow them to be spontaneous and relaxed. These children are often aptly described as having a love affair with the world.

## SEPARATION: THE ESSENTIAL DEVELOPMENTAL PROCESS OF THE COUNTER-DEPENDENT STAGE

Mahler's research is useful in charting the course of development during the separation process in the counter-dependent stage.[4] She found four distinct substages in this process: differentiation, early practicing, rapprochement, and object constancy.

During the differentiation substage (from six to eleven months), children begin to see themselves as separate from their mothers and fathers. At first this occurs in very small ways. Children explore their parents' faces, grabbing at their noses and ears, or pull themselves to the edges of their laps to see the world beyond them. Then children start to crawl, but always within sight or earshot of their mothers or fathers.

In the second substage (from eleven to sixteen months), children begin to stand upright and eventually to walk. This allows them to explore territory farther and farther away from their mothers and fathers. Parents soon find that their children can climb to incredible heights and will roam unbelievable distances as they explore their worlds. Children need to be told yes at least twice as often as no during this stage; this supports their exploratory behavior. Parents should "kid-proof" their environment instead of restricting their children's movements, so they will develop safe, optimal exploratory behaviors.

The third substage (from sixteen months to two years) is marked by a rediscovery of mother and father, as more separate individuals, as children return from exploring the world. Children begin to realize their separateness and feel scared and vulnerable. They may shadow their mothers or fathers, not letting them out of sight. Also, a battle of wills begins when they start demanding their parents' immediate attention or presence. Angry outbursts and temper tantrums, too, mark this period, although these can begin earlier. Temper tantrums release frustration and tension from children's bodies and permit children to feel peaceful and calm again, ready to forgive and be forgiven. A reassuring hug, smile, or understanding words from their parent tells them they are still loved, and this is all that's necessary to prevent a developmental trauma. Most parents get caught up in these power struggles and sometimes find it hard to forgive and forget. Holding on to resentments can cause trauma, as children feel emotionally abandoned in the process.

The fourth substage (from two years to three years) requires children to learn to reconcile their intense longings for the bliss of oneness with an equally intense need for separateness and individual selfhood. This eventually precipitates the developmental crisis of psychological birth. These conflicting forces battling inside children can be resolved only through the experience of object constancy: the ability to see self and other as separate objects with both good and bad qualities. When children venture too far away and become afraid, or when they fall and bump an elbow or knee, they expect mother or father to be right there to provide comfort. When this happens, the injury is just an "owie," but if the parent fails to understand or provide comfort, a developmental trauma can occur.

Without the full development of "I'm okay, you're okay" object constancy, children see a parent as "good parent" when he or she is available, and as "bad parent" when he or she is not available. They essentially split the world into good and bad. Ideally, three-year-olds have developed enough object constancy to hold on to positive images of their mothers or fathers while away from them at preschool or while visiting friends. Children with object constancy may long for the presence of their parents, but they do not fantasize that their parents are bad or have abandoned them and no longer love them. Healthy three-year-olds have built up sufficient "good parent" and "good self" experiences that allow them to function separately from their parents. Children can even have angry or hateful thoughts toward their parents or themselves and not be overwhelmed by these feelings, if they have been able to bring their self-centered anger under control.

Reconciling good parent/bad parent splitting during the separation stage is essential for completing the psychological birth. In addition to solid object constancy, this reconciliation requires the presence of both a nurturing father and a nurturing mother to provide a buffer for the child when the other is not available. Sensitive, nurturing parents can help children differentiate themselves from their mothers and fathers, maleness from femaleness, and masculine from feminine without splitting.

Both parents must take an active role in the bonding and separation processes. At the time of the psychological birth, the role of both parents is to provide some nurturing support for children while setting limits to their exploration. At the same time, they provide nurturing support for each other while children experience internal conflict between wanting to maintain symbiosis with the parents and wanting to explore the world. If the father is absent either emotionally or physically during this "terrible twos" period, it's unlikely that the child will complete the psychological birth on schedule.

## WHEN THE PROCESSES BREAK DOWN

There are several places in the bonding and separation processes where things can break down. It's important that both parents have maximum skin-to-skin contact with their child immediately after birth, during the bonding process. This helps the father securely bond with the child, so that he can support the separation process when it begins. Children separated from their parents during the first twelve to twenty-four hours following birth miss the optimal time for bonding. Although it can and does occur later, it requires more effort for the parents to supply the necessary sensory contact and to repair any trauma.

The bonding process can also break down if the father or other close family member is not available to support the child during the first few months. Feeding the child during the night breaks up the mother's sleep and can leave her exhausted. If she's breastfeeding, she needs help with the housework during the day so she can sleep when the baby does. If she's bottle-feeding, she needs someone to occasionally take the night shift. The physical recovery from pregnancy and delivery requires deep sleep, which is difficult to get without outside help. When she doesn't get this sleep, the mother becomes exhausted and doesn't recognize the first flutterings of the baby's opening heart and cues indicating that he or she is awakening to the world around him or her. Everything becomes a blur, and the child can experience a developmental trauma.

Another critical factor in these two early stages is the degree to which the mother and father have completed their own bonding and separation processes. Most of us were raised by parents who did not complete their own essential developmental processes themselves. As a result, they were unable to provide us with the proper emotional support, information about who we are, and relational skills that we needed to complete this important work. That is why so many people still experience co-dependency.

Parents who haven't completed their own separation process may fear both closeness and separation. Their fear of closeness may create anxieties about being engulfed by their child and losing their own somewhat fragile sense of Self. On the other hand, a fear of abandonment may erupt when their child pulls away and refuses parental support during the separation process. Both of these things frequently happen between child and parent. The two conflicting sets of needs and fears cause parents to send out conflicting messages to their children about separation, often interfering with the completion of this normal developmental process.

Once parents have bonded with their child, it's important for both of them to be physically and emotionally present during the separation stage. Their presence and the support they provide during the first several years of a child's life are critical in making sure that the child doesn't get stuck in co-dependency. Our companion book to this one, *The Flight from Intimacy*, offers much more information about this critical developmental stage.[5]

## CASE EXAMPLE

Madeline came to me (Barry) complaining of a bizarre set of physical symptoms for which her physician could find no cause. She had an intense burning in her chest, a loss of hearing, dizziness, constipation, and skin rashes. She also reported having highly co-dependent, conflictual relationships. As she related her personal history, I learned that she had been physically and sexually abused as a child. Her mother had beaten her, and her father had raped her during a drunken episode and then left the family.

Madeline had believed that she was such a bad person that she had caused her father to leave. Her mother had actually told her that she was the reason her father had left. When I asked her about her birth, she related that, from what she had learned, her mother had suffered complications during delivery and almost died. Her mother saw her for the first time two weeks after Madeline's birth. She also learned that her father came to see his wife during this two-week period but didn't even look at his child. He was unable to face the possibility of his wife dying and his having to raise a child alone.

Madeline's lack of early bonding with either parent was part of what precipitated their physical and sexual abuse of her. People securely bonded with their children do not physically or sexually abuse them.

My work with her involved both bonding and separateness issues. Initially, we worked on bonding and building trust. Then I began to help her separate herself psychologically from me and then from her mother. At first, she was so identified with her mother that, when she looked in the mirror, she saw her mother, not herself. I asked her to list all the positive and negative ways she was like her mother and all the positive and negative ways she was *not* like her mother. In her first list, she listed mostly the positive ways she was like her mother ("We have the same smile") and a few negative ways ("We both hate ourselves"), but she could not think of one way she was different from her. Each time we met, I encouraged her to come up with at least one way she was different. Gradually, she began to see how she and her mother differed, and she built a positive, separate self-image. The more she was able to see herself as separate, the more her physical symptoms disappeared. Madeline will have to work hard to maintain object constancy, but she gained some valuable tools in therapy that will help her continue working to break her co-dependency in relationships.

## SUMMARY

Co-dependency and counter-dependency are part of a larger developmental struggle between oneness and separateness. Understanding this process is essential for seeing how the inability to become separate contributes to co-dependency issues. Our developmental approach emphasizes that, once you understand how co-dependency is created, you'll find it possible to break free of its trap.

# 5. The Causes of Co-dependency

Co-dependency is most commonly caused by traumatic bonding breaks at the time of birth and during the first six months of life. Newborns have nervous systems acutely sensitive to sounds, touch, and smells, and they are able to recognize their parents' voices, faces, and odors. They arrive already attuned to their parents' energy and become stressed when separated from their parents too frequently or for too long. Many parents, unfortunately, don't know this and may still be operating from antiquated beliefs about infants' needs and abilities.

Parents don't know, for example, that babies are happiest when carried on their mothers' bodies or otherwise kept very close to them during the co-dependent stage of development. Ignorance fosters a casual parental attitude about the importance of the mother-child relationship and the father's role during this period. The net result is that parents are often not emotionally and physically supportive during the period when their babies need them most.

Bonding takes place as parents care for their babies. During the first days, weeks, and months after birth, newborns go through many cycles of waking and sleeping, which are determined primarily by hunger, the need for comfort and nurturing, and the need to avoid discomfort. These cycles of waking and sleeping are regulated by babies' nervous systems and their need to relieve tension in their body. When they feel the first pangs of hunger, they begin making small noises and movements. As the internal tension grows, so do the noises and movements. Eventually babies' escalating tension reaches a point where they release a very clear cry indicating that they have a need. As soon as the parents feed or hold the baby or change the baby's diaper, the baby relaxes. The figure below illustrates the bonding cycle.

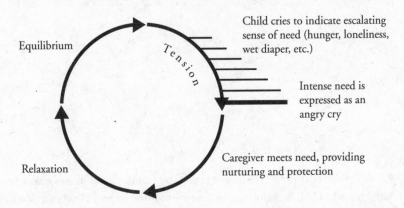

THE BONDING CYCLE: The child's needs are consistently met, and he or she stays connected to the caregiver.

Because newborns' nervous systems are still developing, their cries don't give the parents much information, so parents may have to try a series of trial-and-error interventions. As parents and baby become attuned to each other more deeply and the parents learn to recognize nuances in their child's cries, they meet the baby's needs more quickly and effectively. This helps the child relax more quickly and go into a deep state of equilibrium. Then the cycle starts all over again.

The sleeping and waking cycles can be very short in newborns, particularly if they are small — sometimes only two hours. This disrupts the parents' regular sleep cycles, so they often don't get the REM sleep they need in order to maintain their energy and sense of well-being. Outside support for both parents during this time is very important, as their bodies and psyches are experiencing deep hormonal and psychological changes. Outside support can prevent parents from becoming overly fatigued, cranky, and emotionally unavailable during this important period of development.

The most important aspect of bonding, however, is parents' ability to synchronize with their baby's emotional states. During periods of play and excitement, mother or father and child have unified experiences of elation and stimulation. In this process, the parents and the baby produce hormones that have an elevating effect, such as oxytocin, and neurotransmitters, such as dopamine. The parents learn how to help the baby reregulate his or her emotions through eye-to-eye, ear-to-ear, skin-to-skin, and brain-to-brain attunement. These experiences of biological synchrony between baby and parents or other adult caregivers are at the heart of the bonding process. Repeated rounds of exhilarating play and of comfort create a sense of safety for children, which helps them develop curiosity and the ability to trust.

One of the recently recognized causes of the shaken baby syndrome is angry or frustrated parents or caregivers who can't cope with their babies' persistent crying. Many newborns cry because they're releasing tension related to birth trauma and may actually be suffering from birth-caused dislocations of shoulders, necks, and hips. Dr. G. Gutmann, a German medical researcher specializing in the treatment of traumatic birth syndrome, discovered that over 80 percent of the infants he examined shortly after birth were suffering from an injury to the cervical spine.[1]

Parents have more difficulty becoming attuned to babies who have suffered traumatic births. They feel frustrated and incompetent when they are unable to provide comfort and relieve their children's pain. This often causes them to disengage from their children. Some parents may even perceive their children as disliking them because the parents are unable to comfort them at these times. All of this disturbs the process of emotional attunement and may cause a developmental trauma.

The concept of developmental trauma is a breakthrough in the field of mental health. This trauma happens when trusted adult caregivers don't emotionally attune themselves to infants and don't respond to their day-to-day needs for nurturing, protection, safety, and guidance in timely and appropriate ways. Children experience this loss of emotional attunement as an overwhelming emotional state, and as abandonment, which creates long-term changes in their bodies and brains and produces symptoms of post-traumatic stress.

The concept of developmental trauma challenges us to think more broadly about what is traumatic. Parents typically believe they are parenting their children the way everyone else does. More likely, they are parenting the way they were parented.

Developmental trauma is created in infants and children unconsciously and without malicious intent by adult caregivers unaware of children's emotional needs. These "ordinary" events, particularly ones occurring during birth and the first six months of life, form the foundation for children's mental health and also shape their lifelong development. Developmental trauma not only affects children's nervous systems but also reduces children's ability to form secure relationships as adults.

## CO-DEPENDENCY AND DEVELOPMENTAL TRAUMA

Trauma permanently imprints children's cellular memories and nervous systems. Children learn to respond in certain ways to specific cues and signals, which activates the adrenal stress response. If, for example, a mother slips away without saying good-bye when she leaves her son in the care of someone else, he may cry and fuss every time she leaves the room. This is a sign that he has been sensitized to her unannounced departures. Eventually, these kinds of experiences get hardwired into children's brains, bodies, and characters. Adult mental health is rooted in these early emotional and relational experiences. Common causes of developmental trauma include

- the inability of parents or adult caregivers to meet children's needs for nurturing, protection, safety, and emotional attunement;
- emotional coldness, unresponsiveness, or remoteness by mothers or other primary caregivers;
- persistent disregard of children's basic emotional needs for comfort, stimulation, and affection, particularly in times of stress;
- the inability of parents to help children reregulate their emotions in a timely manner;
- persistent disregard of children's need for physical touch, particularly skin-to-skin contact;
- repeated changes of primary caregivers that disrupt or prevent secure bonding;
- premature, repeated, and overly long periods of separation from mothers or other primary caregivers;

- undiagnosed and/or chronic or recurring painful illnesses such as colic or chronic ear infections;
- extended periods of crying when the parents do not provide comfort;
- betrayal by trusted caregivers in which the adults use children to meet their own needs for love, touch, emotional support, security, and protection;
- inconsistent or inadequate child care;
- chronic maternal depression or physical illness during children's first six months;
- premature birth and invasive life-saving medical interventions;
- prolonged physical separation from mothers at birth;
- maternal use of drugs and/or alcohol during gestation and nursing periods;
- invasive medical procedures such as ultrasound and amniocentesis during the gestational period; and
- drug-induced labor and birth.

Intergenerational factors are also primary causes of developmental trauma. Research on the neurobiology of attachment indicates that the early experiences of female infants with their mothers influence how they will respond to their own infants when they later become mothers. Relational trauma serves as the primary mechanism for transmitting intergenerational parenting styles and behaviors. It also influences mothers' ability to respond to children's needs for emotional attunement and relational synchrony.[2] If a woman experienced long periods of intense crying as an infant, for example, she is likely to be unresponsive to her own child during periods of prolonged crying and screaming. This intergenerational pattern of neglect can be difficult for adults to identify and treat, because the source of it is buried so deep in their psychobiological wiring.

Perhaps the most common cause of co-dependency is an intergenerational phenomenon known as the reversal process. Here parents and other caregiving adults unconsciously use children to meet their own needs. Rather than the adults caring for the children, the children take care of the adults. The adults discourage their children from developing their own interests and identity and encourage them to stay close and take care of them.

This "parentizing" process is particularly prevalent in parents and other adult caregivers who were abandoned or neglected as children. In this situation, it's common for parents to care for children until they are old enough to become self-sufficient, and then to expect them to begin caring for the parents. Children, sensing their parents' unstable condition, may decide that the only way to survive in this situation is to take care of their parents' needs and try to ignore their own needs. They believe if they do a good job of taking care of their parents' needs, then the parents may be available again to care for the children's needs. Parentizing is very common in oldest children.

Another version of reversal happens when a parent looks into the eyes of his or her newborn baby and sees him or her not as a separate human being but as extension of the parent. They project their own unfulfilled wishes and dreams on the child and expect him or her to become the successful doctor, lawyer, sports figure, musician, or other notable person the parent always wanted to be. As a result, the parent focuses only on the child as an object of his or her own unfulfilled dreams and ambitions, and programs the child to live these dreams in order to earn the parent's love. This is also known as conditional love.

Another way that parents engage in role reversal is by giving their children things that the parents wanted but didn't get. Parentized children also learn to perform and make their parents look good so that their parents will love them. The parents' focus is on meeting their own emotional needs rather than on meeting their children's needs.

Because so few adults are aware of parentizing and role reversals, many parents traumatize their children with these patterns. The reversal process is very difficult to identify and heal, because parentized children look like well-behaved and dutiful children to outside observers. However, the children almost always know when parents are engaging in reversals with them. Nonetheless, they often believe that if they don't sacrifice themselves for their parents, the parents will not or cannot take care of them and they might not survive. This co-dependent programming is rampant in a narcissistic culture such as the one that currently exists in the United States.

If the reversal process is not healed, it will be transferred into other adult relationships. If it's not healed there, it will show up when a couple has a family. If it's not healed at the family level, families will collectively imprint it on the functioning of organizations and even nation-states. Recognizing and healing the effects of this reversal process is essential to advance human evolution at all levels.

## THE BIOCHEMISTRY OF DEVELOPMENTAL TRAUMA

Children's biochemical states are determined by whether their social and emotional needs are being met. There are direct correlations between infant post-traumatic stress and child, adolescent, and adult stress disorders.[3] The most common cause of early relational stress is children's inability to regulate their emotions when adults are not available or able to soothe and comfort them. Frequent or sustained episodes of emotional and relational stress during the first six months of life can damage the long-term growth of parts of the brain that regulate emotions.[4]

Even events that seem inconsequential can trigger terrifying and painful emotional memories from the past that have been imprinted into the circuits of children's nervous systems.[5] Identifying and healing very early traumatic experiences involving the loss of connection to caring adults is difficult, because these memories are hardwired into the brain. In adults, it requires some "rewiring" of the brain to clear the blockage. Some of the new trauma reduction and elimination treatments are designed to do exactly this. We discuss some of these in the next section of this book.

When the body becomes flooded with stress hormones, this interferes with the brain's ability to think clearly. First, the brain uses its most sophisticated resources — logic, reason, and problem solving. If this fails, it goes to the next level of sophistication — fighting and fleeing. If neither of these is effective, the brain uses its most primitive response: freezing. In this moment, people are immobilized in a state of shock.

## CONSEQUENCES OF DEVELOPMENTAL TRAUMA

The term "developmental trauma" can sound abstract and may not truly convey the extent of pain that it involves. Here's a list of concrete behaviors that children and adults display as a result of early developmental trauma:[6]

* attachment problems: uncertainty about the reliability and predictability of the world, distrust and suspiciousness, social isolation, interpersonal difficulties, and difficulty becoming attuned to other people's emotional states and points of view

- biochemical disturbances: hypersensitivity to physical contact, analgesia, somatization of trauma in the physical body, increased health and medical problems, and hypervigilance to try to avoid being triggered into a traumatic reenactment
- affect or emotional dysregulation: easily aroused, high-intensity emotions; difficulty de-escalating emotions; difficulty describing feelings and internal experiences; a chronic and pervasive depressed mood or sense of emptiness or deadness; chronic suicidal preoccupation; and overinhibition or excessive expressions of anger
- dissociation: distinct alterations in states of consciousness, amnesia, being "spaced out," and depersonalization
- impulse-control problems: poor modulation of impulses, self-destructive behavior, aggressive behavior, sleep disturbances, eating disorders, substance abuse, oppositional behavior, and excessive compliance
- cognitive disturbances: difficulties in regulating attention, problems managing life situations, problems focusing on and completing tasks, difficulty planning and anticipating, learning difficulties, and problems with language development
- poor self-concept: a lack of a continuous and predictable sense of self, low self-esteem, exaggerated feelings of shame and guilt, generalized sense of being ineffective in dealing with one's environment, and belief in being permanently damaged by a trauma
- narcissistic disturbances: unwillingness to admit mistakes; need to be the center of attention; grandiose and inflated self-image; drug, alcohol, or food addictions; loss of connection to one's feelings; a lack of empathy; and a sense of entitlement to be treated specially by everybody

These problems fall along a continuum, from mild to severe. The critical point in this discussion is that "subtle and ordinary" trauma caused by ignorant and unconscious caregivers during the first six months of life is a major cause of adult co-dependency.

## BREAKS IN THE BONDING CYCLE

It's common now for very young children to be cared for by strangers who are not securely bonded with the child and who may not be interested in or even capable of synchronizing with them emotionally. When young children are separated from their parents for periods that are too frequent and/or too long for their young nervous systems to handle effectively, their nervous systems go into overwhelm and they experience a developmental trauma.

Figure 5.2 shows how children are traumatized when their parents are not able to become attuned to them energetically and meet their needs for nurturing, protection, and safety. They go into shock, collapse, and look as though they are falling asleep. We call this trauma reaction "falling into a black hole." In this deep place, they lose contact with the world around them and believe they will not survive.

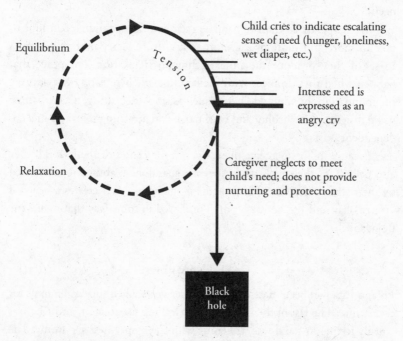

THE TRAUMA TRAP: The child's needs are not consistently met, and he or she loses connection to the caregiver.

The black hole stores memories of traumatic relational experiences involving abandonment, neglect, and abuse that children split off from their conscious awareness. Young children typically have only a few memories stored in their black holes, but they may accumulate a very complex and compact system of compartmentalized traumatic memories as they grow older.

After numerous episodes of falling into the black hole, children learn coping mechanisms that help them slow the fall or even avoid it. They find substitutes for the missing nurturing, love, and emotional support to help them regulate their emotional states. Very small babies, for example, learn to suck their thumbs or fists or use pacifiers and soft blankets as substitutes for the physical comfort and emotional synchronization they need from their mothers or caregivers. Oral substitutes developed during the co-dependent stage of development help soothe traumatized and emotionally stressed children. Because the relational component is missing, however, the substitute never completely satisfies the deep yearning for personal and emotional connections.

In a desperate attempt to regulate their emotions, children continue to take in more and more of the mother substitute or try other substitutes to see if they produce the inner feelings of relaxation and peace that happen when they connect with their mothers. These early behaviors lay the foundation for adult addictions such as smoking, eating, masturbating; using drugs such as alcohol and marijuana; and attaching to others in a co-dependent way.

Because infants perceive themselves as the center of their world, they also believe it's their fault when they are abandoned, abused, or neglected by their adult caregivers. This judgment against the Self creates a belief of "you're okay and I'm not okay" or "I'm flawed in some way that makes me unlovable."

## CASE EXAMPLE

Ed and Rita had been married twenty-three years when they came to us for counseling. The last of their children was leaving home soon, and Rita was already feeling lost and was struggling with the empty-nest syndrome. The primary complaint about the relationship came from Rita, who wanted more intimacy with Ed.

Rita, the oldest of five children, had made a career out of taking care of others. Her mother had grown increasingly frail with the birth of each child and had come to depend on Rita to help her. Rita married Ed at the age of nineteen and had worked to support the two of them while he finished his college education. The first of their three children arrived when she was twenty-two. After the birth of their third child, she found herself busier than she had ever been with her routine of cleaning, shopping, doing laundry, and attending the children's school activities. Because she was devoted to the children and their interests and devoted to supporting Ed in his corporate career, she had not developed interests of her own or personal relationships. Her home and family had been her profession.

Ed had been involved very little with his family. His business commitments required him to travel frequently and to work long hours. He had grown up as an only child in an emotionally distant family with parents who had not married until their late thirties. Ed learned early in life to play quietly and entertain himself. While he knew his parents loved him, he never felt close to either of them.

In working with Ed and Rita, it became obvious that Rita had been parentized and was a people-pleaser and co-dependent. Ed, on the other hand, was counter-dependent. Rita had always perceived him as a warm and loving partner who expressed his devotion by providing well for the family. She tended not to see his detachment or his need for isolation, which was easy for her to overlook with her great dedication to the children and her home. Neither partner recognized that they had suffered from developmental trauma as children and lacked vital skills for shared intimacy, until they found themselves living without children.

We were able to help them recognize their very different backgrounds and patterns of relationship and how these were contributing to their intimacy issues. We also helped them understand how the presence of the children had distracted them and camouflaged their problems, and why they had been able to make their relationship work as long as it had. With the children gone, Rita was coming face-to-face with not only her co-dependency but also the reversal that had robbed her of her childhood.

Rita's newly revealed co-dependency was also creating some difficulty for Ed, who was experiencing Rita's demand for more intimacy as an invasion of his psychological space. He had become uncomfortable with Rita's desire for a closer relationship and wanted her to find a job or something else to keep her occupied. He really was not eager to form a closer relationship with her.

This left Rita with a number of options. She could persist in trying to pull Ed closer. She could explore her need for a closer relationship by going to work or developing personal friendships. Or she could even explore whether she wanted to stay in her relationship with Ed. This is where therapy with Ed and Rita stopped, as Rita explored her options.

## SUMMARY

Relationships between one co-dependent and one counter-dependent partner are very common. A person who has emotionally distant parents often marries a person who is more dependent and emotionally needy, while a person with overly dependent or clinging parents seeks out a mate who is more detached. This attraction of opposites is often an attempt to heal unresolved developmental trauma involving bonding and separation. Relationships between such opposites, however, often have more conflict, because these early issues recycle frequently and press for completion. At the core of recurring relational conflict is usually a reenactment of developmental trauma involving one or both parents. It's useful to frame such a conflict as an opportunity for growth rather than as something bad or dysfunctional.

# Part 2
# THE RECOVERY PROCESS

# 6. The Elements of Recovery

The theme of this part of the book is that *full recovery from co-dependency is possible*. The resources necessary for recovery are a willingness to change, the courage to look at your life in new ways and learn new skills that help you clear away early trauma, and a willingness to ask for help from others. The resources we've used that are the most effective in recovering from co-dependency are

- your willingness and ability to work on yourself alone, as well as with your partner, your therapist, or your support group;
- your ability to create committed, conscious, and cooperative relationships to jointly work on co-dependency and counter-dependency issues;
- your work with a therapist who understands co-dependency, who has worked through it personally, and who knows how to treat it; and
- your participation in groups, classes, and workshops where you can get the support of others who are serious about healing their trauma and changing their co-dependency patterns.

Your willingness to work on yourself is the most critical element. It's easy for people with co-dependency issues to give the responsibility for their healing over to someone else — someone they believe knows more than they do. Partners, therapists, and support groups can inadvertently become enablers for those who are working on themselves.

Our twelve-step process of recovery is more hopeful and more effective than the traditional twelve-step processes many people use to address addictions such as alcohol, eating, smoking, and drugs. We describe the most powerful healing element in the first step: working on yourself.

## WORKING ON YOURSELF

This book provides many self-inventory quizzes and awareness activities that you can do by yourself. They can help you learn more about yourself and your co-dependent behaviors.

Completing written exercises is one common way of working on yourself. This includes filling out questionnaires or inventories that help you identify your problems more clearly. Keeping a journal or diary can also be a big help in locating patterns over time. Art, dance, and other expressive therapy methods are also very helpful.

There are other activities as well that can help you build stronger self-esteem. One of these is breath work, which helps clear negative patterns of disease and tension lodged in the body. More information on how to use this tool is given at the end of chapter 14. Another powerful individual tool is mirror work. Learning to love yourself involves being able to sit in front of a mirror and say loving things to yourself. More information on this tool is given in chapter 15. Both of these tools can be combined with affirmations, which are highly positive self-statements that can be written down or repeated verbally. Affirmations are recognized as an effective way to change self-limiting beliefs and perceptions, which are very common among co-dependents.

Each chapter in this part of the book describes one of the steps of recovery and offers specific tools for working that step through. We've divided the tools into categories. Some are for use in committed relationships, some are for your use as a client in therapy, others are for use in support groups, and some are for you to use while working on yourself. The majority of the tools are most effective for working on yourself or with a partner.

## CHOOSING A PSYCHOTHERAPIST WHO UNDERSTANDS

Psychotherapy is an important healing resource in the recovery process. People with co-dependent patterns may find themselves repeating behaviors over and over again and may finally seek therapy for help in identifying their persistent self-defeating patterns. They realize that they can't see the forest for the trees and need someone more objective to help them put their puzzling behavior in a meaningful context.

The most important thing is finding the right therapist. Look for someone who has done his or her own personal work. Not all therapists have broken free of their own co-dependent patterns. If they haven't cleared them away, there is a high probability that they will re-create a co-dependent relationship with you. Ask your therapist about his or her co-dependent patterns, addictions, and early traumas to see how he or she has dealt with them. If you get an answer like, "That's not really relevant for my work with you," or some vague reply, you may want to look for another therapist. Remember that 98 percent of the population, including therapists, have co-dependency issues.

Therapists who are consciously working to overcome their own co-dependent tendencies can be valuable role models as well as a source of practical help in breaking free of co-dependency. Such therapists will be interested in helping you expand your view of yourself and your behavior and in teaching you to see your own expanded possibilities. They will be careful not to rescue you, and they will help you assume more and more responsibility for your life.

## SUPPORT GROUPS, CLASSES, AND WORKSHOPS

When you are in the process of breaking free of the co-dependency trap, you might assume that you are the only one with the kinds of problems you have. Support groups whose members are struggling with problems similar to yours can provide a broader perspective for your struggles and perhaps offer you a range of possibilities from which to choose. Many support groups in the addictions field are based primarily on the Alcoholics Anonymous twelve-step model. Groups such as these are often a place to begin if you're not sure how to spot your co-dependency patterns.

There also are support groups offered by Adult Children of Alcoholics, Al-Anon, and Co-Dependents Anonymous. Co-Dependents Anonymous groups are usually run informally. People do not have to give their last names or tell where they work. They don't have to say anything at all if they don't want to. And they don't have to pay to attend, except perhaps for a donation to cover coffee and room rentals. No one has to sign up, register, or answer questions. All they need to do is attend; by their presence at the meeting they acknowledge that they have co-dependency issues.

Meeting formats vary with each group. Some have no leader, and anyone can talk or discuss feelings and problems. Others have a designated leader who may share information about a personal problem and relate it to one of the program's steps. Sometimes groups select a theme related to one of the steps and invite anyone who wishes to personally comment on it to do so. Sometimes individuals interested in going further with the theme are encouraged to do homework on it. An informal network often develops among members so they can call each other when they need support.

Also look for courses and workshops on co-dependency offered by churches, schools, mental health groups, and civic organizations, which often sponsor very reasonably priced classes and provide a lot of information on the nature of the problem. Their most useful aspect is that they provide opportunities to meet others who are struggling with co-dependency.

## THE THREE C'S: COMMITTED, CONSCIOUS, AND COOPERATIVE RELATIONSHIPS

Another resource for breaking free of the co-dependency trap, and perhaps the one most overlooked, is intimate relationships with a high degree of commitment, consciousness, and cooperation. These relationships may come in many forms and may be composed of best friends, business partners, siblings, parents and children, or the two partners in a couple.

"Commitment" can be defined in many ways. For our purposes, the most common aspects of commitment include the willingness of both individuals to stay with the relationship and not run away when conflict emerges, their willingness to change, and their willingness to be emotionally honest.

"Consciousness" refers to the degree to which people are aware of their behavior and understand what motivates it. "Cooperative" means a willingness to help each other during the healing process. Many co-dependent relationships are competitive rather than cooperative in nature. In a cooperative relationship, people freely teach and learn from each other instead of withholding information or using it to manipulate and control the other.

A conscious, committed relationship can provide a strong therapeutic context for people who wish to break free of the co-dependency trap. It provides an arena where relationship trauma can be healed, old patterns broken, and new patterns developed. This is love and intimacy at its highest and best.

Most people typically define intimacy as only those warm, close, and maybe sexual times that are blissful and serene. We have expanded the definition of intimacy to include the times when partners are struggling to break out of co-dependency patterns and are right there supporting and loving each other unconditionally when they feel vulnerable, sad, hurt, angry, or hopeless. This is the kind of intimacy that heals old wounds and "wholes" the spirit. Many people are only now discovering who they really are and who their partners of many years really are. This can be an exciting and sometimes scary adventure that opens both partners to the depths of human love and intimacy.

No therapist or support group can provide enough of the bonding required to break free of co-dependency. In committed relationships of any kind, partners learn how to bond with each other and then separate in a straight, clean, and healthy way. This is how the psychological birth is finally completed.

## A NEW TWELVE-STEP PROGRAM
## FOR RECOVERING FROM CO-DEPENDENCY

Recovering from co-dependency is a process with predictable steps. While the order of these steps may be different for each individual, we suggest reviewing and reflecting on each step. Some people may find they need to do more in-depth work on some of the steps. For example, the first step, which involves recognizing the extent of the co-dependency patterns in your relationships, can take considerable time and effort. What makes it so difficult is that co-dependency may be so pervasive in your close relationships that you may not recognize it as dysfunctional behavior. As a friend of ours said when we described a co-dependency pattern, "What's wrong with that?

Everybody acts that way." Other steps also can require intensive work. Learning to feel your feelings more fully and to express your feelings in effective ways, for example, usually requires some focused work.

Here are the twelve steps that we recommend.

1. *Recognize co-dependent patterns.* There are many ways to avoid recognizing co-dependency in yourself. Experiencing co-dependency can be like being asleep: you dream that things are a certain way, and even if they aren't that way, you keep dreaming they are. Because almost everything around you has co-dependent overtones, you may not be aware that there is a better way to live.

   For you, denial may have been a safety mechanism you learned in order to survive. If you really saw or talked about what was happening in the family in which you grew up, you might not have survived childhood. You may have been taught not to notice what was happening to you and to other people in your family in order to maintain the appearance that yours was "one big happy family." Of all the things you were taught to ignore, the denial of your own feelings has the most devastating effects on you and your relationships. Co-dependency is a feeling disorder.

2. *Understand the causes of the problem.* There is much disagreement in the literature about the actual causes of co-dependency. Some claim it's the result of a genetic weakness, while others claim it comes from contact with alcoholics or an alcoholic family. Our thesis is that it's caused by developmental trauma during the first six months of life, and that this prevents full bonding. It is also a systemic problem created by growing up in a dysfunctional family and co-dependent society.

3. *Unravel co-dependent relationships.* Once you understand that co-dependency is caused by trauma and incomplete relationship processes, it is possible to recognize these recycling in your present relationships. In co-dependent relationships, your psychological birth is always pressing for completion. Once you recognize what is not complete, you can, with additional support and new skills, complete your bonding and consciously finish the separation process.

4. *Reclaim your projections.* When you attempt to become separate by defining others as wrong or bad, you usually use projection as a

coping mechanism. You are able to see in other people the parts of yourself that you don't like — anger, the tendency to be controlling, and self-centeredness — and you may pass judgment on, or blame, people with these behaviors. You may also twist reality so that you can be "right" or "good" and justify your behavior by defining others as "wrong" or "bad." Reclaiming these projected parts of yourself often requires loving confrontation and the committed support of others — a group, family members, friends, partners, a spouse, or a therapist. Projections are building blocks in the wall of denial. The blocks tend to fall away slowly, until your wall of denial falls and you can see and accept all of who you are.

5. *Eliminate self-hate.* If you haven't become separate from your mother or your family, and you've tried to separate by defining her or them as wrong or bad, you've probably defined yourself as wrong or bad as well. If you've denied having these negative feelings, they may still control your life. It's necessary to uncover, claim, and transform these negative perceptions. They're based on illusions and are the result of incomplete separation. By understanding that these projections are a source of low self-esteem, you can correct them.

6. *Eliminate power plays and manipulation.* Lacking the full natural power that comes from completing the psychological birth, you are likely to use power plays and manipulation to get what you want. The drama triangle (the rescuer, persecutor, and victim game) is a common way to manipulate others while remaining passive (for a discussion of the drama triangle, see chapter 12). As you find more effective ways to get people to cooperate with you, your need to control others will diminish.

7. *Ask for what you want.* One of the simplest, most straightforward ways to get what you want is to ask for it directly in such a way that people who have it to give are delighted to give it to you. Most people don't ask directly. For example, a person who has plans to go out may say to his or her partner, "I might be needing the car later," and then feel disappointed when the other person doesn't read his or her mind. Or someone might say, without negotiating, "I'm taking the car tonight!" so that the other person gets angry and says, "No!"

8. *Learn to feel again.* Children raised in dysfunctional families learn very early to deny their feelings and perceptions about what is happening in their families. One of the most frequently denied feelings is anger, even though people in co-dependent relationships feel angry much of the time. Anger must be "justified" before they can safely express it. Someone must be blamed or made the scapegoat for all the family's unhappiness and problems. Children often are used in this way. As an adult, you must learn to recognize and express the feelings you learned to deny in order to survive your childhood. People *cannot* recover from co-dependency without reclaiming their feelings.

9. *Heal your inner child.* If you grew up in a co-dependent family, you were taught to focus on what others wanted and needed rather than on what you wanted and needed. You were forced to create a False Self in order to please others and to hide your True Self, including your innocent, vulnerable inner child. Your inner child suffered from developmental traumas unconsciously inflicted by supposedly caring, loving people. They may have laughed at you, teased you, not respected or listened to you, physically beat you, or ignored your most important needs. To keep from feeling hurt, it may have been necessary to hide your traumas from the outside world. In the process, you also may have hidden them from yourself. Recovery involves reconnecting with and healing your inner child.

10. *Define your own boundaries.* Everyone has a psychological space or territory that belongs to him or her alone. It consists of one's thoughts, feelings, behaviors, and body. Most people who come from co-dependent families had their psychological space violated so often as children that they are no longer even aware when it happens now. Most people with co-dependency issues have very little sense of their personal boundaries and almost no skills in defining and protecting themselves when they are violated. It's essential to learn how to define and protect your boundaries in effective ways if you wish to break your co-dependency patterns.

11. *Learn to be intimate.* Those with co-dependency issues often both fear and desire intimacy. The fear is often that they will be abandoned, controlled, hurt, engulfed, or trampled by those with whom

they are intimate. Breaking co-dependency requires finding others with whom to safely bond. People often need reparenting experiences with a therapist or another supportive adult who can supply the missing information, touch, nurturing support, and unconditional love necessary for completing the bonding stage and supporting the psychological birth.

12. *Learn new forms of relationship*. Most people who have lived with co-dependency patterns have little or no awareness that they are missing the richness of life. They may be vaguely aware that "there has to be more to life than this," which allows them to begin taking risks to change. What replaces co-dependency is interdependency, where two or more people are autonomous enough to be able to cocreate life together and are able to support the highest good in each other.

## CASE EXAMPLE

Bill and Sara had been married for about eight years when Sara began to feel the need for change. She had been a people-pleaser all her life and did an excellent job of taking care of Bill's needs. In fact, her total sense of worth as a person depended on taking care of Bill. She had come from an alcoholic family and had watched both her mother and her father die from alcohol-related illnesses. She had been raised by an aunt and uncle who also drank heavily. Bill was naturally very surprised when Sara announced to him one day how unhappy she was, because he had thought only he was unhappy. They had been having more and more fights, because Bill felt controlled by Sara's caretaking. His mother had also been a caretaker who controlled him and invaded his space.

Bill felt that he couldn't do anything successfully on his own. His mother had always undermined his self-esteem by taking over if he made a mistake. He had started his own business several years earlier, and he kept the financial aspects of it private, fearing that Sara might criticize how he managed it. The business did not fully provide Bill's share of their joint expenses, so Sara used her salary to cover the shortages. With Bill withholding information on the business, Sara distrusted him even more.

Things came to a head when Sara announced that she didn't want to have sex with Bill anymore. She had lost her sexual feelings early in the marriage but had continued to have sex with him because she thought this was what good wives should do. They had tried couples therapy briefly, but Bill had felt threatened by the therapist. Sara had also tried group therapy for co-dependency but found it mostly educational. Both had read the popular literature in an attempt to sort out what was wrong with their relationship.

Sara made an appointment to see me (Barry) because, she said, she wanted a male therapist to help her better understand men. She readily admitted that she was very co-dependent and needed to know how to break her co-dependency. I took a cognitive approach with her at first, explaining the causes of her co-dependency and showing her where she seemed stuck. She had decided to separate from Bill for a while to sort out the problems. I suggested that, although she would be getting her own place, the best way to work on breaking co-dependency would be with couples therapy. She agreed to ask Bill if he would be willing to come with her for three sessions to see if it might work.

Both of them showed up at the next session to work with Janae and me. Bill seemed scared and resistant at first. By the end of the session, however, he began to see how therapy could help. Both of them committed to working together on their co-dependency. Sara had complained about Bill's intrusion into her space, so we helped Sara set boundaries and negotiate an agreement with Bill that he would not come to visit her without calling first. She could decide whether she wanted to see him. This was the first actual personal boundary she had ever set in their relationship, and we both impressed on Bill the importance of his keeping the agreement in order to build trust.

As homework, Sara agreed to make a list of her wants and needs and to come prepared to ask Bill for these things at our next session. She also agreed to go talk to her aunt and uncle and get as much information as she could about her mother, who had died when Sara was ten, and about her father, who had died when she was seventeen.

As Sara and Bill entered our office for their next session, we could see something had changed. Sara was animated and jovial, while Bill seemed much more relaxed. Sara quickly announced that she had experienced some major breakthroughs. She had recently visited her aunt and uncle. While she was asking them questions about her childhood, her uncle had blown up and pounded his fist on the table. She had started to cry, and suddenly all the sadness and anger she had been holding in for so long had come pouring out. She was able to tell her aunt and uncle what it was really like for her growing up, and though they were shocked, they listened intently as she poured out her feelings.

That night she had gone home and, for the first time, had written out a long list of things that she wanted or needed from Bill. She arrived ready to ask Bill for them in a clear way, knowing that she deserved them. She reported having renewed energy and lots of insights.

Bill also had some breakthroughs of his own. For the first time, he had recognized how controlling and invasive his mother had been. More important, he had recognized that he had been projecting his mother onto Sara. He announced that he was going to ask his brother, an accountant, to help him get his books in order and then share the information with Sara so she could support him in his business. They also announced that they were going to take a co-dependency class at a local church so they could work together in breaking their co-dependent patterns.

Bill expressed his fear of losing Sara. He asked her how long it was going to take until she would have sex with him again. She looked right at him in a loving way and said, "As long as it takes me to clear away my blocks so I will *want* to have sex with you again. I won't do it out of guilt or obligation anymore. The more you cooperate, and the more I find out I can trust you to keep your agreements, the shorter the time it will take. I love you and I want to work this out with you." Bill breathed a sigh of relief and agreed to work with her to do his part in building trust.

It seemed appropriate at that point in the session to talk to them about surrender. I said, "The core issue for both of you is surrender, which has a masculine and a feminine form. Bill, you need Sara to help you develop the feminine form, which is the willingness to receive without resistance. This may be very difficult, particularly when you are projecting your mother onto Sara. Sara, your issue is learning the masculine form, which is the willingness to take charge of your life without guilt." Sara quickly announced, "You know, I haven't felt guilty since I talked to my aunt and uncle. I feel free from it now, and I hope it doesn't come back."

Sara and Bill have a good chance of breaking free of the co-dependency trap if they continue to work together on their interlocking patterns. Their committed relationship is an ideal place to do much of the healing they need to do. Couples therapy will also help them learn new skills and tools. Their class on co-dependency will help them see they aren't alone in their struggle and will give them a safe place to discuss their relationship. Their therapy and reading materials are providing support and skills for working on themselves. The time during which they are living apart can provide much-needed personal space for developing their independence and finding effective ways to identify their co-dependency patterns and work on themselves. This will help them become stronger, more separate individuals with higher self-esteem who can weather the stormy seas ahead as they break free of their co-dependency.

## SUMMARY

Individuals in a relationship that has not yet reached the interdependent stage of mutual cooperation and commitment may find that it takes longer to make progress. Even with breakthroughs, such as the one described in the case example, it requires a lot of steady and disciplined work to break free of co-dependent relationship patterns. When you have a committed, cooperative relationship in which both of you are working on breaking free of the co-dependency trap, it can still take anywhere from two to five years of work to get beyond your major co-dependency patterns.

# 7. Facing Your Problem

As with any pattern of co-dependent behavior, the severity of the symptoms can range from very subtle to glaringly obvious. In co-dependent relationships that are basically harmonious, the symptoms can be subtle. They can be simple things such as which person drives, who speaks first, who manages the money, and how parenting responsibilities are shared. These behaviors, symptoms of the rigid cultural roles of a dominator system, are more difficult to identify because they are so unconscious. Recognizing and changing these behaviors requires that you closely examine your daily interactions with your partner. Reversing roles for a while in a specific task, such as cleaning the kitchen or servicing the cars, is a useful way to create both awareness and new patterns. After a period of reversing roles, you may then want to negotiate a specific behavior when it arises. For example, as you both head to the garage, one person might say, "Will you drive?" or "I'd be glad to drive."

In relationships involving psychological or verbal abuse, the symptoms are more obvious. People engaged in abusive relationships are often long-term victims. They may suffer from years of neglect, abandonment, parentizing, humiliation, and reversals because they fear rejection or fear for their lives. In such instances, their denial is a primary way to keep from experiencing their pain and suffering.

## THE ROOTS OF DENIAL

Denial is a defense mechanism for avoiding unpleasant or painful things such as shame and the fear of loss or abandonment. Denial allows you to avoid seeing and feeling what's really going on both outside and inside you. Denial is an especially useful tool for small children who find themselves in the midst of rejection, chaos, violence, drunkenness, abuse, neglect, or abandonment. Denial can make the pain and fear go away, at least for a while. The purpose of denial is self-protection and survival.

In co-dependent families, denial also prevents conflict. If people spoke the truth, confrontations would be inevitable. This might cause explosive changes in an already fragile family system. As a result, families may believe that denial is the only way to preserve the co-dependent family structure. Members often have neither the awareness to see the problem nor the skills to work it through. They learn not to rock the boat, even if they must deny their own needs and develop a False Self to display to the world.

You may have developed a False Self because the person you really were simply wasn't acceptable to the adults around you. When, as a child, you innocently spoke some truth and found yourself being punished, you soon learned to be quiet or to say only what was expected. Through trial and error you discovered the unspoken rules about what was permissible. You learned to discount the unspoken messages and base your behavior on what kept the peace.

### Discounting and Counting

Discounting is a tool that parents and families use to make sure that children and others in the family system ignore their internal world, their needs, wants, feelings, ideas, and abilities, and individuals can use it on themselves too. It entails either undervaluing or overvaluing yourself or others and can also involve selectively forgetting important information. Ultimately, it involves either discounting yourself, discounting others, or discounting a situation.

Counting is the opposite. It entails supporting your own needs, wants, feelings, ideas, and abilities, as well as those of others. It allows you to be responsible for how you respond to people. This means that other people don't "make" you feel anything, and that you determine how you feel and respond to what others do and to situations that you encounter.

The following chart lists some common forms of discounting and counting:

|  | *Discounting* | *Counting* |
|---|---|---|
| *Other* | • Interrupting<br>• Using sarcasm and fantasy<br>• Not looking at someone who is speaking to you<br>• Not giving reasons for actions | • Listening<br>• Talking straight<br>• Looking directly at people<br>• Saying, "This is why I did _____." |
| *Self* | • Accepting what others say without question<br>• Losing or breaking things and destroying property | • Asking yourself, "What do I think about this?"<br>• Valuing, appreciating, and being responsible for property |
| *Situation* | • Forgetting to do things<br>• Giving up; blaming<br>• Believing the problem will go away | • Keeping agreements<br>• Looking for solutions<br>• Looking at the facts |

## "For Your Own Good"

Having to repress your feelings, thoughts, and dreams, and suppress the fragile parts of the person you were becoming, is a form of developmental trauma that well-meaning adults inflict during early childhood. Many of the messages and forms of discipline that taught you to deny your real self were given by parents and other authority figures who believed they did it "for your own good." As a child you probably found it hard to believe that you needed harsh punishment, criticism, humiliation, shame, ridicule, and neglect. But because you regarded your parents and teachers as intelligent, all-knowing protectors, you accepted their judgment. You believed them when they said it was good for you, so you felt you must have deserved it.

This form of parenting, which supports the denial mechanism in codependent families, uses the vicious cycle of cruelty.[1] This phenomenon involves a pattern in which the devastating effects of cruelty are passed on from one person to another as a way of getting revenge. Examples of this are bullying and child abuse. Children who are bullied and abused almost always grow up to become bullies and abusers. Those who pass on the cruelty to someone weaker are attempting to release the feelings of anger and rage they were unable to express when they were being cruelly victimized themselves. Adolf Hitler is an example of an abused child who used the vicious cycle of cruelty to an extreme degree. His father beat and abused him while also indoctrinating him in the "evilness" of the Jews. This helped set the stage for his hatred of Jews and his need for revenge as an adult.[2]

It's important for you to recognize the "for your own good" incidents in your childhood and see them as acts of vicious cruelty unintentionally inflicted by well-meaning people who were unconsciously acting out their unhealed experiences of trauma while giving you false information. But it's also important to remember that your unconscious parents did the best they could with what skills and awareness they had. This point is illustrated by the fact that many people make oaths as children that they will never treat their children the way they were treated. Yet, in disciplining their own children, they are shocked to find themselves employing the same punishments and frequently even the same words used to punish them as children.

### Dishonesty: A Form of Denial

Dishonesty is another mechanism co-dependent families use to enforce dysfunctional behaviors. A lack of honesty in parent-child interactions undermines children's ability to trust both themselves and others. This causes them to distrust their inner world of self-experience by complying with the external world's unfair expectations and believing its false messages. Eventually children's realities begin to split in two, and they must choose between them. Because the external world has more power and authority, and because children have a strong need for bonding and affection, they will almost always choose the external reality. At this point, they must do something with their feelings and internal experiences. Shutting them down by denying them is the most common reaction. If parents, family, and friends were also forced to make the same choice when they were children, they almost always demand this type of behavior in the next generation of children.

This split allows children to discount themselves or the situation during a crisis. In a typical discounting response, they might

- minimize the situation ("It's no big deal");

- pretend something isn't happening ("This can't be happening; I must be crazy");
- repress their feelings ("I don't really care");
- avoid their feelings by sleeping, obsessing, working more, or engaging in other compulsive behaviors ("I'm not aware of anything"); or
- numb themselves with drugs, alcohol, food, or other addictive substances ("Give me something to help the pain go away").

## *Self-dishonesty: Another Form of Denial*

Separating yourself from your feelings and pretending to feel something you do not is a form of lying to yourself. Lying to yourself sets the stage for lying to others. In a family where all members have been trained in self-deception, you can expect wholesale lying. The results are dishonest relationships and family secrets. Family secrets alone can keep you stuck in your development process.

Nothing can make you feel crazy quicker than being lied to. Each of us has a deep place inside ourselves that recognizes truth. When our brains receive information that does not match our inner truths or experiences, we suffer from a "short circuit" that literally makes us feel crazy. In such instances of cognitive dissonance, we require a great deal of self-confidence in order to trust our internal knowledge more than the external reality of our parents or other authority figures. Most children do not have a sufficient reservoir of self-confidence or life experiences to defend themselves against denial-based realities. As a result, most children experience life as chaotic and crazy.

## *The Happy-Family Syndrome*

Dishonest people eventually must lie to the world in order to maintain the lie within themselves and within their family systems. Families in which there is bullying, alcoholism, sexual abuse, or violence have rigid rules about not telling what really goes on at home. Members are frequently threatened with additional abuse or violence if they tell family secrets, and they learn to put up a good front despite the chaos at home. Children learn to live a lie that further extends their crazy-making experiences. While living this lie, family members are somewhat aware of the discrepancy between what really happens and what everyone pretends is happening. In the larger community, such families may be perceived as stable and upstanding.

A second form of the happy-family syndrome entails living a fantasy. This form usually afflicts an individual and may or may not affect others in the family. Individuals afflicted with the happy-family fantasy are extremely difficult to treat in therapy. They may seek help because of some life crisis, like a divorce or a job loss. These people typically recall their childhood as almost idyllic. They describe the family and their childhood experiences in such glowing terms that it begins to sound like a television series, such as *The Brady Bunch* or *The Cosby Show*. Such descriptions indicate that people have created fantasy-world memories to help them deny the dissonance between their internal feelings and external experiences.

### Denial in Relationships

A child who is inadequately bonded or who has been abandoned, abused, or neglected often moves through life looking for people who will provide the nurturing, security, and affection he or she didn't receive. This need makes the child dream that some kindly person — perhaps a teacher, a minister, a handsome "prince," or a grandparent substitute — will appear. When such a person does appear, the child projects the needed nurturing-parent qualities onto him or her, whether or not this person is capable of playing the role. This phenomenon, also known as infatuation or idealization, serves a valuable psychological function for dreamers fantasizing that their long-unfulfilled needs will finally be met. The dreaming phenomenon also keeps the dreamer disconnected from the old feelings of being poorly bonded, abandoned, abused, or neglected. The dreaming or idealization may go on for many years in spite of information and experiences that totally refute the dream.

An example of this kind of dreaming is a woman seeking a warm and affectionate husband. During their courtship her man is attentive and caring, and she believes her dreams have come true. She continues to dream he is warm and attentive even after it becomes obvious that he is alcoholic and abusive. Her dreams support her through the rough times when he stays out all night, comes home drunk, or hits her. She is able to make excuses that explain his "uncharacteristic" behavior, so that her "dream come true" can continue.

This kind of dreaming and denial in relationships keeps dreamers from actually meeting their needs, and it creates a new reservoir of repressed feelings. It can also support co-dependent behaviors in both individuals and families, sometimes permitting life-threatening situations, such as battering, to develop. In these situations, the dreamer may continue to project positive qualities onto the partner until a crisis finally breaks the dream, forcing the dreamer to finally see what's happening.

## BREAKING THROUGH DENIAL

It's important to remember that the various forms of denial are part of a cultural pattern that has been handed down from generation to generation. Well-meaning parents and other adults who are unaware of what children really need pass on the denial patterns they inherited. If you find yourself participating in this process, do not judge yourself. You too are doing the best you can, and you'll be able to do better now that you know there's a better way.

In order to break the pattern of denial, you must complete several important tasks. All of them are designed to help you find your real self — your real feelings, needs, wants, ideas, thoughts, and dreams. These tasks include

- learning to recognize and refute discounts;
- learning to give "counts";
- listening reflectively;
- asking for and receiving feedback on how others see you;
- discovering holes in your awareness;
- accepting your inner world of experience as valuable;
- recognizing the dream or vision you have of your relationship and checking it against reality;
- asking your partner what his or her dream or vision is for your relationship and checking it against your own; and
- determining if you are addicted to a person; to a substance, such as chocolate, tobacco, or coffee; or an activity, such as overeating, by living without it for five straight days without major discomfort.

## TOOLS FOR FACING YOUR PROBLEM

We've successfully used each of the tools described in the following pages to break through denial in our own relationship, and we've shared them with our clients. Breaking through denial can be a real challenge, because telling ourselves the truth often stirs up feelings of shame. And telling the truth to those closest to us stirs up our fears of being abandoned. While each tool is effective in its own right, using all of them will give you the best results.

### Tools for Working on Yourself

- Keep a journal that you use daily. Write down what you've experienced in your interactions with people during the day. Record your feelings, reactions, and dreams.
- Learn to recognize and honor a signal in your body that tells you when you hear dishonesty in either yourself or others. You may experience it as a tightening of a muscle, as a knot in your stomach, or a pain in your head. When this signal comes, be ready to acknowledge it and spend some time reflecting on the situation to discover the specific untruth.

### Tools for Therapy

Look for a therapist who has broken free of his or her own co-dependency issues, as such a person can be a valuable ally for you. Because co-dependency is a relational issue, having an empathic and understanding person to assist you in breaking free can help you find a healthy way to fill in any missing developmental pieces.

- Use a reality approach that examines the information available from your past to create a story of what really happened to you as a child. Gather information about past and present relationships to bring into a therapy session to use in creating the story.
- Learn how to sequence, or break down, old, dysfunctional patterns of behavior into steps. Look at each step to see where there might be a hole in your awareness about what happens when the pattern is replaying. Use sequencing to find out where the pattern of behavior takes a dysfunctional turn. This is the place where you, your partner, or both of you will need to change your behavior.

### Tools for Support Groups

A support group can be either a twelve-step group or a therapy group. Twelve-step groups are traditionally facilitated by members who are further along in their recovery, while therapy groups are facilitated by trained mental health professionals. Support groups typically focus not on clearing the causes of co-dependency but on building a community of healthy friendships. Therapy groups focus more on deeper emotional work and can be less costly than individual therapy.

• Make a contract with the group. Ask the group to confront you each time you discount yourself, others, or the situation in any way.

• Learn to recognize when you rescue or persecute others and to recognize when it's being done to you. Watch group dynamics and discuss your perceptions with group members.

• Learn to recognize your need to be a victim. Ask group members to help you do this. When you complain about something, they can stop you by asking, "What do you want?" Learn to do this for others in the group who play victim.

• Ask group members to give you feedback when you employ "counting" behaviors in the group. This helps reinforce the gains you're making.

### *Tools for Committed Relationships*

We believe that a committed relationship is the most powerful means for healing relational traumas associated with co-dependency. You'll find an indepth discussion of committed relationships in chapter 18.

• Create a "No Discount Contract" with your partner. Make an agreement not to discount each other. In your contract you'll both agree, for a specific length of time (several weeks or a month), to avoid discounting. Determine what consequences you each want if you forget. Your contract might stipulate things such as the following:

   • "When you tell me what you don't like about me, say it in a way that I don't feel put down."

   • "If I discount you, I want you to remind me by _____ _____."

   • "This contract is in effect for \_\_\_\_\_ week(s)/month(s). At that time we will decide if we want to renegotiate and/or continue it."

- Create a common vision for your relationship. Set aside a day with your partner when you won't be interrupted. Take a trip, send the children out with a babysitter, unplug the phone, or take a picnic to a quiet spot. Working individually at first, write down your dream for yourself — what you'd like to do personally and professionally in the next year. Then share your individual dream with your partner. Look for areas of mutual interest, and then create a shared dream or vision.

- Develop reflective listening skills. During conversations with your partner, stop periodically to summarize what you've heard him or her say. For example, tell your partner, "What I'm hearing you say is..."

- Create a ritual or activity that recognizes the end of the old form of relationship that you've had. For example, fill a small box with reminders of the past and bury it. Or place the reminders or slips of paper that describe the old patterns on a funeral pyre and burn them. Another possibility is to find small rocks or stones that represent old ideas or ways of behavior and throw them into a creek or pond one at a time. As you throw each rock, say, "I release _____ (old pattern) as a way of being together with _____ (partner's name)." Activities like these can help our brains release the dysfunctional patterns we've stored there.

### CASE EXAMPLE

Sandra and Russ came to us for counseling just weeks before their divorce was to become final. They'd been married seventeen years and had four children. They'd been active in the Catholic Church since childhood and had centered many family activities on parish events. For nearly ten years, they'd led marriage enrichment weekends for other couples, and they had what seemed to be an ideal family life.

Sandra worked part-time to supplement the family income so that they could send the children to parochial schools. She was active in scouting and catechism class and saw her professional role as that of mother and wife. When she described her life with Russ and her children, her story was filled with happiness and contentment. Russ had been a supportive partner who, until recently, had been the perfect husband and father. They had experienced a few rough spots, and Sandra had been shocked when he suddenly announced that he wanted a divorce and was moving out.

Russ, who owned a small business, sat slumped in silence as Sandra told her story of their relationship. Obviously depressed, he began to tell his side next. From the very beginning, he had felt misgivings about trying to create Sandra's happy-family dream. Even as a child he'd felt rebellious and resentful at Catholicism's strict rules. He never wanted four children, and had come to resent the financial burden that the children's private schooling had become. Russ explained that he'd tried hard to fulfill his part of the happy-family dream. He confessed that he felt lost and exhausted. He'd tried his best to do all the things that were supposed to make people happy, and this hadn't worked. He was at the point where he felt he would die if he didn't get out of the trap soon.

In talking further with Russ and Sandra, it became clear they came to counseling with very different dreams. Sandra wished that the session would end in reconciliation so the happy-family dream could resume. Russ, on the other hand, was clear that he had come for divorce counseling. He wanted support in helping Sandra see how desperate he was to get out of the dream that was killing him.

Further inquiry into the couple's history revealed that Russ had periodically tried to tell Sandra that the relationship wasn't working for him. Each time this had happened, however, Sandra had managed to persuade him that it was working, by either discounting, making him feel guilty, or persuading him that the realization of the dream was right around the corner.

Denial in this relationship was rampant. Russ had continually denied the severity of his own experience until he finally felt his death was imminent. Sandra had repeatedly denied the information she'd received from Russ telling her that their marriage wasn't working. She'd denied both the verbal and the nonverbal information he gave her. She was able to avoid seeing Russ's slumped, defeated posture, his increasing thinness, his sunken eyes, and obvious depression. Sandra's need for her own happy-family dream to come true was so strong that she was still dreaming, in this session, that it would happen.

Russ was firm about his plan to continue with the divorce and to maintain his separate living quarters. He indicated that he had little to give as a parent and really needed time alone to think and find himself.

We saw clearly Russ's determination to end the relationship and believed his statement that he felt as if he were dying. As therapists, our task seemed to be to help Sandra break through her denial by making sure she fully received and accepted Russ's information and feedback.

When Sandra saw that the session was indeed divorce counseling and not marriage counseling, her armor of hope shattered. She began to weep softly as we asked Russ to repeat his feelings to her until she really took them in.

The final part of the session focused on helping Sandra to accept Russ's decision and to see that her perception of the recent years of their marriage had really been a fantasy. This was very difficult for Sandra. Each time the reality of divorce and the end of her dream penetrated her denial, she broke into sobs of despair. We quietly supported her feelings of grief and sat with them both until they seemed to reach a mutual reality. They looked briefly at each other and got up to leave, and then it was over — both the denial of unhappiness in the relationship and the old relationship itself.

## SUMMARY

Denial is one of the most difficult human conditions to deal with. The more we stuff away our old pain and feelings, the more difficult it is to break through denial. It's important to look truthfully at the past and our parents to realize that everyone did the best they could. This way, we don't get stuck blaming them. It's also important to develop conflict resolution skills so we can work through the conflicts that emerge when we tell the truth and break the happy-family illusion. With good tools and skills, these conflicts can become doorways to creating real intimacy in a family. For more information on resolving conflicts from a developmental perspective, see our book *Conflict Resolution: The Partnership Way.*[3]

# 8. Understanding the
# Causes of Co-dependency

To identify the sources of co-dependency patterns in your adult relationships, begin by reviewing your early childhood to see where the roots of the problem exist. Most people don't remember much of what happened during early childhood. You may remember a few selected events, but chances are, if you compared notes with others who were actually present at these events, they would remember them quite differently. Even so, several important facts about human behavior make the task of remembering workable:

- It isn't important that you remember actual events. Your memory may not be congruent with what actually happened, but your belief about or *perception* of what actually happened is what drives your behavior.
- It's important to identify the feelings that go with your perceptions. Your feelings are a more accurate record and are stored as cellular, or body, memories.
- All the information about your past is usually present in your current behavior and relationships. Your existing relationships contain replays of traumatic events and unresolved issues from your earliest relationships.

- This means that all the causes of co-dependency stemming from bonding traumas during the first six months of life are present in your current relationships and are pressing for completion.

This phenomenon is easier to see when you look at your existing co-dependent patterns the way M. Scott Peck does. When people "fall in love," says Peck, they experience a kind of regression, or falling back in time. He describes it this way: "In some respects — but certainly not in all — the act of falling in love is also an act of regression. The experience of merging with the loved one has its echoes from the time when we were merged with our mothers in infancy."[1]

The following examples illustrate this phenomenon. As an infant you nursed at your mother's breast or were held and given a bottle. At that age, time did not exist. You could comprehend only the blissful present. Compare this scenario with the words of a client describing her co-dependent relationship: "We don't see each other very often, but I yearn to be close to him. When we get together, time seems to stand still. When we make love, I forget about his drinking and all the times he's yelled at me. I want the good feeling between us to last forever. But it doesn't, and he starts drinking again."

When you wanted to be fed as an infant, you cried. Sometimes, however, your mother couldn't respond immediately. Waiting for her must have seemed like an eternity to you, even though it may have been only a few minutes. Now consider another client's words and notice the similarity:

> I called Melody on the phone and there was no answer. I knew she sometimes did shopping after work and didn't get home right away, but I felt anxious, like she was unavailable for me. At first I thought, "I'll call her in about an hour," but five minutes later I called again, and kept calling every five minutes for the next hour. I was frantic. All kinds of thoughts went through my head. Was she angry at me? Was she out with someone else? Was she in an accident? I couldn't let go of these thoughts.

The roots of co-dependency are easy to understand. You started out as a helpless infant who could not survive without your parents' care. Nature created a symbiotic relationship between you and them, which provided you with at least three things: it kept you alive and cared for, it gave you the illusion that you would always be safe and cared for, and it gave you the illusion that you were very powerful. Understandably, you held on to these beliefs as long as possible, despite a competing desire to become a separate person and despite your parents' attempts to wean you from this co-dependency.

In almost every case, parents are not able to become perfectly attuned to their children. So your need to spend more time in this blissful state probably was not met. Your parents had other things to do and had their own needs, worries, and problems. They may have become depressed or physically ill or had certain beliefs about child rearing that frustrated your need for oneness. They may have believed in schedule feeding, or that responding to your cries too often would spoil you. Whatever happened that interfered with getting your needs met for extended periods of timeless bliss, it's likely that you still have some unmet needs for it that you only vaguely remember.

The need for closeness and for extended periods of timeless bliss are normal needs that can be met in close adult relationships. What complicates the process, however, is the belief that you must re-create a co-dependent relationship in order to meet these needs. Many parents don't know how to teach their children to separate, while others, because of their own needs to hold on to their children, undermine their children's efforts to become separate. If you never became psychologically separate and autonomous, then the relationship you'll be inclined to create as an adult will be a re-creation of the original symbiotic one you had with your parents.

People who didn't become emotionally separate often feel a more desperate need for a return to this blissful state of oneness. You'll hear them say: "I don't feel alive unless I'm in a love relationship with someone," "I don't feel complete as a person without her. She makes me feel like a whole person," "I would die if I ever lost him. My life wouldn't be worth living. I could never be happy again," or "When I'm not with him I feel very insecure. When we cuddle up together, I feel really safe."

Co-dependency grows out of the fantasy that your mother or father, on whom you counted to make you feel good or safe or secure, *now* exists in the person with whom you have a relationship. Our whole culture, especially popular music, films, and television programs, reinforces this fantasy. Your goal in life is to find ways to hold on to that person and make him or her love you the way you need to be loved or cared for by your mother or father. Unconsciously, you're seeking help in completing your unfinished bonding process with your mother or father.

Of course, you are not conscious of this dynamic, and therefore it never works over the long haul. It leads to manipulation, control, and suffering rather than to enduring love. What's missing from this scene is a full awareness of the source of your problems and the tools for correcting them. Unfortunately, most people don't see these problems until they're already deeply enmeshed in a co-dependent relationship, or after they have gone through numerous relationships with unsatisfying outcomes.

The most dysfunctional co-dependency behaviors frequently don't show up until a couple becomes close enough, and feels safe enough, for their patterns to surface. Couples can live together for years and not encounter them. Once they get married, however, the commitment of the marriage contract often creates enough safety that the behaviors begin to surface. A marriage relationship can also trigger memories from childhood for the first time. Add to this the unrealistic cultural fantasies about couple relationships, which are supported by the mass media, and you can see why co-dependency persists for so long.

## TOOLS FOR UNDERSTANDING THE CAUSES OF CO-DEPENDENCY

Barry's book *Breaking Family Patterns* provides many excellent tools for understanding the systemic causes of co-dependency.[2] It presents information on twelve patterns of dysfunctional behavior learned during childhood and recycled in adult relationships. The book contains both self-awareness activities to help identify the patterns and useful tools and skill-building exercises for breaking those patterns.

### *Tools for Working on Yourself*

- Examine your anger and resentments. Make two lists. At the top of one list, write, "I resent my mother for..." At the top of the second list, write, "I resent my father for..." After you have completed these two lists, you may have a clearer idea of the issues you're dealing with. Then at the top of a third list, write, "I resent my partner for..." After completing the third list, you will likely see that many of your current resentments have their roots in childhood and represent unsolved conflicts from that time. Another list you might compose may be headed with: "I resent myself for..." You may be blaming yourself for many of the same things you blame others for.

- Make a list of the things about yourself and others that you remember your mother or father disapproving of when you were a child. Then place a check mark (√) next to the things you disapprove of in yourself and an *X* next to the ones you disapprove of in others. Unfortunately, we inadvertently take on the beliefs, values, prejudices, and fears of our parents. Are you still very sensitive to a certain kind of disapproval from your partner that reminds you of how your parents disapproved of you? This represents wounds from childhood that can be healed with the help of your partner. Chapter 17 discusses how to heal such wounds within committed relationships.

## *Tools for Therapy*

Therapy can be a good place to examine in depth what really happened to you as a child. You may have created a happy-childhood fantasy for yourself to help you avoid the awful reality of it. A therapist who understands the dynamics of co-dependency can help you correct any distorted perceptions of your childhood you might hold and support you in creating a more accurate perspective about it.

A therapist can also help you identify beliefs you might have created about yourself when you were a child and determine whether to keep any of the beliefs ("I can't do anything right," "I'm ugly," "I'm no good") that still rule your life and your relationships. Because many people have poor self-esteem or weak object constancy, they have trouble maintaining a positive self-image in the face of criticism or perceived mistakes. A good therapist can really help you heal your traumas, build your self-esteem, strengthen your object constancy, and design homework activities to help you be more successful.

## *Tools for Support Groups*

- In the groups you attend, notice who reminds you of your mother or father. Identify characteristics in others that you have trouble dealing with, and see if these other people remind you of your parents. Notice how you react to these people. This will tell you how you might have reacted to your parents.

- Ask group members to role-play conflict situations with you. Try role-playing conflicts you had with one of your parents, and learn to make new and more effective responses to this parent. Ask other group members to coach you in making better responses.

### Tools for Committed Relationships

- Separately, you and your partner can each make a list of traits that describe your own mother and father. The list should be their traits as you remember them from childhood. If there were other significant adults who helped raise you, such as a grandparent or even an older sibling, make a list of that person's characteristics as well. Try to list at least ten traits for each person.

After you've finished writing your list, do the following:

1. Place a check mark (√) next to the traits you see in yourself.
2. Place a plus sign (+) next to the positive traits and a minus sign (–) next to the negative traits.
3. Place an X next to the traits you see in individuals with whom you have intimate relationships, such as your husband, wife, lover, or best friends.
4. Discuss together the patterns that emerge from the lists. Ask yourself the following questions and compare your answers:

    - With which parent do I most identify? Which parent do I see most in my partner?
    - Do I see more of the positive or negative traits of my parent(s) in myself? Which do I see in my partner?
    - Who did I have the most conflict with while growing up — my mother or father? How do the traits I adopted from my parents relate to that conflict? Do I have similar conflicts with my partner?

This exercise can generate a good discussion between you and your partner regarding the unfinished business that may be cycling in your current relationship. Remember the law of human development: anything left unresolved or incomplete in your life will persist and press for completion. If you and your partner can begin to see that your current conflicts are rooted in the past histories of each of you, then you may be able to identify what is pressing for completion in your relationship. Without this kind of awareness, it's almost impossible to break free of the co-dependency trap. You will likely continue to recycle these unresolved issues over and over again.

## CASE EXAMPLE

Cara and Rick had been married for thirty-seven years when they first came for therapy with us. Cara was very unhappy with Rick and their relationship. Rick seemed to be unaware of any problems and came along at Cara's insistence. In the initial therapy session, Cara began by explaining why she was unhappy. When Rick heard her describe their relationship problems as being his fault, he responded by blaming them on her. What became apparent was that both were highly invested in being "right" and making the other one "wrong." The first sessions were like a battleground. It looked as if we weren't going to be able to help them resolve their problems. Each of them took a turn blaming the other and then collapsing into helplessness and hopelessness.

What we decided to do was support their helplessness and hopelessness. We started saying things like, "This sure looks to us like a hopeless situation. We have never seen a relationship that was so hopeless." This was a risk, because they might have taken our words as permission to leave the relationship. However, we didn't think this would happen, because they had been married for thirty-seven years, which indicated some staying power, and they were highly co-dependent and could probably survive a dysfunctional relationship better than doing without the relationship.

The strategy began to work. However, it wasn't until we also asked them to recall other times in their lives when they felt helpless and hopeless that the crucial information began to surface. Cara said she remembered feeling helpless and hopeless many times as a child. She admitted that she still feels that way in her relationship with her father. She described him as judgmental and a perfectionist and said that, no matter what she did, he would find something wrong with it. While growing up, she felt criticized and emotionally abandoned by him. She desperately wanted his approval and praise for her accomplishments, but she never got it. No matter how hard she tried, he continued to criticize her.

Cara's story seemed to trigger similar memories in Rick. He said, "You know, my mother was a lot like that. I tried everything I could to please her, and it never worked. Finally, when I was eighteen, she had to go to a mental institution." With tears in his eyes, Rick continued, "I tried to help her, but she still went away. I felt as if it were my fault that she went crazy. I just didn't know what to do to make her feel better. Everything I tried was the wrong thing."

Now we understood why it was so important for each of them to be "right" when they had conflict. All their lives they'd had this deep-seated fear of being wrong. Each had a strong unfulfilled need to be seen as "right" by his or her partner. One of the first things we asked of Cara and Rick was that they request positive feedback from each other. They needed to know it was possible to be right in the eyes of their partners. Their first efforts at this process were clumsy, and it was difficult for each of them to take in the other's compliments and kind words. Initially, they discounted what was being said, which was evident in subtle ways, such as body twitches and a slight turning away from each other. With our support, they continued talking to each other until they were able to absorb some of the positive feedback.

The next step was to help them become more separate in their relationship. One area where they were especially co-dependent was household chores. Cara had a list of things she wanted Rick to do around the house. Because he was retired and she still had her business in her home, she was always busy. Rick, however, wanted to relax and putter around the house.

In order to please Cara, Rick would agree to do the things on her list. Then he would become afraid that he would do them in the wrong order or not be able to do them to her satisfaction. Filled with the fear of being criticized for doing the wrong thing, he would then withdraw and watch television or take a nap. When Rick did this, Cara would nag him about the unfinished items on the list. This would remind Rick of his critical, controlling mother and he would withdraw even further, until a major conflict erupted between them. The intensity of the conflict helped restore contact. We were able to get Cara and Rick to prepare separate job lists. Cara agreed that she would do the things Rick wasn't willing to do, or they would pay someone else to do them.

Another problem was that Rick felt left out when Cara worked long hours, so he asked her to do more fun things with him. In addition, Rick began doing more things on his own. They began cooperating with each other more on day-to-day activities and gradually developed more goodwill and feelings of mutuality between them. For about a year, they returned to therapy whenever they got stuck. Since then they have been functioning well on their own.

## SUMMARY

When couples understand the source of their co-dependency patterns and learn specific tools for working on them on their own, they're able to do a lot of the healing themselves. It's easy to see how Cara and Rick could have continued indefinitely in their co-dependency patterns, making themselves and each other miserable. When partners stop blaming each other for their unhappiness, they're able to move closer together and deepen their relationship. Once they release the need to control each other, they can use effective, cooperative ways to meet their needs and wants.

# 9. Unraveling Co-dependent Relationships

The next step in the recovery process is to identify the co-dependency patterns in your current relationships. Co-dependency is so common that you may sometimes find it difficult to distinguish from the more functional patterns of a relationship. The following are *key* indicators that you're in a co-dependent relationship:

- Even though you have a lot of objective evidence that the relationship is not good for you, you do nothing to change it or to break the co-dependency patterns.
- You find yourself making excuses for your partner or yourself designed to hide the truth from yourself and others.
- When you think about changing or leaving the relationship, you feel afraid and cling to it even harder.
- When you take some preliminary steps to change the relationship, you suffer acute anxiety and physical symptoms that can be relieved only by reestablishing the old co-dependency patterns.
- When you do begin to make changes, you experience an intense longing for the old patterns, or you feel scared, all alone, or empty.

## RECOGNIZING CO-DEPENDENCY

The following are some common characteristics of people with co-dependency issues:

- Co-dependent individuals use an external frame of reference. They focus all their attention on what their partners are or are not doing.
- They use a relationship the same way someone might use alcohol or drugs. They are "addicted" to the other person and believe they can't function independently without that person or the relationship.
- They cannot define their own psychological boundaries — they don't know where they end and others begin. They rescue other people and take on the problems of others as their own.
- They are people-pleasers who try to control other people's perceptions and make a good impression on them.
- Co-dependent individuals don't trust their own ideas, perceptions, feelings, or beliefs. They defer to the opinions of others and don't offer or stand by their own ideas and opinions.
- They try to make themselves indispensable to others. They will knock themselves out to do things for others that the others could do for themselves.
- They play martyr. They learn to suffer, but to do it gallantly. They put up with intolerable situations because they think they have to.
- They are skilled at controlling others. They try to control everything, but fail because it's an impossible task.
- Co-dependent individuals are out of touch with their true feelings. They distort them and express them only when they create a situation where they feel justified in doing so.
- They are gullible. Because they aren't in touch with their own feelings, they lack discernment. They are poor judges of character and see only what they want to see.
- They lose contact with their spiritual selves and often are cut off from the spiritual side of life.
- They are fearful, rigid, and judgmental.
- Black-and-white thinking dominates the lives of co-dependent individuals. They can think of only two options for solving any problem.

## FAMILY ROLES

There are also certain roles that people with co-dependency issues get stuck in that restrict their lives even further. Roles are behaviors designed to fill specific functions in a family — usually a person plays a certain role to keep the family system balanced. We've listed the four most common co-dependency roles, with descriptions of the price a person pays for playing it.

*The family hero.* These people are often high achievers and act overly responsible. They are the leaders — football stars, straight-A students, and cheerleaders. They are often older or eldest children who take life seriously and are overly responsible. For them, everything is work, and they become self-disciplined and task-oriented. *The price they pay*: They are tense, rigid, and need to be in control in order to feel comfortable in relationships. They often become obsessive and perfectionistic, always concerned about measuring up and being productive. They are unable to feel their feelings and tend to separate themselves from others and become isolated and lonely. They usually find co-dependent people to take care of or be responsible for.

*The loner.* These people are easy to get along with because they are adept at adjusting and being flexible. They usually don't rock the boat. They avoid leadership positions and stay on the sidelines. They don't get emotionally involved with anything and are careful not to draw attention to themselves. They may feel a sense of powerlessness. *The price they pay*: They are emotionally blocked and don't know what they feel. They don't meet their own needs, rarely ask for anything from others directly, and feel isolated and lonely. They are usually depressed and unable to make decisions. They tend to choose people with co-dependency issues who cause conflict in their relationship. This keeps them from becoming too close.

*The caretaker.* These people spend most of their time taking care of other people's emotional needs. They are often warm, sensitive, caring people who know how to listen. They often find themselves taking care of others financially as well. *The price they pay*: They don't meet their own needs and often feel too guilty to receive anything freely from others. They give to others at their own expense and seek out people who are "takers" and emotionally needy. They don't experience much intimacy and usually marry someone they can take care of emotionally and/or financially.

*The rebel.* These people often act out the dysfunctional patterns of other family members. They get negative attention from parents, teachers, and the law. They frequently meet their need for self-esteem by acting against authority. *The price they pay:* They have a poor self-image, they fail in school, and they are labeled as the "sick one." They lose contact with their deep feelings of emotional abandonment, which they cover with anger. They harbor feelings of resentment and often try to get even with their parents by doing everything opposite to the way they think their parents would want it. They seek out mates who will allow them to act out their anger and resentment with them. They are often physically and verbally abusive to their mates, who tolerate their behavior.

## TOOLS FOR UNRAVELING CO-DEPENDENT RELATIONSHIPS

Unraveling your co-dependency patterns requires a systematic approach that will not just help you feel better but will actually change your life. The tools that we describe here will help you see things that you probably have not been aware of before. The activities for working on yourself require time for remembering, reflection, and meditation, so we encourage you to create some "retreat" time for yourself. This can be a regular block of time each day or a period of time away from your home and day-to-day responsibilities. Retreat time can be a very useful tool in helping you build boundaries for yourself as you discover who you really are at a soul level.

### Tools for Working on Yourself

The following tools can help you bring some of the unfinished business of your childhood to the surface:

- Make two lists. On the first list, write all the things your parents, teachers, or other adults *didn't* say or do to or for you that you now realize would have done you some good had they said or done them.
- On the second list, write all the things your parents, teachers, or other adults did and said to you while you were growing up that you now see didn't do you much good and in fact were harmful to you in some way.

- After completing the lists, examine them with the following information in mind. The first list represents unresolved co-dependency issues. These are things you are still waiting for someone else to provide for you. You will have to take charge of these needs and either ask your parents to meet them now, or, if that isn't possible, ask other people to help you meet these needs.

    The items on the second list represent unresolved counter-dependency issues. These are things for which you haven't forgiven your parents. These are the things holding you back and contributing to your difficulties with intimacy. You will have to let go of these things if you intend to complete your psychological birth.

You will remain stuck in your development process until you address the items on both lists. The ultimate form of being stuck is waiting for someone else to change or provide something for you so you can feel better. You may have a very long wait.

I (Barry) remember doing this exercise and coming up with a long list of things I wish my parents had said to me, such as "I love you just the way you are." On a visit to them some years ago, I brought out my list and asked them to tell me, in their own words, all the things I had wanted to hear. They were delighted to do this. I actually tape-recorded what they said in case I needed reinforcement later. Hearing their words helped me let go of some of my resentment and hurt, and helped me to take charge of my own healing process.

### Tools for Therapy

One of the most valuable tools you can learn through therapy is to become an objective observer of your own behavior. This enables you to step outside yourself in the midst of a conflict and witness your behavior. The steps in this process are as follows:

1.  Learn to recognize the signals when you are overreacting or having a flashback. Usually something traumatic in the situation makes you regress to the time of a developmental trauma. You may find yourself flooded with feelings that are *greater than* the present situation calls for. You may feel anxious, afraid, panicked, outraged,

rejected, ashamed, confused, or sad. Also, you may notice body signals such as increased heart rate, sweating, a pain in your stomach, tightness in your chest, or light-headedness.

2.  Take several deep breaths and calm down first, before you react any further. Ask yourself, "Am I in any danger in this situation?" If you feel like there's some danger, remove yourself from the situation before you try to analyze what happened. Take a walk or time-out in another room in order to calm down. Remember to let time pass, and notice if you feel better.

3.  Learn to observe yourself. Say to yourself, "I am reacting to an old feeling from another time." Or say something to acknowledge what is happening. "I am feeling angry as can be, and I don't know why." Then ask yourself, "What in this situation might have caused me to overreact?" and "What is the trauma in this past situation?" Your therapist can help you role-play the past event so you can access some of the feelings and yet remain somewhat detached. Men should remember that anger often covers up sadness or fear, and women should remember that crying often covers up anger and fear. Look for the deepest feelings you can find.

4.  Figure out what you needed in the past situation. Ask yourself: "What do I want from my partner in the present that will help to heal the past?" "How can I get my partner to cooperate with me to do this healing work?" and "Do I need to be held and comforted, or do I need to express my anger and resentment?"

### Tools for Support Groups

It's difficult to clear these patterns without support from friends. Having a network of friends willing to support your efforts to break free of the co-dependency trap is useful in completing this step in the recovery process. Friends frequently don't know what to do, and they feel left out when you're changing and not sharing your process with them. Some regular contact with friends can help you avoid slipping back into self-defeating patterns. If you don't have friends who will support your changes, you can use an established support group such as Co-Dependents Anonymous or Adult Children of Alcoholics.

We have personally utilized men's and women's support groups for our own healing. These are generally leaderless groups that meet regularly. Members share about their issues and get feedback from others in the group. You can also ask group members to provide ongoing support for the changes you're making.

### Tools for Committed Relationships

Many times we literally hypnotize ourselves by the words we use to describe our behavior. They can either trap us in co-dependent behavior or free us from it. The purpose of the following partner exercise is to help you and your partner become more aware of hypnotic word-blocks. "Have to" phrases tend to trap us and "choose to" phrases tend to free us.

- You and your partner can individually make lists of things that each of you feels you *must* do to make the relationship work. Then in turn, each of you can state how you feel about each task. Begin with "I have to..." For example: "I have to do the laundry for the family, and I feel burdened by this."
- Now sit facing each other, maintain eye contact, and talk directly to each other. Take turns saying to each other the sentences you wrote on your list. Notice how you feel when you say each sentence. Partners need not make any response to comments but can just accept what is being shared by saying "thank you."
- Now repeat the process, but this time change the beginning of the sentence to "I choose to..." Again pay attention to how you feel when you say each sentence, and see if your feelings about each specific task change as a result. Discuss the results with your partner. Ask yourself, "Am I allowing myself to be trapped by my own words?" Ask your partner, "Do I have to do this to please you, or am I free to choose not to do this if I don't want to?" Also ask your partner, "Are you willing to make, and be responsible for, your choices?"
- By changing your wording, you may also discover alternative choices that you may not have previously considered. The goal is to consciously choose your own life experiences rather than feeling controlled by "have to" phrases.

Cara and Rick, the couple mentioned in the case example in the last chapter, used this tool successfully to examine their lists and minimize the control games attached to their lists. Rick went through his list of things that Cara had given him to do, and decided which ones he felt he wanted to do and ones he felt he did just to please Cara. They renegotiated the ones that she wanted him to do but that he didn't. They agreed to pay someone else to do the chores that neither of them wanted to do. This was an option that neither had thought of before. Also, they agreed that, in the future, Rick would make his own lists of things he was willing to do and then check the list with Cara for input. This considerably reduced the control games between them.

## CASE EXAMPLE

Jane was a bright, attractive single woman when she met and fell in love with Jack. They were living together and planning marriage when Jane came to see me (Barry).

She explained that she loved Jack very much but was disturbed by his drinking. She said she grew up with an alcoholic father and didn't know whether she was just overreacting or whether there might be a pattern emerging. She also explained that she had been in several destructive relationships previously and had discovered alcoholic behavior in the men she chose. So she was afraid to trust her own judgment.

After asking her some questions to find out more about Jack, I learned that he was resistant to therapy and anything that involved self-analysis or self-awareness. Jane really wanted a man who was willing to work with her to heal her own wounds and build a deeper, intimate relationship. She wanted to know if she had picked the wrong person for this kind of relationship.

I suggested she ask him to come to therapy with her for one session to help her determine what to do about the relationship. I said that this would be a way of determining how serious he was about building that kind of relationship. She agreed and said she'd let me know what happened.

The next day I received a call from Jane, who was in tears. She said she'd asked Jack to come with her to therapy, and he had become so angry with her that he'd packed his things and moved out of their apartment, telling her he never wanted to see her again. She was shocked. As we talked, she calmed down and began to see how lucky she was that she hadn't gone ahead and married this man. She thanked me for helping her get clear about what she wanted and for helping her discover Jack's level of commitment to the kind of relationship she wanted.

I had one other session with Jane to help her see the early warning signals of co-dependency and alcoholism. She was still very gullible and knew that she had been attracting alcoholic and co-dependent men partly because she hadn't worked out her unfinished business with her father. She is now addressing this in a support group and working on herself. I expect that at some point she'll return to therapy to work more on this process.

When you aren't aware of how your co-dependent patterns relate to unfinished business from your past, you're likely to subconsciously draw people into your life to help you complete these patterns. Obviously, when Jane met Jack she had no idea how similar to her father he was. It was only when they had gotten close enough and were planning a more permanent relationship that she became aware of the similar pattern. Fortunately for her, she consulted with someone who could help her test out her fears. Many people don't become conscious of these patterns until they've been married for many years. Then it can take a long time to break free of the patterns or the relationship, if their partners aren't willing to work on breaking them.

## SUMMARY

Recognizing patterns of co-dependent behaviors is a transformative experience. It sets in motion a process of change that is difficult to stop. Turning your back on that process would be similar to trying to put toothpaste back in a tube after you've squeezed it out.

You'll probably see co-dependent behaviors in others more easily than you recognize them in yourself, and that's okay. Once you *can* identify your own co-dependent behaviors, particularly their sources in your family of origin role, you'll be able to work with your whole family system to unravel those behaviors and reweave the fabric of your life. The important thing is to trust your inner wisdom and guidance, and follow your own path of recovery.

# 10. I Have Met the Enemy and It Is I

In chapter 7, we discussed the fact that you had to develop a False Self in order to please your parents and participate in the denial that went on both in your family and in yourself. In developing this False Self, you learned through interactions with your parents and other adults that certain parts of you were unacceptable to them, so you overdeveloped other parts of yourself that were acceptable.

Joni is an example of a child who had to do this. As a little girl, Joni liked being outside with the boys in the neighborhood, swinging on the ropes and racing bicycles. These were behaviors her father and mother disapproved of. Each time they found Joni outside behaving like a tomboy, they called her back inside to play quiet games with her sisters and watch TV. Her father and mother made it clear to her that girls did not behave like tomboys, and that what they wanted from her was quiet, passive behavior. Eventually she learned to repress the more outgoing, adventurous part of herself and adapted her behavior so that they would love her and approve of her. In other words, she became a nice, quiet girl.

As she grew older, she found herself irritated by some of the girls in her class who talked tough, entered competitive sports, and acted adventuresome. Occasionally one of these girls would bully her or ridicule her for her quietness, making her life miserable. She often felt helpless and defenseless in responding to their harassment. Joni, who saw these girls as strange, was unaware of how much she envied them and their adventurous ways.

## THE ENEMY: A PART OF MYSELF

To understand the dynamics of the situation just described, it's important to realize that you're made up of many different parts:

- the part that loves
- the part that hates
- the part that obeys
- the part that rebels
- the part that is happy
- the part that is sad
- the part that likes to control
- the part that likes to be controlled
- the part that is deceptive
- the part that is truthful
- the part that is feminine
- the part that is masculine
- the part that is an adult
- the part that is a child

Each part of you may have somewhat different desires, dreams, fears, and ideas. These parts often behave like an internal family, competing against each other as they attempt to be recognized and meet their own needs. For instance, your adult part may recognize that you need to get up and go to work in order to pay your bills, while your child part may want to stay home from work and ride your bike over to the park for a picnic. This sort of conflict between parts is one we're usually aware of and can deal with effectively.

A more difficult situation occurs when you don't like a certain part of yourself or think that others find it unacceptable, such as the part of you that needs to receive love and affection. As a result of childhood traumas that kept you from meeting this need, you learned not to let people see this part. You may have stopped asking for and even hoping for affection. You eventually "split off" this part, and the needs associated with it, from your awareness.

Once a part has been split off, a strange thing begins to happen. People who have active parts similar to the ones you have split off seem to arrive to trouble you in your life, as they did Joni. Whatever traits you refuse to recognize in yourself you'll see in other people. If you've split off the part of you that needs to receive love and affection, you may find yourself surrounded by people who want love and affection from you. Or if you deny that you like being in charge and managing things, you may find a lot of people trying to manage and control you. As the adage states, "What you resist, persists."

The more completely a part is split off from your awareness, the more forcefully it will come in search of you. When you meet this distant part of yourself in other people, you may experience them as the enemy. The enemy may appear in your life as a dominating boss, a shiftless employee, a distant wife, or a rebellious child. You may find yourself embroiled in some persistent conflict with an enemy — perhaps a dominating boss, for example — and decide to switch jobs. You may find your new boss is easy to get along with, but that a co-worker whose desk is near yours turns out to be dominating. This phenomenon is called "projection."

## PROJECTION

Projection occurs when you recognize split-off parts of yourself in other people but don't recognize them in yourself. When you are projecting, you may have trouble distinguishing between your internal world and the external world.

Roger, for example, had difficulty with an impending separation and divorce. He'd been reacting with calmness and grace to his wife's decision to leave him. Within one week, however, he had a series of catastrophes, one after another. It was not until a cat fell through the sunroof of his car and urinated on the backseat that he began to see the relationship between the catastrophes of his internal world and what was happening in his external world. He was able to see that his wife was "pissing" on him and that he indeed was "pissed" that she was leaving him. He decided to deal with his anger toward her immediately.

Projection is complicated by the presence of co-dependency and the inability to feel and act separately from other people. By seeing in others the very qualities that you refuse to acknowledge in yourself, you not only can avoid taking responsibility for your own feelings but also can avoid taking charge of your life.

Another important characteristic of split-off parts is that the more they are ignored or denied, the more strength they gain. They gather energy until they reach a critical point. Then usually one of two things will happen: You may act out the split-off part unexpectedly. (For example, if your anger is split off, you may erupt in a fit of anger. It will just "happen to you" without your being truly aware of it.) Or someone else may act out the part for you, and you'll get to see it in the other person.

Split-off parts always remain outside your awareness. If, for instance, you repress your anger and always try to be soothing or agreeable, you'll experience yourself as a pleasant person. The people you interact with, however, may experience your anger in subtle ways. They may notice your tight jaw, frowning brows, pointed remarks, tense body posture, or sarcasm and sharp tone of voice. You may be totally unaware of these signs of your anger.

Men and women project their unacceptable parts onto each other in relationships in a somewhat predictable pattern. Men are socialized to develop their masculine side and ignore their feminine side, while the opposite is true for women, who are taught to be feminine and not develop their masculine side. It's important to remember that both positive and negative parts can be projected. It may be just as difficult to "own" your angelic parts as it is to own the more devilish ones.

In male-female relationships, there is a progression of stereotypical projections that begins around puberty. It starts with the first attraction to the opposite sex and moves through a series of stages. Each stage involves a deeper level of distorted projections and gradually becomes more psychologically complex. The progression usually peaks by midlife, when people eventually become aware of their deeper projections. The progressions for men and women generally follow the sequence shown in the sidebar "The Progression of Masculine and Feminine Projections."

| THE PROGRESSION OF MASCULINE AND FEMININE PROJECTIONS | |
| --- | --- |
| *Projected Feminine (Men)* | *Projected Masculine (Women)* |
| Shallow Woman | Jock |
| Nurturing Woman | Big Daddy |
| Madonna | Father God |
| Goddess | Hero |
| Martyr | Warrior |
| Witch | Warlock |
| Wise Woman | Sage |

By midlife, if you have done sufficient internal work to heal your developmental traumas through relationships, therapy, support groups, and individual inner work, you reach the interdependent stage of development. Once this integration occurs, you become more conscious of your projections and the projections of others.

In the interdependent stage of development, each person is able to consciously use projections to help heal old wounds. For example, if you need more nurturing, you can ask your partner to temporarily become your projection of the Nurturing Woman and give you what you need. Being able to do this is an important part of reclaiming the True Self.

Once you understand how people mirror your projected parts, it becomes easier to reclaim your projections. You just need to observe which people and behaviors upset you the most. The people you once thought were "the enemy" will transform into "a lost part of yourself." Once you can do this, you are ready to begin loving yourself and others more fully.

## INTIMACY BEGINS WITH LOVING YOURSELF

Accepting negative feelings such as jealousy, greed, impatience, fearfulness, and anger can be difficult. Families usually provide little experience and few tools for coping with these emotions. It's important to recognize that these parts of yourself are not only useful but even valuable at times. Anger, for example, tells you there's something you need that you're not getting, and fear helps you protect yourself. Chronic victims, for example, tend to be angry at their persecutors or rescuers, but what they really feel is fear of being abused or invaded again. The anger can serve to keep people at a safe distance, but it also prevents victim types from experiencing much intimacy.

These emotions are also useful for giving others feedback about their behavior. Everyone needs to know how their behavior affects others. If you repress your anger and fail to give people information about the impact of their behavior, they don't see the consequences of their actions. Without feedback from others, it is very difficult to change one's own co-dependent patterns. It's important, both for yourself and for others, to love, accept, and use with discretion *all* your parts.

In seeking out split-off parts, you may discover them hiding somewhere inside you. Jerri, the oldest of six children, was suffering from depression when she came to me (Janae) for therapy. In reviewing her childhood, I realized that she "grew up too fast" and played the role of surrogate parent to her younger brothers and sisters. Jerri shared with me several recent dreams in which she was trying to kill a little girl. As she and I worked on interpreting her dreams, she discovered her own split-off child, who felt as though she were dying. Further exploration revealed that, in her dreams, Jerri was really trying to kill this inner child. Jerri brought some photos of herself as a child to therapy for me to look at with her. We noticed the expression on her face, her body language, and how disconnected she seemed from other people in the photos. This helped her access her feelings about being lost and alone as a child. She began nurturing her inner child by rocking herself, by taking time to do things just for herself, and by consciously allowing this part to come out more.

Loving your projected parts is the first step toward loving yourself. Only then will you be able to love others and live richly in relationships.

## FORGIVENESS

The word *forgive* literally means *to give back*. The process of forgiveness involves giving back to your parents and others the things they did and said to you that you now see were harmful to you. In the process of reclaiming your lost parts, you may discover feelings of anger, hatred, or resentment, especially toward your parents or even toward yourself. Sometimes our anger, sadness, and fear are things that belong to our parents, which we took on. These must be given back to them. Finding these feelings and expressing them is an important part of healing childhood wounds and traumas. You have good reason to feel these emotions. Only after you've learned what caused you to lose vital parts of your real self, and have felt the feelings connected to this great loss, can you forgive.

True forgiveness does not deny the truth of your feelings or deflect them. It faces them head-on. It's especially important that you acknowledge any feelings of hatred you have for your parents. This is an important step on the path to true forgiveness. When your hatred and anger are expressed completely (not necessarily directly to them), these often transform into feelings of sadness and pain at your having been ignored, abandoned, or used. This leads to the real healing: a genuine understanding of who your parents are and why they treated you the way they did. Only then can you begin to feel the empathy and sympathy needed to truly forgive them. It enables you to see *them* as imperfect — as people who were responsible but not guilty. They did the best they could with what they had. They need healing as much as you do.

One last part of forgiveness is to forgive yourself. It's important to do this so you don't unconsciously create an internalized, abusive, parental part that continues to mistreat you. If you find you're more critical of yourself than others are, then you have probably adopted an angry, hurtful, internalized parent that is part of your False Self. Give back to yourself the traits of your True Self, and replace those of your False Self. This allows you to reclaim all the positive parts of yourself that you were forced to split off.

## INTEGRATING INTERNAL PARTS

Once you've identified lost or split-off parts, learned to love them, and forgiven yourself and your parents, the next step is bringing the parts together in your everyday life. Integrating these parts will be useful in several ways. First, you'll no longer need to defend against encountering them in others. Second, you can use these parts in productive ways to love or protect yourself or to meet your needs. Third, since many of these lost parts are connected to emotions, they'll help you become a rich, full, feeling human being with a whole range of human responses to life.

For instance, if your ability to feel tenderness and compassion returns to you, you'll be able to express these deep emotions during intimate moments with others. You'll be able to express joy when something wonderful happens, such as when you receive a warm letter from an old friend. When your child uses the car without asking and gets in a fender bender, you'll be able to get appropriately angry. When your spouse flirts at a party, you can state clearly that you feel jealous and afraid. All feelings become valued and have appropriate places for expression.

Once you can be fully present in life with all your parts, you can live a life richer than you ever imagined. You'll find that the energy you once used to repress these parts is freed up, and you feel more vital and alive. You'll feel more relaxed and content and have a lot more hope. When feelings are allowed to surface in the moment rather than being repressed, the tension doesn't get trapped in your body. Your life becomes an authentic expression of who you are.

## TOOLS FOR RECLAIMING LOST PARTS

The process of reclaiming your split-off parts can be tricky. First, by definition, a split-off part is largely outside your ordinary awareness. Second, the parts of yourself that you split off and hid from others are usually connected to some developmental trauma, and so if a split-off part is exposed or activated in some social or relationship situation, your first response is likely to be to fight, flee, or freeze. It takes a good deal of self-reflection to spot your own split-off behaviors and to react in a new way. The following suggested activities can help you reclaim these lost parts of yourself.

### Tools for Working on Yourself

- Have *parts days*. As you dress each day, choose clothes that reflect different parts of yourself. Select clothes that really help you see the differences between your parts. For example, when you'll be outdoors hiking, wear your boots, Western-style shirt, and a bandanna. On special occasions, wear dressy clothes with jewelry or a tie, makeup, and leather pumps or dress shoes. On casual weekends, wear an exercise suit and sport shoes. Take time to reflect each day as you dress to go out as a different part of yourself. Write in your journal about these differences.

- Work on self-forgiveness. Make two columns on a sheet of paper, and in the first column write statements of self-forgiveness about the things you've been berating yourself about (such as "I forgive myself for believing that I was a bad person"). Use a response column on the right side of each forgiveness statement to record any resistant thoughts and feelings about forgiving yourself (such as "I have done some pretty awful things in the past"). Write responses for those forgiveness statements — ones that you can complete without resistance. Then go back and work with your points of resistance. It may take some time to get through this exercise without resistance, so be patient.

### *Tools for Therapy*

- Prosecute your parents with the assistance of your therapist. You may want to prosecute your parents separately — without their presence — because their perceived "crimes" may be different. If you would like to do so, stage a courtroom scene, asking your therapist to play the judge. You can act as the prosecutor. Read a previously compiled list of things you believe your parent did that hurt you or caused lasting wounds. Allow yourself to fully feel your rage and anger at how you were treated. If necessary, imagine your parent watching you pound on a pillow or beanbag chair while you yell at him or her and purge repressed emotions from your body. Following the prosecution, you'll need to defend your parents. Again, your therapist can play the role of judge while you become the defense. In this process, you'll act as different witnesses, including

  - your parents at different stages of their childhoods;
  - the parents of your parents;
  - other people who played a significant role in your parents' childhoods; and
  - your parents as adults trying to raise you.

This exercise can provide surprising information about how your parents grew up, the difficulties and wounds they experienced, and how their experiences affected your childhood. Once this is complete, it's easier to feel compassion and to forgive both your parents and yourself.

## Tools for Support Groups

- Have a *parts party*. Review your internal parts, listing as many of them as possible. Identify them by name, such as *my sexual part, my child part, my wife part,* and *my employee part*. Then think of a famous person who portrays that part to the point of exaggeration. For example, if your girl child part is precocious, wise, and outspoken, you might portray her as *Olive*, the young girl in the *Little Miss Sunshine* movie. Or if you have a *preachy* part, you could portray it as *Billy Graham*. Go to your group with your list and ask group members to take parts that match their personalities. Then ask the parts to interact as *characters*. For instance, *Olive* would talk to *Billy Graham* while other parts talk in pairs or groups. After five minutes, have the pairs or groups switch to talk with new parts. Do this for a half hour or longer so you can see the different ways your parts relate.

   During this role-playing, notice any conflicts or inabilities to communicate between some of the parts. Try observing the whole scenario from outside the group. The parts should not interact with you. You should sit quietly at the edge of the group making notes about what you're seeing and how you're feeling. Stop the action when it has gone on long enough. The next step is to let each person describe his or her experience as that part. Notice any information they give that might be useful for your self-awareness.

   The last step is to have your group create a circle. Then put yourself in the middle of it. Look at each part (person) directly and tell it why you need it and what positive things it does for you. Then tell the part that you love it and will use it wisely. Do this with each part until you are completed. This last step is *very* important, as it allows you to take back each part and integrate it into your daily life. It also allows the player to release the part so that he or she doesn't leave the party carrying your part around inside. Co-dependent people are good at doing that.

- Have *parts nights*. As a group, brainstorm the parts of yourself you have the most trouble accepting. Then make a list of the parts most common to the group. Rank the parts as 1, 2, 3, and 4 in the order that you'd like to explore them. Use each part as a theme for a meeting. Arrive at your group with everyone dressed in masks, outfits, or costumes that portray this part. Use the meeting time to learn more about this troublesome part. You can draw what this part represents to you. You can also interact with other *parts players* in a theme drama. Use each other to help exaggerate your individual experiences. Use the last one-third of the meeting to discuss and share your experiences about expressing this part.

## Tools for Committed Relationships

- Make a list of all the things you wish your opposite-sex parent had said to you or done for you while you were growing up. These are the things you're still waiting for someone of the opposite sex to do for you. Decide which things you can do for yourself, which ones you would like to ask your partner to do for you, and which ones you're willing to ask others for. Then ask your partner if he or she would be willing to do or say these things at a specific time.

- Review the list of masculine and feminine projections in this chapter. Then make a list of things your partner says or does that remind you of any of these parts. Share your lists with each other, using them as discussion tools.

## CASE EXAMPLE

Amy arrived at our office bruised and with fresh stitches around her eyes. Her loose teeth were wired to hold them in place while they healed. Her body was somewhat slumped as she walked in hesitantly and sat down. She held her head down and twiddled her fingers nervously as she began to tell the story of her near encounter with death.

She had been riding her bicycle near her home one evening about dusk and had stopped for a traffic light. Suddenly she felt both herself and her bicycle being dragged forcefully off the street and into a nearby parking lot.

Her assailant began beating her unmercifully about the upper body, face, and head. She began screaming wildly and continued to scream and resist until she realized how much stronger he was. The blows dazed her, so that she screamed and resisted less. She knew that he planned to kill her.

Suddenly, another man ran up and scared the assailant off. She was overcome with both relief and grief. The rescuer called the police and an ambulance, and she was taken to the hospital emergency room for treatment. With information from the rescuer, the assailant was eventually caught and sent to prison.

For Amy, however, this was not enough. Amy believed that the attack was an important message for her. She believed that she had somehow drawn this experience to herself, and wanted to focus her therapy on the lesson behind it.

Over a period of weeks, she shared a lot about the recent years of her life, especially her relationships. One significant part of her story involved her breakup with her boyfriend. She also revealed a history of co-dependent relationships in which she was the clinging person. As we pieced together a history of family relationships, her patterns became clearer.

Amy's parents were both severely dysfunctional. Her father had been an alcoholic, and her mother had been an invalid with multiple sclerosis. Her mother had died when Amy was ten. Amy, who was always closer to her father, clung to him even more after her mother's death. Her father, incapacitated from grief, soon became severely alcoholic. When Amy was seventeen, he killed himself.

Amy soon married an older man and had two children. After eight years, she divorced him and married again. This marriage also failed, so she stayed single but had several live-in relationships.

Just prior to her attack, she had been in a valued relationship with Larry. As they became closer in their relationship, all their old feelings and issues from their past relationships started surfacing. Both got frightened at the closeness of the relationship and the old feelings, which contributed to their breakup. Following the breakup, Larry immediately found a new girlfriend to live with him.

Amy was devastated. She drove by Larry's house incessantly, often sitting outside to watch him and his new girlfriend. On several occasions, she got so angry she broke windows by throwing rocks at them. She banged on their door, shouting profanities and insults and attacking them whenever possible. She experienced moments when she was totally consumed by rage and hatred. She eventually cooled down and tried to resume a life on her own. It was at this point that she was attacked while riding her bike.

Amy was able to see the similarity between her attack on Larry and the attack on herself. It became obvious to her and to us that the parts she had split off were her anger, rage, and hurt, which had expressed themselves through her attacker. She also realized that the breakup with Larry had replayed the abandonment patterns of her mother and father. She admitted that she hadn't been able to express her rage and anger when they died. She believed, however, that she'd released a lot of old feelings in her rage at Larry. She realized that these parts had been split off for so long that she'd finally exploded in what she'd believed was a justified attack on Larry. Only after her assailant had beaten her half to death was she forced to look at her own "attacker" part.

Eventually Amy was able to vent more of her anger at her parents for abandoning her and to then reclaim the attacker part. She learned to express her feelings of anger more immediately, rather than let them build up until they exploded.

Amy's experience is an excellent example of how you can use the people around you as mirrors to show you your split-off parts. The people with whom you are in conflict become symbols of your internal parts. Recognizing them as parts of yourself allows you to work on the conflict internally and then to claim your part of it. Developing the ability to work internally will noticeably reduce the way you experience external conflict and also defuse the intensity of your conflicts.

## SUMMARY

Reclaiming the parts of yourself that you have tried to hide from others — and have effectively hidden from yourself — is an important skill. The most common way that people try to hide seemingly negative aspects of themselves is by projecting them onto others. They can see and criticize what others are doing while remaining totally unaware that what they see is a split-off part of themselves. Hidden parts of ourselves also reflect self-judgments that seem to show up only when we make a mistake or do something we think is stupid. Reclaiming split-off parts requires a lot of deep self-reflection, so give yourself the time necessary to complete this important part of breaking free of the co-dependency trap.

# 11. Eliminating Self-hatred

Self-hatred has its roots in the dominator culture. The first and most important cause of self-hatred is the lack of secure bonding experiences and parental support for developing independent thought and action. People who have completed these two essential developmental processes generally have strong self-esteem and are capable of loving both themselves and others.

The second cause of self-hatred is the parental disapproval syndrome, a mechanism used by parents and teachers in a dominator culture to punish children for behaviors such as critical thinking and assertiveness, which are inconsistent with dominator values. The dominator culture uses rejection and disapproval as methods to extinguish these unwanted behaviors. This leads children to develop a negative self-image, low self-esteem, critical self-talk, and self-hatred. In consequence, they generally disapprove of themselves just as their parents and others disapproved of them.

As a result of the repressive system you grew up in, you became a judgmental person who disapproved of yourself and others. You likely developed the same biases, prejudices, beliefs, and values as your parents. You may also have internalized your parents' beliefs and attitudes, and may criticize, humiliate, and verbally abuse yourself when you make a mistake, long after your parents or teachers have stopped doing this to you. Your internal dialogue or self-talk may even repeat the same words, phrases, and bad names they directed at you while disciplining you.

## BLACK-AND-WHITE THINKING

Chapter 4 presented information on the fourth phase of the separation process: object constancy. Object constancy is the ability of children to see their parents and themselves as good and bad when the children are separated from their parents. This ability develops when children have had enough "good parent" experiences to carry them through periods of separation. Weak object constancy keeps the separation process or psychological birth from happening on schedule. As a result, children stay stuck in the third, or "splitting," stage, where the world around them is filled with either all-good or all-bad people. There are no gray areas. The dominator culture supports this divisive form of thinking by teaching people to use a comparative frame of reference. It teaches them to see others as being in some way better or worse then themselves.

If children have poor object constancy, and their parents are unavailable for any reason, the children will see themselves and their parents as bad. Children's inability to view themselves as separate from their parents causes them to lump together their feelings about their parents and themselves. This "bad parent = bad child" pattern contributes to all-or-nothing, black-and-white thinking and behaviors and helps create a pattern of "bad child" and self-hatred.

When you make a mistake or fail to do something perfectly, this kind of thinking can trigger your negative thoughts and self-hatred. Because it's difficult to be perfect and meet everyone's expectations, you may spend most of your life seeing yourself as bad and experiencing self-hate. Unless you can change this, it will be impossible to experience self-love without becoming perfect. Since being perfect is next to impossible, people often cope in one of two ways. They may try to pretend they're perfect, or they may develop a need to be "right" about everything. The emphasis on winning and on excellence, which very few people achieve in a dominator culture, destines many to a life of failure and defeat.

## SELF-LOVE

Self-love begins when you're able to gain object constancy and see yourself as having both positive and negative parts, all of which are lovable. Self-love is almost a taboo in our dominator culture because it's associated with self-ishness and masturbation.

Self-love and self-nurturing, characteristics of partnership societies, are expressed in the daily relationship that you have with yourself. They are expressed by taking good care of your body, getting adequate exercise and rest, eating nourishing foods, maintaining good grooming habits, and wearing attractive clothing. Creating quiet time to meditate, pray, and reflect helps you love your spiritual self. Going to therapy, finding community in support groups, and spending quality time with your partner helps you create harmonious social relationships.

Self-love, as it is expressed in your relationships with others, is evidenced by your ability to set appropriate boundaries. You can say no to abuse, to invasions of your space, to being used, to drugs, to being controlled and manipulated, to guilt and shame, and to exposing yourself to negative people. "I'm worth it!" is an important attitude for self-love, and it requires you to give your needs status equal to that of others' needs. To begin loving yourself may require that you replace negative messages from your childhood with more positive ones. Then you can create life situations in which you experience acceptance and approval, high self-esteem, positive self-image, and positive self-talk.

## SELF-TALK

Desire and fear, the two great motivators in a dominator culture, can be used to propel or compel you to take action. They are embedded in advertising to influence your thoughts, words, and actions. Your thoughts are creative. You learn to think in words and phrases that you believe will affect your life either positively or negatively, depending on whether your dominant thoughts, or self-talk, are positive and based on desire, or negative and based on fear. In either case, you may feel compelled to act in accordance with the externalized standards, unable to really think for yourself. As a result, you may not know what really makes you happy — only what you've been told will make you happy.

Negative self-talk locks up your mental resources, your beliefs, and your actions. Negative thoughts can form "brain chains" that run inside your mind in a continuous loop. They can have a devastating effect on your life by creating cycle after cycle of negative experiences. Positive self-talk, unless it's based solely on desire, can release your mental resources, beliefs, and actions. It has a freeing, expanding effect on your life that helps create cycles of positive experiences.

The most important thing about self-talk is that it fuels the performance cycle on which your actions are based. Self-talk creates beliefs. Beliefs create performance. Performance creates more self-talk.

To create positive self-talk, it's very important to remember that you need to move *toward* something. You focus on the condition that you want to achieve, rather than on what you want to move away from — what you fear or don't want. For instance, if you think to yourself "I refuse to be co-dependent," you're still focusing on the state of being co-dependent. Thinking "I am interdependent" focuses your thoughts on the concept of interdependency, your real goal.

Since the dominator culture accepts negative self-talk as its standard, shifting out of the negative-self-talk habit takes greater effort. When people offer you some of their negative thoughts, disagree with them mentally, or internally, and then create a positive self-talk statement to neutralize the negative one. For example, when your partner says, "This relationship is nothing but trouble," you can respond with: "Problems are an opportunity to get closer together." Positive self-talk supports positive self-esteem.

## SELF-ESTEEM

Self-esteem is the deep down, inside-the-skin feeling you have about your own worth. Positive self-esteem means accepting yourself, totally and unconditionally, fully realizing that you have strengths and weaknesses and positive as well as negative qualities. You are lovable without having to be perfect. To establish positive self-esteem, concentrate on your positive attributes — your good qualities and your successes.

Self-esteem begins early in infancy. Children who are loved unconditionally and have their bonding needs met in timely and appropriate ways develop self-esteem. Between the ages of one and fifteen, as children become separate, they normally hear the words "no," "don't," "you can't," "better not," and "shouldn't," from fifteen thousand to twenty-five thousand times. Messages such as these from authority figures create a base of negative self-talk that eventually generates limiting beliefs and limited performance. To neutralize this negative programming would require at least fifteen thousand to twenty-five thousand positive messages!

The two most powerful tools for creating positive self-esteem are asking for what you want and being willing to receive what you want. If you have blocks in either area, you must work your way through them so you can have positive experiences.

Self-esteem affects the way people interact in the world. According to Harris Clemes and Reynold Bean, people with high self-esteem[1]

- feel good about their accomplishments;
- act positively on their own behalf;
- assume responsibility for doing their share;
- tolerate frustration if things don't turn out as well as they would like;
- approach new challenges with eagerness and enthusiasm;
- feel able to influence their environment; and
- display a wide range of feelings.

People with low self-esteem

- avoid difficult situations;
- are easily led or deceived;
- are defensive and easily frustrated;
- don't know what they feel; and
- blame others for their own feelings.

Stanley Coopersmith found four components necessary for the development of positive self-esteem in children:[2]

- Acceptance of children by adults, parents, teachers, and other authority figures. This helps reinforce bonding and creates feelings of being valued.
- Clearly defined and enforced limits. These should be as few as possible to create a balance between experimentation and safety, exploration and invasion, and assertive and passive or aggressive behavior in the child.

- Respect by adults for children as persons. It's important for their needs and wishes to be taken seriously. This gives them psychological space for growth and also for privacy and separateness.
- Parents and other adults with high self-esteem serve as models. Children need models from whom to learn. Also, adults with high self-esteem are better able to accept children, to define and enforce limits, and to respect children's boundaries.

As an adult you may still need to work on these four things to fully develop high self-esteem. You may still need experiences of acceptance, limits, respect, and love from companions with strong self-esteem. Building self-esteem is also a developmental task, so you may need to review your childhood for traumatic experiences that need healing.

## AFFIRMATIONS

Affirmations are high-quality, positive statements that you think or say about yourself, such as "I am a lovable and capable person." They can be written or spoken and should not contain any qualifiers such as *sometimes* or *under certain conditions*. They should also be stated in present time, as if they have already happened: for example, "I am able to care for myself and meet my own needs."

Affirmations are a special kind of self-talk that can be used to change the "tapes" that run inside your mind. When a situation involves feelings, experiences, or people that remind you of your unfinished business, it may trigger bad feelings and snap you emotionally right back into the old stuff. The "old tapes" phenomenon helps this happen. For example, if a controlling older woman happens to criticize you at work, you might flash back to a time in your childhood when your mother used the same tone of voice and facial expressions as she spoke to you. As a result, the criticism triggers a memory of a developmental trauma, and you may feel helpless to defend yourself but not know why.

Affirmations can also be used to change negative thought patterns. Once you've identified a negative thought pattern, you can convert it into something positive. Then you can "splice" this new tape into your internal tape player and replace the negative thought pattern with a positive pattern. With persistence, you can eventually edit out the negative messages and fill the tape with all positive affirmations.

Louise Hay uses affirmations, mirror work, and support groups as primary tools for working with clients suffering from both cancer and AIDS.[3] She has had remarkable healing outcomes with both patient groups. Many people go into remission after this kind of work. Her work also focuses on self-love, working with beliefs, and the relationship between self-love, beliefs, and the onset of illnesses.

## TOOLS FOR LEARNING TO LOVE YOURSELF

Patterns of self-hatred can be hard to break, but you can teach yourself to love and accept yourself instead of hating your imperfections. This is important work, because persistent negative beliefs show up in your negative self-talk and keep you stuck in co-dependent behavior patterns. Doing this work will help you break free of the co-dependency trap.

### *Tools for Working on Yourself*

- Take charge of strengthening your self-esteem. Find ways to improve your appearance, perhaps through exercise, diet, a change in hairstyle, or new clothes.
- Listen to subliminal tapes designed to change your limiting beliefs about yourself and what you can achieve.
- Write and use personal affirmations using the following guides:
  - Be personal: say "I."
  - Use the present tense: "I am."
  - State your change as a goal: "I am healthy."
  - State your target clearly: "I am healthy and I weigh 135 pounds and run two miles every other day."
  - Do your affirmations when you first rise each morning and just before going to sleep *every day*!
  - Visualize the end result of your goal as having already happened when you say your affirmation.
  - Write your most important affirmation on a note card, and carry it with you so you can repeat it during free moments of your day.

## Tools for Therapy

- Ask your therapist to do the first exercise described under "Tools for Committed Relationships" below.
- Role-play the process of changing negative self-talk statements into positive ones. To practice this skill, use the negative comments — about work, the weather, or a person — that you might find in your more casual relationships.
- Discuss setting your own limits as a means of increasing your self-esteem. Examine the issue of limits — how they were set and enforced in your childhood. Look for gaps or holes in completing that component of self-esteem. Create methods for setting your own limits.

## Tools for Support Groups

- Group self-talk. If your group has been together as a group long enough to know each other more intimately, spend part of a meeting giving each other positive feedback. Let one person be in the "love seat" while each member gives the recipient two or three minutes of supportive messages. Allow time for this person to really take it in.
- Find new options. Long histories of "brain chain" responses and negative self-talk create experiences of limited options. Ask group members to volunteer information about situations where they have habitual responses and feel powerless to do anything else. As a group, brainstorm as many new options as possible for each member's situation.

## Tools for Committed Relationships

- Make a list of the things you find most difficult to accept about yourself. Your partner can write a separate list of such things about himself or herself. Then share your lists and discuss any feelings that come up. To do this, take turns with your partner, working with one item on your list at a time. Rewrite statements about difficulties as statements of acceptance — for example, "I accept my growing baldness/wrinkles as part of who I am." Then read your statement of acceptance to your partner and have him or her affirm it: "I also accept your growing baldness/wrinkles as part of who you are." After you have worked with one of your items, switch with your partner and ask him or her to follow the same process with one of the items on his or her list.

- Contract with each other to identify instances when you use negative self-talk and black-and-white words or statements. Listen for such words as *always* and *never* and statements that indicate catastrophic thinking, such as "Well, I guess it's all over. We may as well call it quits."

- Discuss with your intimate partner sensitive self-love issues such as masturbation and feelings of selfishness. Explore your beliefs and feelings about having separate interests, taking time alone, and giving yourself sexual pleasure. These are areas where co-dependency often is the strongest.

## CASE EXAMPLE

Kate came to me (Janae) for therapy at a time when she found herself unable to make a decision about leaving her secretarial job. Her present job offered security and adequate pay but also a lot of stress and little opportunity for personal growth or advancement. A new job she was considering would pay about the same but offered less job security. It would also be much less stressful and would present more opportunity for personal growth and advancement.

Further exploration into Kate's background revealed a conflict between achievement and living a traditional feminine role. She had grown up in a rural area where most women lived highly co-dependent lives. She'd had no feminine role models for becoming an achiever, even though her high school years had been full of accomplishments. Her strong drive for achievement seemed partly based on a deep need for parental approval and love. As the oldest child, she'd experienced abandonment when the younger children had arrived. She had soon learned that achievements and counter-dependent behaviors won her strokes and approval.

Kate's father and mother had given her two conflicting messages that seemed to be playing out in her job dilemma. The first message was, "Be an achiever and be independent if you want our love and approval." The second was, "Good women should take care of the people around them. They shouldn't be too smart or be selfish." Part of Kate felt she should stay at the old job and take care of the dysfunctional people with whom she worked. She felt responsible for them and for her work duties. She was afraid to risk leaving her secure position, and yet she yearned for the growth possibilities at the new position.

In therapy she discovered that she had split off vital parts of herself in order to gain her parents' love. She found it difficult to love herself and to believe in her own needs, dreams, and ideas, because this conflicted with the other message, that she should take care of others. As we worked together on this dilemma, I provided a lot of mirroring and support for her achiever part, helping her see that she could choose to do these things for herself as a form of self-love. In order to provide a role model, I also shared my own story about having similar issues and told her how I'd worked through them.

Kate worked diligently on herself, seeking to understand her family patterns and to express her feelings of anger and resentment at the double bind inherent in the conflicting messages from her parents. She did take the new job and, within weeks, was making leaps in self-esteem and responding positively to the personal growth opportunities it offered.

Kate was also able to support her need for self-love and self-determination by reframing her history of frequent job changes, seeing in her history not a "lack of achievement" and "instability" but her "mastery of each new job." She also saw herself on the path to involvement in global projects and was able to view each job as preparation for this global work. She returned to college and began to chart a much broader course for her life, continuing to create a feminine support system for herself and her new dreams.

## SUMMARY

Learning to love and accept yourself unconditionally is the single most important task of healing patterns of self-hatred. At the deepest levels, healing co-dependency is actually nothing more than removing the barriers that prevent you from seeing and experiencing your True Self. With the proper tools and a clearer understanding of yourself, you can take steps forward in your evolutionary journey toward wholeness and a full recognition of who you are at a soul level.

# 12. Giving Up Power and Control Games

That people with co-dependency issues will try to control others is predictable. They do this by engaging in what we call "one-up" and "one-down" power plays. They nag, scream, beg, bribe, protect, rescue, accuse, cry, run after you, run away from you, seek revenge, whine, act hurt, lie, threaten suicide, lecture, insult, try to please, act helpless, hover over you, complain, lock you out, impress, condemn, bargain with you, curse, threaten to kill you, get drunk, wreck the car, throw things, break things, get sick, throw themselves on the floor, hide in a closet, talk about you behind your back, never admit they're wrong, leave, come back, leave again, drive recklessly, take drugs, overeat, work long hours, fail to get out of bed, tell people what to do and what not to do, analyze, deny, project, rationalize, suppress, and anything else they can think of to *try to control the behavior of someone else*. The goal of all their behaviors is the same: to get others to take care of them.

## PASSIVITY:
## THE MASTER GAME OF CO-DEPENDENCY

Passive persons are masters at dominating and controlling the behavior of others from a "one-down" position. They know all the moves — the dominator culture has taught them well. Passivity results from the same thing that causes co-dependency: the failure to securely bond and then become psychologically separate from one's parents. Passive people behave the way they do because they never learned how to get what they want in direct, active ways. They use passivity to control others in order to maintain a co-dependent relationship. If you understand passivity and how it works, you can learn to stop using passive behavior to try to get what you want.[1]

## PASSIVE BEHAVIORS
## AND HOW TO EFFECTIVELY CONFRONT THEM

The following categories of passive behavior are present in people with co-dependency issues. In each category is a brief discussion of reasons why people might use behaviors in that category and some suggested ways to effectively confront these behaviors.

### Behavior 1. Doing Nothing

Passive people may say, "I don't know" a lot when faced with a problem. They may not answer questions directly. They may engage in long silences before answering simple questions.

*Reason for the behavior.* They hope you'll do their thinking for them. They've learned that appearing weak and helpless gets someone else to think for them.

*How to confront this passive behavior.* When you encounter individuals who have made contracts with you to confront them on their passivity, or someone you'd like to be closer to and whose passivity is getting in the way of this, you might say things such as the following to them: "I believe you have the information, nurturing, help, and so forth that you need, so why don't you think about what you're telling me and what I'm suggesting, and then let me know what you want to do." "You may need some time to think about it." "If you need information that you don't have, you can ask for it." "Think about what you need from me (or others) and ask for it."

### Behavior 2. Overadaptation

This behavior entails requests for overly detailed instructions by people who engage in compulsive attempts to make sure they do everything right.

*Reasons for the behavior.* People who use this approach are afraid of being wrong. As a result, they've learned to do as they are told. They did not, as children, learn reasons for doing things, and they usually have faulty cause-effect thinking. They wish to pass the problem on to another person to solve, so that if the solution is wrong they can't be blamed.

*How to confront this passive behavior.* Make sure your partner (or other person) sets his or her own goals, and that these take into account what's appropriate for the situation, his or her own feelings, and other people's feelings. You can help by asking questions or making comments such as: "What are your reasons for doing that?" "People have reasons for doing what they do. I expect you to think about what you want to do and why you want to do it."

## Behavior 3. Agitation

In this category are nonproductive, repetitive behaviors such as tapping a pencil, chewing on an eraser, pacing back and forth, and talking incessantly without saying anything new.

*Reasons for the behavior.* These actions are attempts to avoid solving a problem. People use them in order to wait someone out, anticipating that the other person will get so uncomfortable that he or she will solve the problem.

*How to confront this passive behavior.* Encourage the individual to address the problem. Say something like: "Stop and think about what you want" or "Rather than doing that, put your energy into solving the problem."

## Behavior 4. Incapacitation or Violence

Actions in this category include incapacitation responses such as stomachaches, fainting spells, seizures, and other physical ailments. Or an action could take the form of violence: having a tantrum, kicking or hitting someone, or breaking something.

*Reasons for the behavior.* This is a more desperate attempt to get someone else to take responsibility.

*How to confront this passive behavior.* Take whatever steps are necessary to restore order or control. When a person is out of control, you may need to take control in a very direct and appropriate way. Immediately *after* a blowup, when a person has discharged some energy, is the best time to get him or her to do some new thinking about the problem. Just before or during a blowup, this approach usually doesn't work. Confront the person with a statement like: "It's not okay for you to solve problems that way" or "Think about what you could have done differently to solve the problem."

## HOW TO AVOID RESCUING

One of the most important interpersonal communication challenges for people with co-dependency issues is to learn how to recognize and avoid rescuing. Every time you help another person, the potential exists for playing the rescuer, persecutor, and victim game (also known as the drama triangle). This is how the dominator culture maintains hierarchical, or "one-up" and "one-down," relationships. Rescuers maintain power by doing things for others, without being asked, that the others are perfectly capable of doing for themselves. Rescuing contains implied messages such as "I can do it better than you" or "You are weak and helpless and can't do it for yourself." The victim usually feels the subtle put-down and then may get angry at the rescuer. Then the victim switches to the persecutor role and the rescuer becomes the victim, who may say something like "I was only trying to help." What helps keep this game going is competition for the victim role, which is the only way people with co-dependent behavior patterns know how to meet their needs in a dominator culture. There are various effective ways to avoid rescuing your partner. See the sidebar "How to Avoid Rescuing" for a list of tips.

The rescuer acts superior to the victim. The role of the victim is to be powerless and inferior to the rescuer. Playing either of these two roles will inevitably lead you to accumulate feelings of resentment that will eventually draw you into the persecutor role. The intensity of the emotions expressed in the persecutor role usually stays in direct proportion to the intensity of the emotions you felt in the rescuer or victim roles. Here are ways to avoid persecuting your partner:

• Avoid behavior that places you in a one-up position. Avoid talking down to your partner, and don't give advice unless it's requested. Don't interrupt. Maintain equality in all spheres, except those in which you both agree that you have more experience and expertise.

Strive to reduce any inequality by sharing with your partner what you know about the subject.

- If you feel angry with your partner, check to see if you might be engaging in rescuing behavior by doing more than 50 percent of the work. Also check to see if you did something you didn't want to do, but did anyway, for fear of hurting your partner's feelings. This can apply to listening to people in general when you're bored, continuing to do something when it feels unproductive, doing things you don't want to do either because you don't like the person, he or she bores you, or you're tired. The responsibility is half yours. The angrier you are at your partner, or the angrier he or she is at you, the more likely it is that you've either rescued or persecuted him or her. Remember, no one can play this game with you without your full participation. If you get angry with your partner or other people often (more than once a week), look to see what *your* part in the problem is and do something about it.

---

## HOW TO AVOID RESCUING

- Don't help your partner without a verbal contract to do so. You can make such a contract by asking, "What do you want from me?"
- Don't ever believe that a person is helpless, unless he or she is unconscious. Encourage him or her by saying, "I know you can solve that problem. Would you like to discuss it further?"
- Offer support to people who are feeling helpless in discovering their own power: "Think about some ways you could solve that, and then talk to me."
- Don't do more than 50 percent of the work on the problem or task. Make an agreement with your partner that he or she will do at least 50 percent of the work at all times. Tell your partner, "This is what I'm willing to do — what are you willing to do?"
- Don't do anything that you don't really want to do: say, "No, I'm not willing to do that."

- Don't *allow* feelings of resentment to accumulate in your partnership. Share held resentments as soon as possible and encourage your partner to give constructive feedback to you.
- Don't invite persecution or rescuing from your partner. Some people, in order not to be one-up on their partners, interact from a one-down position. This can be done by dressing sloppily, being sick a lot, not keeping agreements, or being passive.
- What keeps the game going is competition for the victim role. Many people believe being a victim is the only way they can meet their needs. To break this game, you must be willing to ask for what you want 100 percent of the time and to negotiate to get it.

## ONE-UP/ONE-DOWN POWER MOVES

The following list identifies some of the common power moves that people with co-dependency issues make in an attempt to dominate or control their partners:

- Poor timing. Pick a fight during a favorite TV show or just as your partner is going to sleep or is leaving for work. The idea is to keep your partner off balance and limit his or her ability to respond.
- Escalation. During an argument, move from the topic and start questioning your partner's personality or making other statements that distract your partner. Use phrases like "you always" or "you never."
- Sandbagging. Throw in as many problems as you can think of. Dig up old conflicts and make them related in some way.
- Asking why. Put the other person on the defensive immediately by asking something like: "Why didn't you . . . ?" or "Why were you so late?"
- Blaming. Blame it all on the other person. You're right, they're wrong, and why won't they admit it?
- Pulling rank. Rather than standing on the merits of your argument, remind your partner that you have more education, money, or experience.
- Labeling. Label your partner's behavior as childish, neurotic, or co-dependent. This is a great way to obscure the issues when you feel shaky about your position.

- Leaving. This prevents any resolution of a problem. You can walk out of the room, leave the house, threaten to leave, or just refuse to talk.
- Avoiding responsibility. Saying you don't remember, or you must have been drunk or too sleepy, is a way to avoid a conflict.
- Playing martyr. By taking refuge in hopelessness, you can use one-down power to manipulate your partner. You can say, "Yes, you're always right; I am a hopeless case," or you can threaten to kill yourself.
- Using money. This is a common way to control a spouse. An old favorite is: "When you make as much money as I do, then you can complain."

## TOOLS FOR GIVING UP POWER AND CONTROL GAMES

Because people aren't taught effective, healthy ways to get their needs and wants met, they rely on games and dysfunctional methods. These less effective ways involve the use of power plays, control, and manipulation, which eventually take their toll on a relationship. These games can produce a lot of conflict in relationships and cause people to feel stuck.

### *Tools for Working on Yourself*

Here is a six-step assertiveness process that is helpful in breaking power and control games.[2]

1.  Prepare yourself. The first step in creating a clear, assertive message is to write it down and then review it. Make sure that it respects the personal boundaries of the other person, that it's a persistent concern, that the two of you have built a base of trust, and that you can meet your needs by sharing this message. Make an appointment to deliver the message, and choose neutral ground on which to do it, if possible. Timing is important, so avoid scheduling it when either of you is tired or rushed.
2.  Deliver your message. Communicate your message directly, maintaining eye contact. Breathe fully, using a calm yet firm voice.
3.  Be silent. Wait for a while after communicating your message to allow the other person to think about it and to speak what's on his or her mind.

4. Engage in active-listening defensive responses. If your partner starts to defend himself or herself, you'll need to shift gears and actively listen to his or her defensive response. Make an observation such as: "You're feeling wrongly accused of that" or "You seem hurt by what I said."

5. If your partner starts to defend himself or herself, use a recycling process. Restate your message, follow it with silence, and listen again to any defensiveness until you get the feeling that your partner understands your message. It can take several repetitions to get to this point. Persist.

6. Focus on the solution. This is usually a negotiation process. You must ask the other person for what you want and then be willing to negotiate the conflict until both of you are satisfied with the solution. When you have agreed, restate the agreement to make sure you both understand. Also, arrange some way to check in with each other later to make sure the solution is working. This is important, as it assures that neither of you agrees to something that doesn't really work.

### Tools for Therapy

Control and power games arise out of poor self-esteem and weak object constancy. Therapy can help you develop a program to improve your self-esteem. Four main skill areas determine your level of self-esteem:[3]

- Contact skills. People with high self-esteem make effective contact with themselves and others.
- Acceptance skills. People with high self-esteem accept differences between themselves and others. They respect the right of others to be different, and they take seriously their own feelings and behaviors, even when these are different from those of others.
- Influence skills. People with high self-esteem make things happen for themselves and others and are able to effectively stop unwanted things from happening.
- Constancy skills. People with high self-esteem maintain a fairly constant positive image or good feeling about themselves, even in the face of failure.

Complete the "Self-Esteem Questionnaire" at the end of this chapter to help you determine the areas where you might need help in therapy. A good therapist will be able to develop a plan to help you shore up any weak skill areas.

### Tools for Support Groups

Support groups can provide you with an opportunity to rehearse scenarios in which you have trouble maintaining your position or staying out of game behavior. One of the most difficult things to do for those with co-dependency issues is to say no. They often need the support of others in learning effective ways to say no. Role-playing or rehearsing a situation where a resolute no is called for can help you stay out of co-dependency. Here are some effective ways to say no:

- The reasonable no. When you say no, give a very clear and succinct reason for your response. In answer to a request to go out drinking with the boys, you might say, "No, thanks. I'm serious about staying with my twelve-step program."
- Active listening, then no. First you respond to the request, and then you say no. For example, if your partner wants to go to the movies and you want to watch TV, you might say, "You look like you were really counting on me going to the movies with you tonight. Is that correct?" Then follow it with, "I'm sorry, but I'd like to watch my favorite TV show tonight. Would you be willing to go without me this time?"
- The rain-check no. Here you can say no for now but request that you be asked again. Your partner asks you to cook dinner tonight, and you have plans to go to a meeting. You can say, "I have plans tonight, but I'd be willing to cook tomorrow night. Would that work?"
- Broken record. This is useful in cases where people refuse to take no for an answer. In these cases, you may need a one-sentence refusal statement that you repeat over and over like a broken record, no matter what the other person says — for example, "I don't have any money to loan you." It's good to develop your statement ahead of time and rehearse it, so you can firmly hold your ground while you repeat your message.

*Tools for Committed Relationships*

- Game-breaking responses make it easier for partners to stop power and control games. Such responses make it hard for the other person to continue the game. Two very effective game-breakers for people who try to give you advice or information that you don't want or need are: "Thank you, I wasn't aware of that" and "Thank you, I am aware of that."

- It's also important that partners set ground rules for handling conflict. The sidebar "Ground Rules for Establishing Partnership Relationships" lists five ground rules necessary for establishing and maintaining a cooperative relationship.[4]

## GROUND RULES FOR ESTABLISHING PARTNERSHIP RELATIONSHIPS

- No scarcity. Both partners must believe they can get what they want if they cooperate with each other.
- Equal rights. Both parties agree that each has an equal right to get his or her needs and wants satisfied, and that each shares equal responsibility for creating a cooperative relationship.
- No power plays. Both parties agree to enter into problem-solving discussions and not use power plays or games to get what they want.
- No secrets. Both parties agree to be honest with each other and not keep secrets.
- No rescues. Both parties agree not to do things for each other without asking. Both agree to ask for what they want and to negotiate differences.

## CASE EXAMPLE

A conflict that Cara and Rick brought to couples therapy provides a good example of how to stop power and control games. They were at an impasse on a conflict concerning Rick's driving habits. Cara was critical of the way he drove, claiming that she was afraid to ride with him anymore. The more she had criticized him, the more Rick had resisted and denied her accusations.

Finally he'd refused to drive anymore, and had insisted that Cara do all the driving from that point on. She'd agreed reluctantly but wanted to find a better solution. Rick consented to discuss it only in therapy. Cara complained that, while driving, Rick drifted out of his lane and didn't look properly when he wanted to change lanes. She claimed that they had nearly been in two accidents recently because of his inattentive driving habits.

By helping Cara rephrase her message, and by reflecting Rick's feelings, we were able to help them explore possible options. We discovered that Rick frequently needed Cara's help when changing lanes in heavy traffic because of a blind spot between their car mirrors. However, he did not ask her for help, because she was frequently knitting or reading while they drove. He tried to make lane changes by himself, but he admitted that it was difficult for him to see because of the blind spot. He agreed to ask her for help when they got in traffic, and she said she would be glad to help if he asked her.

One additional problem remained, and that was Rick's tendency to drift over into the other lane. He admitted that sometimes he let his mind wander while he was driving, and that the car sometimes drifted over the center line. He recognized that it happened occasionally on the open highway. Cara said that she got scared when the car started to drift and often would yell at Rick to bring his attention back. He objected to her yelling at him, because it made him feel bad and often led to a fight between them. What eventually emerged in our dialogues was that Cara and her family had been involved in a bad automobile accident when she was a child, and it had left her traumatized. No one was killed, but she and several other family members had been injured. She said she still had fear of that happening again. Rick, on the other hand, was never in an accident and tended to react to Cara's fear as if she were telling him he didn't know how to drive. Cara's comments reminded him of his critical mother.

We looked for a better way for Cara to connect with Rick, should he want her assistance in driving. What Rick said would work was for Cara to reach over and touch him on the arm when she started to get scared and say, "Rick, I'm getting scared. Would you focus more attention on your driving?" He felt relieved by this simple solution.

Cara and Rick developed a cooperative rather than a competitive way to handle driving and recognized that this could actually bring them closer together while they were driving. Rick said, "I might even enjoy driving again," as he smiled at Cara. As they drove away from the session, we noticed that Rick was again at the wheel.

## AWARENESS ACTIVITY

The "Self-Esteem Questionnaire" can help you locate specific areas where your self-esteem may be weak.[5] Fill it out, score it, and then develop a plan for improving yourself in weak areas.

## SELF-ESTEEM QUESTIONNAIRE

Rate each of the items below from 1 to 4, depending on how consistently you're able to perform each behavior.

1 = I am hardly able to do this.
2 = I am sometimes able to do this.
3 = I can do this fairly often, but could improve in this area.
4 = I can do this often and in a manner with which I am satisfied.

### Area A: Contact Skills

_____ I'm able to ask for help or can ask someone for something I need without feeling inadequate, shameful, or guilty.

_____ When I'm with another person, I feel fully present. My thoughts don't drift away to other things.

_____ When I talk to others, my words and voice match how I feel inside.

_____ I take an active part in groups and enjoy being involved.

_____ When I like someone, I can show them directly how I feel.

_____ I'm aware of how my body feels, what parts are tense, when I need rest, and I seriously try to supply what my body tells me it needs.

_____ Contact subscore

## Area B: Acceptance Skills

_____ I can express my ideas without waiting to hear what other people think.

_____ I can base my actions on my feelings and let myself experience them as an important part of me without getting stuck with, and without hanging on to, any of them.

_____ I take time to show my own taste and interests in such things as the way I decorate my office, how I dress, and how I express myself verbally. These expressions of myself are more important than what others think of me.

_____ There are times I choose to be alone, to withdraw from others and be by myself — resting, reflecting, meditating, or doing something else I enjoy. At these times I don't feel I have to be productive.

_____ I take time to do imaginative and creative projects.

_____ I can share my point of view even when others' views differ from mine.

_____ Acceptance subscore

## Area C: Influence Skills

_____ I can handle a great deal of pressure without physical upsets and headaches.

_____ I am able to set firm and clear limits for myself and others without trying to make either myself or others seem guilty or bad.

_____ I can express my feelings appropriately without losing control.

_____ I seek responsibility and enjoy being in charge of projects and activities.

_____ I can make decisions without excessive delay or stress.

_____ I can take risks in new situations and find them challenging and exciting.

_____ Influence subscore

## Area D: Constancy Skills

_____ I feel okay even when others disapprove of what I do.

_____ I can admit my mistakes.

_____ I can listen to positive and negative feedback from others without feeling embarrassed or defensive.

_____ I can speak the truth about my perceptions even when others might not agree with me.

_____ I feel okay about myself even when things I plan don't work out.

_____ I can turn disappointments into new challenges.

_____ Constancy subscore

_____ Total score

SCORING: Add up the numbers for each answer in each subsection, and then add up the subscores to get the total score. Look at each of the subscores and see which ones are low. This will give you some idea where you need to work to improve your self-esteem. Then use the following chart to interpret your total score.

24–48 Low self-esteem in most areas of your life
49–72 Low self-esteem in a few areas of your life
73–96 High self-esteem in most areas of your life

## SUMMARY

Power and control games keep us from breaking free of the co-dependency trap. People with co-dependent behaviors often use one-down power plays to try to control others and meet their own needs, but these efforts almost always fall short of giving them what they really want. The most common power game is the drama triangle. Once you become aware of drama-triangle dynamics, you will likely see them everywhere. You'll find plenty of opportunities to practice the skills needed to avoid drama-triangle dynamics or to extricate yourself quickly when you find yourself enmeshed in them.

# 13. Learning to Ask for What You Want

**M**ost people with co-dependency issues have poor communication skills. In addition to "Don't think or feel" messages in childhood, they received "Don't ask for what you want" messages. As a result, they learned how to choose words that help them manipulate and control, please people, cover up, and remain passive in order to get what they want. Co-dependent communication is full of repressed thoughts, ulterior motives, repressed feelings, low self-esteem, and shame. People with co-dependency issues learn to act happy when they're not. They justify, rationalize, compensate, and deceive. They may also badger, threaten, or be unassertive. Often, the message is, "If you really loved me, you would read my mind, know what I need, and give it to me. If I have to ask, then I can't trust that what you give me comes from love."

Co-dependent communication is indirect, and people are unable to say what they mean or mean what they say. They hope that someone will read their minds, and they work hard at reading the minds of others. All this, of course, keeps them in a victim role and perpetuates their one-up or one-down power plays.

Underlying this passivity is the infantile dream that mother or some other nurturing figure will just know what their unmet needs are. Passive people can go through their whole lives using indirect communication and, consequently, never meet their real needs.

To make the shift from indirect to direct communication, you may need to replace some of your negative self-talk with positive self-talk that supports you in getting what you want. The following are some key positive concepts:

- It's important to ask for what you want.
- Who you are is okay.
- Your feelings and thoughts are okay.
- It's acceptable to talk about yourself and your problems.
- Your opinions count.
- Sometimes you need to say no.
- Telling the truth sets you free.

Once you create beliefs that support these concepts, asking directly for what you want becomes much easier.

## ASSERTION SKILLS

Experts estimate that less than 5 percent of the population can communicate assertively.[1] While this figure is presently shifting, we estimate that 95 percent of the population do not get their needs met, and there is little intimacy in the day-to-day communication of those unduly influenced by the dominator culture.

Assertiveness is the ground between passiveness and aggressiveness. It allows you to communicate in ways that enable you to maintain your self-respect, pursue your goals, satisfy your needs, and defend your rights and personal space, all without dominating or manipulating others. Assertive people stand up for their own rights and express personal needs, values, concerns, and ideas in direct and appropriate ways.

### Knowing What You Want

Wants differ from needs. Needs are the physical and psychological conditions necessary for safety and survival, while wants are things or conditions you desire but can live without. If you confuse needs and wants, you can confuse issues of safety and survival with issues of comfort. You can also have trouble establishing priorities when you have choices to make.

Messages to "not think" and "not feel" also prevent you from reflecting on your inner experiences. This literally trains you not to know what you want and makes learning to be assertive more difficult. You may need to do a lot of journaling in order to discover the differences between needs and wants and to learn what your wants and needs really are. You may be used to adapting to the needs and wants of others and ignoring your own, so be sure to monitor yourself.

### Confrontation

Confronting others or asserting yourself firmly may be necessary to protect yourself, to meet your needs, or to point out discrepancies in what people say or do. Confrontation usually is used in sensitive areas and between people who have a contract for undertaking it, or in threatening situations when you experience an unwanted invasion of your boundaries. Confrontation quickly engages the confronter and confrontee in interaction, so a good rule to follow is: confront only the people you want to get closer to, people who are invading your space without permission, and those with whom you have a contract.

### Asking for What You Want: A Nine-Step Process

This step-by-step process will help you learn to ask directly for what you want or need from another, a vital skill necessary for breaking free of your co-dependency trap.

1. Describe objectively the problem or behavior. (For example, "When you get angry and yell and scream...")
2. Share your feelings about the problem or behavior. ("I feel scared like I did when I was little and Dad yelled at me.")
3. Describe the effects of the problem or issue on you and/or your relationship. ("I want to run away from you and hide.")
4. Pause for a moment to listen to the other person's feedback or perceptions about the conflict. Do not allow yourself to get bogged down at this step by defending, blaming, or escalating. Stop only long enough to listen to short feedback.
5. State clearly what you want from the other person. ("What I want from you is for you to express your anger in words like 'I am angry.'")

6.  Ask the person clearly, "Would you be willing to . . . ?" ("Would you be willing to say that you are angry without yelling and screaming at me?")

7.  Negotiate if there are differences between what you want and what the other person is willing to give or do. ("I need to let off steam when I feel angry; I would like to be able to raise my voice" or "I can handle your raising your voice if it doesn't turn into yelling and screaming, and if you don't direct it at me.")

8.  If you are unable to negotiate the differences, agree to disagree. ("I see that we just don't agree on this issue, and I accept our disagreement. Will you also agree to disagree?")

9.  If the differences are unresolvable and the relationship ends, mark it with some ceremony of completion. Write a letter stating your perception of your unresolvable differences without blame, seeing yourself and the other person as okay. You may choose to mail it or decide to burn it once you have expressed your thoughts and feelings.

This guide will help you ask directly for what you want. Notice that the above steps require action. Thinking, feeling, and reflecting are not enough; they alone will not ensure that your needs are met. Steps 5 through 7 require you to state clearly what you want and then ask for it. They also encourage negotiating to settle differences. Step 8 offers a way to resolve a conflict with someone who refuses to work on the conflict. There are instances when "agreeing to disagree" leaves you feeling incomplete, so step 9 allows you to complete your part of the conflict and move on with your life.

## WHEN CONFLICT RESULTS

If you've been a passive or adaptive person, and you begin asking more clearly for what you want, you may find yourself experiencing more conflict. Conflict is often associated with fighting, compromising, losing, rejection, and humiliation — all negative concepts. It's considered the opposite of romantic love, which is seen as being full of idyllic days and nights unmarred by bickering or unpleasantness. As a result, most people avoid conflict and try to create the romantic dream that Hollywood portrays in movies.

Conflict is not inherently bad. In fact, it can be a constructive force if you're willing to learn conflict resolution skills that bring positive energy into a relationship. Adopting a positive attitude toward conflict is helpful, because conflict is unavoidable unless partners have exactly the same needs, wants, and dreams. How you handle conflict is more important than the context of the conflict. There are three ways to respond to conflict: defend, deflect, or discover.

*Defending* protects you from harm or threats of harm. When defending, it's important that you take care to meet the attack with an amount of force exactly equal to the force of the attack. This will neutralize the attack. If you respond with just a little more energy, you'll escalate the conflict and prolong it. If you meet the attack with too little energy, you may encourage more attacking and set yourself up to be victimized. Either of these latter responses can elicit or create one-up and one-down power plays.

*Deflecting* a conflict may be necessary in some cases. If you're being attacked by someone coming at you with the force of a freight train, you must jump off the track. If your partner in a conflict flips into a rage state during a moment of temporary insanity, the best response is to leave until he or she has cooled down. Deflecting is also useful in responding to people who hook you into conflict and then refuse to work it through with you.

*Discovery* creates an opportunity to learn more about your partner. It can be a time to explore parts or aspects of him or her that are unknown to you. Discovery also offers an opportunity to learn about yourself. Sharing with your partner and taking in feedback may reveal parts or aspects of yourself that you previously have projected or are unaware of. This mutual "uncloaking" can be helpful when couples are ready to discover the source of their conflict. With discovery, you can stop blaming and instead assume responsibility for your behavior. It becomes safe to be open and vulnerable, to risk feeling and expressing your old pain and wounds. When the defensive walls come down and conflict becomes a cooperative matter, real intimacy can begin.

## CONFLICT AS INTIMACY

If conflict is really an opportunity for intimacy, then perhaps now's the time for a new definition of intimacy. While intimacy is usually associated with romance and pleasantness, conflict can also be intimate. In the midst of conflict, people are usually expressing their feelings, so these moments feel more real even though they may also be unpleasant. Conflict can also break down defenses and expose hidden parts of people. When these parts emerge, they often open old feelings and old wounds that want to be healed. When you reach this point in a partnership, another kind of intimacy becomes possible. Being present to hold and emotionally support your partner during such a vulnerable moment creates a sacred space between you. We think of it as "touching souls." Intimacy then includes both romantic experiences and experiences of anger, sadness, grief, and pain. Once you expand your view of intimacy to include all your relational experiences, you'll find yourself able to feel close, even when you're in conflict.

Most people fear conflict because it often leads to separation. As you complete your psychological birth and work through your oneness and separateness issues, you'll find conflict less frightening. You'll also find that, with this larger perspective, intimacy becomes easier.

## TOOLS FOR LEARNING TO ASK FOR WHAT YOU WANT

Co-dependent behavior almost always includes being indirect. Learning to ask directly for what you want is an important skill. This skill, perhaps more than any other, will help you break free of the co-dependency trap.

### Tools for Working on Yourself

Write in your journal about your needs and wants. Make one list of things you need. List them in the order of their importance. Decide how you'll meet these needs. List the things you *want* in the order of their importance. Decide what you're willing to do to satisfy these wants.

### Tools for Therapy

Contract with your therapist to work on assertiveness. Decide which assertiveness issues you want to work on (passivity, phrasing requests, learning to say no). Decide which people in your life are the most difficult to confront. Describe them to your therapist and ask him or her to role-play them while you practice your confrontation skills. Ask your therapist for feedback about your effectiveness and for suggestions on improving your skills. List your most common conflicts in your relationships. With your therapist, review them to identify patterns and look for their sources. Develop effective ways to resolve them.

### Tools for Support Groups

- Discuss with other members in the group the kinds of conflicts you all had in your families while growing up, and list them by category, such as child rearing, money, work, and addictions. Then pick one to re-create together. Ask one member to be the objective observer or facilitator who monitors the re-creation. Have the observer stop the action every five minutes to see how people are feeling and to suggest new responses to old patterns.
- Contract as a group to ask what each person wants. Watch group interactions in order to pinpoint rescues, manipulation, victim responses, complaints, and instances of making assumptions without checking them out. When you hear someone complaining, ask him or her directly, "What is it you want?" This stops people from complaining as a way to manipulate.

### Tools for Committed Relationships

- Discuss with your partner how each of you approaches conflict resolution. Include questions like the following:
  - What are the ways that you defend yourself (for example, blame, denial)?
  - What are the ways that you attempt to change others or control them (anger, threats, withdrawing love, criticism, nagging, sarcasm)?
  - What are the ways that you become indifferent or avoid conflict (work, TV, reading, sports, hobbies, meditation)?
  - What are the ways you rebel when your partner makes a decision you don't like (pouting, not talking, pulling away)?
- Evaluate together a recent conflict between the two of you. Ask yourselves these questions:
  - What did I want from the conflict?
  - What did I get from it?

- Did I ask clearly for what I wanted?
- Was I able to ask for what I wanted in such a way that my partner was delighted to give it to me?
- Were we able to negotiate our differences?
- Were we able to express our emotions clearly?
- Did either of us hurt the other?
- Did I learn something new about my partner or about myself in the conflict?
- Did I reveal something new about myself to my partner?
- What would I do differently?
- Did we end up feeling closer at the conclusion?

## CASE EXAMPLE

Ray is a classic example of a man who cannot ask for what he wants. Growing up in an emotionally reserved family, he had no models for learning directness. He coped with this inability by marrying Mary Ann, who was well trained in "mind reading" and taking care of other people's wants and needs. She trained their three daughters to recognize his food preferences and his daily habits and to anticipate his physical needs. Ray's wife and daughters became adept at observing his nonverbal signals. They would refill his water glass or pass him food before his glass or plate was empty.

Ray found he could meet his emotional needs without asking for what he wanted. When his wife or a daughter failed to take care of some physical need sufficiently, he would explode in anger. Intimidated by his anger, they would repent and pledge to do better. Then they could all hug him and feel close.

This is a life pattern that Ray is unwilling to change. As a result of his addictions to food, work, and power, he maintains superficial relationships with everyone. His inability to express his needs, his addictions, and his lack of self-esteem are evidenced by his poor physical health and increasing obesity.

Not everyone is willing to work through his or her addictive patterns. Sometimes the pain of recovery and the effort required to learn more effective ways of living and relating seem like too much to cope with.

## SUMMARY

Learning to ask directly for what you want and need is perhaps the most important, and sometimes the most difficult, skill to acquire. You'll know that you've broken free of the co-dependency trap when you can ask for something in such a way that people are delighted to give you what you want or need.

# 14. Learning to Feel Again

Co-dependency keeps people disconnected from their true emotions. They allow themselves to express only the emotions known as "racket" feelings, such as anger or sadness, for which they refuse to take responsibility: "She made me so angry" or "He made me cry." Because people with co-dependency issues need to discharge pent-up emotions, they learn to manipulate or blame someone else in order to discharge them. Racket feelings mask deeper and more genuine feelings.

## WHAT ARE FEELINGS?

Because they've grown up in a culture still largely based on the dominator model, most people know very little about feelings. Our culture emphasizes rational thinking functions and virtually ignores the feeling function. Most Americans don't even know what feelings are for. Carl Jung says, "The feeling function is the reason of the heart which the reason of the mind doesn't quite understand."[1]

Human beings experience five basic feelings, with some variations that relate to intensity. We've listed these feelings in the chart "Basic Feelings and Their Definitions."

## BASIC FEELINGS AND THEIR DEFINITIONS

| Feeling | Definition |
|---------|------------|
| Anger | A natural response to being unable to meet your wants and needs. You might not give yourself permission to express anger because you feel scared about the outcome. |
| Fear | Your natural response to perceived physical or emotional danger. You might not be able to think and feel at the same time, and might use fear to cover anger. |
| Sadness | Your natural response to the loss of a person, thing, or relationship, real or imagined. Sadness is an important part of releasing something to which you have an attachment. You might also feel some anger connected to the loss. |
| Excitement | Your natural anticipation of something good happening. Fear and excitement are at opposite ends of a continuum. Some children are denied permission to show excitement. |
| Happiness or Joy | Your natural satisfaction at getting what you want or need, or at doing something effectively. Some people don't know it's acceptable to be effective and happy. |

Sometimes people use other words as substitutes for core feelings, and use them to avoid the basic feelings or to justify their behavior. Words like "frustrated," "guilty," "hurt," "annoyed," and "irritated" usually cover anger. Words like "confused," "nervous," "uneasy," and "tense" cover fear. Sadness is often expressed as being "lonely," "bored," "empty," or "low." Some words represent a combination of feelings. "Depressed," "unhappy," or "upset" can be a combination of anger, fear, and/or sadness. Suffering is usually anger and fear operating in a person who doesn't have permission to express these emotions. It's important to correctly identify your own basic feelings and to use them in your decision-making process.

Feelings are natural, normal responses to your experiences. They can help you form and clarify your values and make decisions. You probably learned early in life to distort your feelings. Elisabeth Kübler-Ross expresses it this way: "We all start out perfect. You begin to see that people become twisted when their natural emotions are suppressed."[2] Alice Miller writes that we stay stuck in infancy and co-dependency for the following reasons:[3]

- We had our feelings hurt when we were small children, without anyone ever noticing.
- Then we were told not to be angry at being hurt.
- Then we were forced to show gratitude toward those who hurt us, because they had good intentions (they didn't mean to hurt us).
- Then we were told to forget everything that happened.
- Finally, we were shown that we could get rid of our stored-up anger by being violent and abusive toward others who were smaller or weaker than us, or we were told to direct that anger against ourselves.

Miller adds, "The greatest cruelty that can be inflicted on children is preventing them from expressing their anger and suffering except at the risk of losing their parents' love and affection."[4] Many children who grow up in co-dependent families are systematically taught to inhibit and repress their angry, sad, and hurt feelings. Frequently they are talked out of their feelings — taught to distrust what they feel and to trust only what others tell them to feel.

If you grew up in a co-dependent family, you probably didn't get your emotional needs met, and you experienced many painful feelings during childhood. To make matters worse, no one listened to your feelings, no one comforted and nurtured you or accepted and respected you, which forced you to cope with these painful feelings all by yourself. In order to cope with this emotional pain, you built defenses against feeling the feelings and shut them out of your awareness. While this may have helped you to survive childhood, it totally disconnected you from your authentic feelings. Without the ability to express your true feelings, you cannot experience the fullness and richness of life.

## CO-DEPENDENT WAYS TO HANDLE FEELINGS

The following list illustrates some of the co-dependent or dysfunctional ways to handle your feelings. These behaviors usually don't help you get what you want or need. If you recognize some of them as your own responses, look for better ways to express your feelings.

- Cry when you're angry.
- Get angry to cover up your fear, sadness, or hurt.
- Get depressed instead of taking action.
- Act strong and block out your feelings.
- Blame your feelings on others. ("You made me mad.")
- Believe that the expression of certain feelings is a sign of weakness. (Men don't cry; women shouldn't get angry.)
- Let the feelings of others control your thoughts, feelings, and actions.
- Let your thoughts block feelings or your feelings block thoughts.
- Express only justified, or racket, feelings, so that you can control other people.
- Give more power to your feelings than they deserve. ("If I started crying, I would never be able to stop," or "If I got angry, I would hurt someone.")
- Believe feelings are bad and should be avoided. Become addicted to a substance or activity to keep yourself emotionally numb.

## HEALTHY WAYS TO HANDLE FEELINGS

The following list offers some examples of healthy, more effective ways to utilize your feelings:

- When you feel angry, scared, or hurt, say so. Ask for what you want from others.
- Use your feelings to help you make decisions.
- Identify each separate feeling and avoid using one to block another.
- Claim your feelings, and take responsibility for actions that result from them.
- Accept that you can think and feel at the same time, and then do it.
- Recognize your racket feelings and avoid using them to manipulate others.
- Stay current in the expression of your feelings, instead of storing them up.
- Embrace your feelings as your friends and allies rather than regarding them as enemies to be avoided.

- Allow yourself to experience your feelings as fully as possible when they surface.
- Remember that there are no "bad feelings," and that there is an important purpose for each of them.

## TOOLS FOR LEARNING TO FEEL AGAIN

In order to eliminate the distortions in your feelings that you learned to accept while growing up and living in a thinking-oriented world, you'll need some new skills to help you understand and express your feelings effectively.

### *Tools for Working on Yourself*

- Create a "feeling journal" for yourself. Make a list of feelings you felt during the day. Record in your journal the circumstances under which you felt each feeling, where you felt the feeling in your body, and how you expressed it, if you did. You may record only the times you felt an emotion or were aware of feeling one but didn't express it. Chart your progress over time. Notice what feelings you're able to identify but can't express. Notice if certain feelings are missing from your list.
- Take inventory of the feelings expressed by various people in your family of origin: your mother, your father, and your siblings. Whose pattern do you most often follow?
- Make a list of the things that happened to you as a child about which you might have been angry, sad, scared, happy, or excited. Next to each entry, place an *E* if you expressed feelings of anger, sadness, fear, happiness, or excitement. Notice in which situations you repressed or held back your feelings. Finally, compare your two lists to see if you're still responding the way you did as a child, or if you've changed your feeling response patterns.

### *Tools for Therapy*

A good therapist can provide the same kind of support for your emotional needs as a cooperative partner. The primary difference is that your therapist may be more skilled in helping you reconnect with your deepest feelings and in providing an opportunity for you to express them in a safe, supportive environment.

Breath work is a powerful therapy that can enable you to regain contact with deep hurt or sadness. Old patterns can become locked into your body, and breath work can help you connect with and release buried feelings. The technique we use is a connected breathing pattern. You "pull" your breath in as you inhale, and then you release it, relaxing as you exhale. Connect both your inhalation and your exhalation so there is no pause between them. Visualize a circle, with the inhalation as one half of the circle and the exhalation as the other half. As repressed feelings begin to loosen, just keep breathing. You may experience shaking or tingling in your arms and legs and a sense of release of tension in your stomach or chest. About forty-five minutes to an hour and a half of this kind of breath work can release many old patterns locked in your body. You may experience an emotional release as well. Following your session, you will feel relaxed and open. You may repeat this as often as you wish.

### Tools for Support Groups

Support groups too can provide emotional support. One important way groups can support your feelings is by giving you feedback. An exercise useful for this is called "the empowerment circle." Each person is given two minutes to tell the group his or her major strengths and resources. Then the group has three minutes to tell the person what strengths they see in him or her. Groups of no more than six people work best.

### Tools for Committed Relationships

- A lot of healing happens at the feeling level. If you're in a committed relationship where you can meet your needs, there are certain things you can ask your partner for. The skills listed here can be transformative in an intimate relationship. They provide what you need in order to complete your psychological birth. Ask your partner

  - to show understanding and respect for your needs and feelings;
  - to listen to your feelings and take them seriously;

- to provide mirroring and feedback so you can see who you really are; and
- to learn from your feelings, as you learn from his or hers.

- Try this exercise: Each person identifies a current conflict circulating in the relationship. Begin the exercise with one of the two conflicts. Each of you can take turns first blaming everything that happened on your partner, and then blaming everything that happened on yourself. Then look at the responsibility (response-ability) you each had in the situation, and notice that neither of you may have been fully *able to respond*. Ask yourself, "What other responses could I have had in this situation?" Next, perform the exercise again, this time focusing on the conflict identified by the second partner.

## CASE EXAMPLE

Cynthia first came to me (Janae) for therapy requesting help with sexual problems in her relationship with Don. She had stopped enjoying sex with him, and then had finally stopped having sex with him altogether. Don was upset and had insisted that she get counseling.

It was obvious from Cynthia's first few words that she was severely impaired in her feelings and was totally fused with Don. Her entire focus was on "getting well" so Don could have sex with her. Cynthia reminded me of a windup doll as she talked. Her body movements were rigid and jerky. Her eyes were somewhat vacant and they gazed into the distance. Her voice was a monotone with virtually no emotions expressed in it. She could have been relating a story about some distant acquaintance, as there were no feelings apparent — only facts.

Therapy with Cynthia was slow and methodical. First, she had to learn to recognize basic feelings. Then she had to learn to identify them in herself. This took several months of intensive journaling, participation in a support group, and discussions with me. Once she had learned to identify feelings, we worked on accepting them.

Cynthia was prone to unexplained episodes of crying. Don was uncomfortable with these outbursts, so she had learned to hold the tears until she was alone in the bathroom or driving her car. Cynthia eventually was able to bring her sadness to therapy, where I could hold her and comfort her. It took almost eighteen months of intermittent therapy, support-group work, and working on herself before she was really okay with her feelings. At that point she found it was safe to express her feelings to Don, and they began working together to address their feeling issues.

This kind of preparatory work is often necessary before people with crippled feeling functions can address co-dependency issues in a relationship. The recovery of one's feeling function is essential to breaking free of the co-dependency trap. If a person doesn't know when he or she is feeling something, or know what he or she is feeling, then this person usually also doesn't know what he or she wants or needs. People can't ask for what they want and need until they know what they want to ask for.

## SUMMARY

Co-dependent behavior patterns almost always contain a distortion of your true feelings, and you must learn how to feel and express these true feelings. Feelings are a big part of your recovery process, and there is no such thing as a "bad" feeling.

# 15. Healing Your Inner Child

Growing up in co-dependent families in a dominator culture, people are forced to give up their True Selves and adopt False Selves in order to survive. In most co-dependent families, the adults are really "playing grown-up," and most of the time they're not available to support or nurture their children.

## NARCISSISTIC WOUNDS

During the first twelve months of a child's life, it's impossible to spoil him or her. Children need to be noticed, mirrored, taken seriously, held, nurtured, sung to, and cherished. This is necessary in order to build a foundation for healthy narcissism, or healthy self-love. Children whose natural narcissistic needs are met consistently between the ages of approximately six months and thirty-six months develop a healthy form of narcissism and grow up to be the truly giving and unselfish people of the world. They're able to show caring and compassion for others in healthy ways and to find true joy in serving themselves sufficiently so that they can then serve others. The important needs to be met during this narcissistic period are as follows:

- Children's needs must be understood and taken seriously by calm, caring adult caregivers.
- Children must receive twice as many yeses as nos and must be encouraged to try new things.
- Limits placed on children's urges must entail no physical punishment, threats, or shaming responses.
- Children's living environments must be "kid-proofed" so they can safely explore and discover their world.
- Children must have nurturing support while learning to regulate their own emotions when they have tantrums or other experiences that dysregulate their emotions.
- Children must have good role models — parents and adult caregivers who show them how to live effectively within socially approved limits.

If your parents' narcissistic needs were not met when they were children, they would have had difficulty responding effectively to your narcissistic needs. They may have unconsciously and unintentionally been influenced by their own unhealed wounds as they parented you. Unparented parents are not able to take their children's needs seriously. They make fun of them, prevent them from expressing their true feelings, and don't respect them as separate individuals with free will of their own. They tease, lie, berate, threaten, isolate, distrust, scorn, coerce, and humiliate their children and invade their personal space. They may use their children as toys or objects to make themselves look good in order to satisfy their ego needs. They withhold or withdraw love as a way of controlling their children and may even torture them mentally or physically. This causes narcissistic wounds in children that are not easily healed. When these children become adults, they can easily be scraped and bruised by an insensitive remark or an unfriendly look.

Even more tragic is the fact that parents of this kind probably believed they treated their children like this for their own good. Perhaps your parents were afraid they'd spoil you. Or maybe they wanted other people to see them as strong disciplinarians, which they thought was the same as being a good parent. In either case, they found ways to justify their harsh parenting. The implied message to their children was, "If you have any problems as a result of our parenting, *it's your fault*. Something must be wrong with you." This is the predominant belief of children who grow up in co-dependent families, and it's also the basis for toxic shame.

Surprisingly, many of us still believe the implied message and accept the cruelty inflicted on us as having been "necessary" or our own fault. We figured out how to cope with our parents' demands in the hope that they would love us.

It's important to change these misperceptions of childhood so that you don't pass them on to your children and grandchildren through the "for your own good" kind of parenting. Some parents think it's necessary to parent their children in the same way that they were parented as a means of proving that their parents really did love them. It's hard to face the fact that they *didn't* and probably *couldn't* love you as much as you needed. Almost all of us made a secret vow to ourselves that, when we grew up, we would not say or do to our children the hurtful things said or done to us. Unfortunately, almost all of us, in the stress of playing grown-up, break that vow and find ourselves saying and doing to our children exactly what was done to us, often using the same methods and words.

The vicious cycle of cruelty provides the "glue" in a dominator society and serves as a mechanism for transmitting traumatic parenting patterns from generation to generation. The only way to stop the cycle is to reconnect with your inner child, clear your developmental trauma, and reclaim both your true feelings and your True Self. The function of defense mechanisms is to protect your inner child from harm. But when you hide your true feelings or True Self from others, you also end up hiding them from yourself. An important adage fits in here: "You can't fix something until you know how it got broken."

The most direct way to learn how things got broken in your childhood is to look for co-dependency patterns in your present relationships. Patterns contain clues about what really happened to you as a child. Even though you can't remember, you're likely reenacting your childhood traumas in your adult relationships — and with your children, if you have any.

Healing childhood trauma often involves reexperiencing feelings such as sadness and grief. When you experience a painful feeling, or a narcissistic wound, think back to times earlier in life when you felt this way. Another important part of the healing process is to mourn the loss of your connection with your True Self and your inner child. The table that follows describes and compares some of the common characteristics of the co-dependent self and the True Self and inner child.

| COMMON CHARACTERISTICS OF THE CO-DEPENDENT SELF AND THE TRUE SELF | |
| --- | --- |
| *The Co-dependent Self Is...* | *The True Self Is...* |
| a false person | a real person |
| a compliant, pleasing person | a free and honest person |
| an artificial person | a genuine person |
| a planner and plotter | spontaneous |
| a withholder | a giver and communicator |
| closed to feedback | open to feedback |
| critical, envious, idealized, perfectionistic | accepting of self and others |
| judgmental | compassionate |
| conditionally loving | unconditionally loving |
| passive or aggressive | assertive |
| rational, logical | intuitive |
| serious | playful |
| unfeeling | sensitive |
| distrusting | trusting |
| unwilling to be nurtured | willing to be nurtured |
| controlling | willing to surrender |
| self-righteous | self-caring |
| contracting, fearful | expansive, loving |
| separated from God and others | connected to God and others |

Because our culture is still largely based on the dominator model, most everyone has learned to hide their True Selves for fear of being hurt or rejected again. In a dominator culture, the more you expose your True Self, the more you risk exposing parts of yourself that others dislike, which can make you feel vulnerable and scared.

As we move toward having a partnership society, many of us are supporting each other in completing our stalled psychological development. Still, it takes considerable spiritual courage to reclaim your True Self and to heal the issues associated with loss. Even though it can be frightening, and you sometimes get hurt by being vulnerable, it's worth taking a chance. You *feel so much more alive* when you connect with and live as your True Self and inner child.

## CONDITIONS THAT STIFLE THE DEVELOPMENT
## OF THE TRUE SELF

Several structural factors that come from our dominator culture may have been present in your family of origin. These factors encouraged you to repress your True Self and develop your false, co-dependent self. They may include

- rigid and compulsive rules;
- perfectionistic, punitive parents;
- rigid and compulsive roles prescribed according to the needs of your parents, who may have said things like: "You're the smart one, and she's the pretty one in this family";
- a lot of family secrets;
- addictions to alcohol, drugs, tobacco, eating, work, sex, and other people;
- a serious and burdened atmosphere in which everyone acts like a victim, and the only humor entails sarcastic put-downs and makes children or outsiders the butts of jokes;
- a lack of personal privacy or personal boundaries, particularly for children;
- chronic illness, either mental or physical, in one or both parents;
- a co-dependent relationship between the parents;
- physical, sexual, or emotional abuse of a child or children by an adult or adults;
- parents who instilled a false sense of pride in and loyalty to the family;
- family members' resistance to outsiders and prohibitions against talking to them about the family;
- prohibitions against children expressing strong feelings;
- conflicts between family members that are ignored or denied; and
- a lack of unity in the family, causing some family members to create subgroups to protect themselves and compete with each other.

## INCOMPLETE DEVELOPMENTAL PROCESSES
## THAT CAN CAUSE CO-DEPENDENT BEHAVIORS

Following is a list of incomplete developmental processes from early childhood that our research has shown us lie at the core of co-dependent behavior. Not everybody who displays co-dependent behaviors has experienced every potential incomplete developmental process, but most individuals will identify with at least some of them. The task of breaking free from co-dependency involves completing the processes left incomplete during early childhood. Examine this list to see if you can identify the processes left unfinished in your early childhood. After you've taken that step, the other parts of this chapter may provide you with some of the tools you'll need to complete them.

A person who experienced the following incomplete developmental processes may develop co-dependent behaviors.

- insecure bonding caused by very little nurturing touch and inconsistent caregiving;
- a lack of support to help develop and trust in inner awareness and resources;
- most parental rewards given for pleasing others; few or no rewards given for independent acts;
- the presence of an enmeshed family relational structure providing few or no personal boundaries;
- a failure to support the completion of psychological birth, causing increased dependency on external rewards from others and fear of abandonment;
- a failure to teach how to effectively regulate emotions;
- a failure to give attention to important developmental needs;
- a failure to recognize and address feelings related to early developmental traumas;
- use of shame- and guilt-based or physical punishment and discipline practices to set limits, which contributed to a loss of self-esteem;
- a lack of appropriate limit-setting, which leads to attempts to manipulate and control others in order to get them to set the missing limits;
- being smothered or invaded by others resulting in fear in intimate situations.

## HOW TO HEAL YOUR WOUNDED INNER CHILD

- Discover your inner child, and learn to listen to him or her speak to you each day.
- Learn to define your own needs and wants.
- Develop effective ways to meet your needs and wants without controlling or manipulating others.
- Identify your developmental traumas and the narcissistic wounds they created. Allow yourself to feel the pain from these in the presence of people who are safe and supportive.
- Learn to heal your developmental traumas and complete your incomplete developmental processes. Some of the tools listed in the next section will help you complete these developmental processes and integrate them into your True Self.
- Create a support system of like-minded people who are willing to form partnership relationships and support each other's growth.

## TOOLS FOR HEALING YOUR INNER CHILD

Developing ways to heal the wounds suffered by your inner child is important work. Doing this will take all the resources you can muster, because it will involve depth work with yourself and breaking patterns of behavior that have kept you from even noticing the pain of these wounds. When you face the feelings connected to these wounds, you will have taken an important step. Remember that healing your inner child requires you to make contact with your feelings and to learn how to express them effectively. The activities suggested in the following sections will give you a place to start.

### Tools for Working on Yourself

- Recall your earliest childhood memory or a recurring childhood dream. Write down as many details about it as you can, using as many of your senses as possible. Describe what you saw, heard, felt, smelled, tasted, and intuited. Then write what you think you concluded about yourself as a result of this experience. This allows you to observe it more objectively. Usually there's an important lesson, pattern, or principle embedded in the memory that you're still mastering in life. You can use this tool to become more aware of what you're learning from it, and then explore ways to integrate it.

I (Barry) remember a client sharing her experience of this exercise with me. She recalled sitting in the grass by herself when she was about two. She looked around, and no one was there. She remembered feeling scared and lonely and confused, and yet she wasn't crying. In the middle of telling this memory, she suddenly burst into tears and deep sobs. When she stopped crying, she told me that she realized that, at that early age, she had decided to take care of others and not cry. No matter how lonely and scared she was, she was going to be a "good girl" and not force her parents to hear her crying out, and would instead deny her own needs.

- Another powerful tool for healing your inner child is mirror work. It involves sitting or standing in front of a full-length mirror and learning to love yourself. Say to yourself in the mirror, "I love you because you're smart." You may have to examine your resistance to loving yourself. This is also a good way to build object constancy and to find new ways to see yourself as lovable.

- The trauma elimination technique is another powerful tool for healing your developmental traumas. This tool is described in detail in the following section.

## Trauma Elimination Technique

My (Janae) years of work in clearing trauma in myself and my clients have proved to me that it is truly possible to clear trauma from your nervous system, brain, and behavioral responses. The trauma elimination technique (TET) is the most effective tool I've used, and it allows you to fully take charge of your own healing process. I also like it because you can use it yourself and need not pay a therapist to help you with it. This empowering aspect is especially important to me because most people who have been traumatized feel helpless and powerless.

I developed TET by synthesizing the best of several trauma healing modalities: the Tapas Acupressure Technique (TAT), Eye Movement

Desensitization and Reprocessing, and Thought Field Therapy. In our extensive use of TET on ourselves and clients, we discovered that it clears trauma not only from present-life experiences but also from other dimensions of reality, such as past lives.

If you wish to use TET to clear traumas from other realities, just set this intention before you begin to use it. If the idea intimidates you, set your intention to clear only present-life trauma. You're always in charge when practicing TET. Use the following procedure.

*Step 1.* Learn the TAT holding pose. Use one hand to lightly touch three points on your face, and place one hand behind your head, as follows:

a.   Lightly touch your thumb just above and adjacent to the inner corner of one eye.

b.   Place the end of your ring (third) finger just above and adjacent to the inner corner of the other eye.

c.   Place the end of your middle finger on an indentation in the middle of your forehead about a half inch higher than your eyebrows.

d.   Place your other hand palm down at the back of your head just below the bump at the bottom of your skull (the occipital ridge), centering it at the midline.

e.   Once you have learned this pose, go directly to step 2.

*Step 2.* Identify the trauma you want to work on, and focus your attention on a picture of this trauma. This should be one particular trauma, and not one that is long-term or recurring. Then complete the following steps:

a.   Notice what thoughts go with this picture.

b.   Identify your belief about yourself that goes with this picture.

c.   Notice what emotion you feel when you see this picture, think these thoughts, and believe this belief.

*Step 3.* Simultaneously hold the picture, thoughts, belief, and feelings while doing the TAT holding pose. Remain in this pose until you feel something happen internally. The feeling is different for each person; it may be a subtle shift of energy, a feeling of relaxation, or a deep sigh. Or hold for one minute, whichever comes first.

*Step 4.* Notice where you've been holding tension in your body related to the picture, thoughts, belief, and feelings, and focus your attention on this place while continuing to hold the TAT pose. Remain in this pose until you feel the shift, or for one minute.

*Step 5.* Return to the picture of your trauma that you began with, and zoom in close to review it with a "magnifying glass," looking for "hot spots" in the picture — the things that still upset you. Zero in on a hot spot and complete the following steps:

a.    Focus on the picture, thought, belief, or feeling.
b.    Do the TAT holding technique until you feel a shift.
c.    Focus on the "storage place" in your body where you hold tension related to this memory while using the TAT holding technique, until you feel a shift.

*Step 6.* Continue returning to the original picture and reviewing it until you can find no more hot spots.

*Step 7.* Drink a glass of water immediately after completing a session. Be sure to drink another eight glasses during the next twenty-four hours to help flush from your body the toxins released by the TET procedure.

### *Tools for Therapy*

Therapy is a great place to work on core issues. It can help you become more aware of your co-dependency issues, identify their sources, and take action to correct the underlying issues. The most important issues for healing your inner child are grieving the loss of your True Self and healing your narcissistic childhood wounds. Group therapy is particularly helpful for this kind of work. Psychodrama and Gestalt therapy techniques can be effective in reclaiming your inner child. Breath work, guided imagery, art, movement, play therapy, and some kinds of bodywork, such as craniosacral work, Rolfing, and other kinds of structural integration, also can help you grieve your losses.

### *Tools for Support Groups*

- Support groups can help you with your healing process. You can contract with the members of the group to give you supportive feedback on your progress in healing your inner child. This feedback can help you gauge your progress.
- Ask each group member to share the ways they do and do not nurture their inner children. It's important to become aware of the

subtle ways you negate your inner child. In a group where each person is doing this exercise, you'll find a lot of ideas, and you can ask for help in eliminating the negative ways you talk to or respond to your inner child.

## Tools for Committed Relationships

- Everybody has a two- to three-year-old child hidden inside who never got enough holding, nurturing, or other care. Working cooperatively, you and your partner can take turns holding, comforting, or caring for each other. The key to this exercise is that you each ask directly for what you want or need: for example, "If I bring you some oil, will you rub my feet for a while?" When you ask directly, it's possible to heal many of the old narcissistic wounds. You'll know that you have healed these wounds when you can ask directly for what you want or need in such a way that people are delighted to give it to you.

- Another way to connect with your inner child is through play. Partners who can play together will find much joy in their relationship. Working cooperatively with your partner, imagine being under ten years of age. Decide on some play activity that the two of you can do together. Take turns playing together as children — swinging on the swings, playing in a sandbox, riding a bicycle together, or climbing trees. This may seem like a silly activity at first, but partners who have done this have discovered a kind of innocent intimacy that they truly cherish.

- Each of you can take a large sheet of paper and list all the invalidating messages your parents, teachers, friends, or other adults gave you as a child. List as many as you can think of. When you're done, visualize the person who originally gave you that message. Notice who most of these invalidating messages came from. This may give you clues to why you may overreact when you hear messages like these from your partner or another adult. Finally, sit facing your partner and read each invalidating message on your list to each other. Speaking directly to the other person's inner child, say, "That is not true of you. I see you as ..." (this is positive mirroring). Take turns reading your lists to each other and getting support for your inner children.

## CASE EXAMPLE

This case example relates to my (Barry's) own work on a recurring childhood dream that helped me reconnect with my inner child. The dream occurred many times during childhood and once or twice since then. In the dream, I am being chased by a monster. I run out of my bedroom and down the upstairs hallway of the house where I grew up. The monster is gaining on me, and I can't run fast enough to get away. I can feel the monster's hot breath on my neck, and he is about to grab me, when I turn the corner of the hall and find myself at the top of the stairs. The only way I can get away from the monster is to leap from the top step. Instead of falling, I fly or float down to the bottom of the stairs. I land on my feet safely, and then I wake up.

I never addressed this dream until several years ago, when I became curious about its meaning. The first thing I did was to pick out some of the key words and speculate on what they might mean. The key words or phrases for me were: "monster," "can't run," "hot breath," "grab me," "turn the corner," "leap," "falling," "land on my feet," and "wake up." Then I located each word or phrase in a part of my body. After that, I listed words of meaning for the key words: "me," "my mother," "animal," "kill," and so on. The following body parts came to mind: legs, neck, hands, and so on.

| Key Words | Meaning of Key Words | Body Part |
|---|---|---|
| monster | me, my mother, animal, kill | legs |
| can't run | too slow to catch on, toilet training, crippled | neck |
| hot breath | red, passion, fear, dog | hands |
| grab me | never, why me, serious | buttocks |
| turn the corner | car, new beginning | eyes |
| leap | fear, look before you leap | face |
| falling | sinking, say good-bye, rocket | arms |
| land on my feet | charmed life, smelling like roses, blessed | feet |
| wake up | call, message, awareness | ears |

Then I acted the dream out in slow motion. At one point, as I am run-ning away from the monster, my left foot and left ankle start to weaken and I almost stumble, but I maintain my balance. Then I asked myself, "What would have happened if I'd fallen down?" The answer came almost imme-diately: "You would have had to face the monster!" I thought, "What would happen now if I turned to face my monster instead of running away?" This was an important shift for me. I saw that as a child I could only run away, but now I was no longer a child, and I didn't have to be afraid to face my monster. In fact, facing my monster might have a lot to do with reclaiming my inner child.

So I decided to turn and face my monster and draw a picture of it. It was a half-human, half-animal thing. It wore a black hood like an executioner, had pointed teeth and deep-set red eyes, and was not at all friendly looking.

I decided then to talk to my monster. I asked him who he was, and he replied, "The executioner. The one who is going to chop off your head. You have been tried, found guilty, and sentenced to death by being beheaded."

Then I asked him, "What was my crime?" He said,

Being born. You came along at the wrong time. No one was ready for you. They thought they were ready for you, but when you came along they found out all too quickly that you were too much trou-ble. So they sent me to chase you away and make you so scared that you wouldn't cause them any problems. They were hoping you would grow up fast before anyone found out how inadequate they were for the job of raising you. You should have known better than to come into this family and upset the apple cart. You used poor judgment. Poor timing. Any other time would have been better. It was the worst possible time.

I worked on this dream some more by making a clay image of the mon-ster's face. Then I painted my own face and became the monster during a therapy group. I also realized that the part of me who ran away and leaped to safety was the part trying to escape my parents' control, as well as the part trying to escape my own need to take care of or please others. In the dream I actually leaped to safety. From this I learned I could be free of my False Self if I took the risk. This led me to remember all the risks I had taken in my life, and how I always landed on my feet. I began to see the dream in a new light. There is a part of me that wants to be free and actually knows how to get free if it's challenged to do so by a monster, or part, that wants to control me or chop off my head. This part is really my inner child. He is so free he can do magical things like fly and always land on his feet. I keep the clay image of my monster on the nightstand next to my bed as a reminder of the role this important ally plays in my reconnection to my inner child.

This example illustrates that the desire to reconnect with our inner child is with us constantly. If we don't pay attention to the urgings of this incomplete process, it will use our dreams to press for completion, as well as any other means available. This may seem like a paradox, but it is through this reconnection with our inner child that we can finally grow up and enjoy life more fully. Otherwise, we're stuck with "playing" grown-up, and we all know that this truly is serious business.

## SUMMARY

Your inner child is a crucial part of yourself that you hid away to protect. Likely you did a good job of protecting it, and now it's time to bring this part of yourself into the light of day. You now have many more resources to help you protect this sensitive, easily hurt part, so you no longer have to hide it. The process of healing your inner child can be a lengthy one, however. Remember that you may have hidden your inner child for many years, and reconnecting with it will take some time. The better you reconnect, the more vital you should begin to feel.

# 16. Building Your Boundaries

Parents who haven't experienced their own psychological births will inadvertently create a destructive symbiotic, or enmeshed, family system of relationships in which each member of the family becomes co-dependent with each other member. What results is a spiderweb-like structure that restrains and represses every member of the family. This kind of symbiotic family system fosters beliefs, values, judgments, and myths that support the structure, and it creates an artificially united front to present to the world. Rebellious attempts to become independent are usually blocked by shame, humiliation, physical abuse, withdrawal of love, and threats of abandonment. The system reinforces the co-dependency with promises of oneness, security, pride, egotism, and superficial attention or approval from the outside world.

Family members often describe this type of symbiosis as an overwhelming experience of suffocation and loss of individual identity. There is simply no space for separateness in this kind of system. Everything family members do is designed to hold the structure together, particularly if the parents are using role reversals to get their needs met. The system is not set up to support individuality and interdependence. The co-dependent family, like co-dependent individuals and co-dependent relationships, has enmeshed feelings, problems, thoughts, dreams, and needs, but it also requires the collusion of a group. Each person's individual self is present in a co-dependent family, but the person is unable to identify with that self or to act to protect it.

## THE CO-DEPENDENT FAMILY

Destructive symbiosis in families may be difficult to recognize as a dysfunctional problem because it supports the "We're one big, happy family" fantasy that was once considered a healthy form of relationship. Once you understand the importance of the psychological birth and becoming a separate person, it's easier to recognize destructive family symbiosis as a dysfunctional form of relationship.

Unhealthy symbiosis often involves legacy issues. They may be expressed in expectations that a son be called "Junior" or follow the family tradition of being, say, a doctor or an athlete. Other legacy issues include expectations that children will live close to their parents' home, have a certain number of children, marry a particular kind of person, have a certain kind of job the family would be proud of, or attend a specific church. Life decisions such as these are not negative in themselves. It is the *absence of conscious individual choice* in such matters, and the spoken and unspoken family expectations, that constitute this issue, as they limit and inhibit the unfolding of the True Self. Unhealthy symbiotic family dynamics are typically unconscious, which means family members are not aware that they're following someone else's program.

Stories of parents who drive their children to be exceptional students or athletes illustrate the adults' unhealthy need to have their children validate their choices and lives. Children whose parents have exaggerated needs for fame, glory, and recognition often grow up to become empty, driven adults themselves. They never feel quite successful enough. In spite of their achievements, they frequently suffer from low self-esteem and perceive themselves as failures.

It's often a feeling of suffocation that motivates individuals to escape from this enmeshment. They may feel as though they're dying. Only then do they dare try to leave the system. Those who choose to stay enmeshed will label them as sick, crazy, stupid, or weird. Those who leave may even be shunned or ostracized by their parents and siblings to protect the shaky family system.

## DARING TO BE DIFFERENT FROM
## YOUR CO-DEPENDENT FAMILY

When you decide to change your life and be yourself, you are also deciding to leave the collective or group mind. The first step in this process, which Carl Jung calls individuation, is separating yourself from the chaos and confusion of your family, especially from your parents.

This may seem like a perfectly logical and appropriate thing to do. Your family, however, may be very unhappy with you. They may even be upset, hurt, or angry with you because you are disturbing the delicate structure of the family web and may cause it to collapse. This danger triggers everyone's fears, so of course they will try to stop you. You may find them using the old enforcement tools such as shame, withdrawal of love, or threats to keep you in your place. They may try to convince you that you're crazy or sick or even try to hospitalize you. They will definitely not let go of you easily, especially if you've been a key figure in the co-dependent family drama.

Outside support at this point is critical, for you may begin to doubt your own sanity. Friends, therapists, and group members are invaluable as allies who can help you cope with your family's parting shots. People who have not built an external support system prior to leaving the system find exiting it much more difficult. One word of caution: you cannot separate emotionally from your family by labeling them "wrong" or "bad." You have to focus on what is right for you without emphasizing what is wrong with them, even if they focus on what they think is wrong with you.

### Who Owns the Problem?

One way that systems keep their members enmeshed is by group ownership of all the problems. When father loses his glasses, everyone must hunt for them. If Suzy comes home with a poor report card, everyone monitors her homework after school. This keeps the whole system in chaos and confusion and maintains the enmeshment. This behavior is a form of group rescue that prevents individual members from being responsible and from experiencing the consequences of their own choices. For example, if father had to attend an important meeting without his glasses as a consequence of misplacing them, he might figure out ways to keep track of them.

There are three categories of ownership to use in distinguishing between what is yours and what is not yours. They help determine responsibility (response-ability):

- mine ("I'm going somewhere, and I lost my car keys")
- yours/theirs ("You/They are going somewhere, and you/they lost the car keys")
- ours ("We are going somewhere, and the car keys are lost")

Each of these categories requires a different response:

- Mine: I am responsible, and I need to respond and take action.
- Yours/theirs: You/they are responsible. I will listen reflectively, offer support if asked, and allow you/them to respond and take action.
- Ours: We both/all are responsible and need to respond by taking action.

Fuzziness about ownership originates in infancy when the child isn't able to respond very well, so the mother, father, and siblings do the responding. This pattern of responding turns into enabling when the child becomes old enough to respond. Prolonged enabling reinforces passivity, victim thinking, and rescuing.

## BOUNDARIES

Undertaking the task of becoming separate and autonomous means you are able to determine the boundary between yourself and others and have an identity of your own.

### The Individuated Family

Individual boundaries define your own body and your own feelings, thoughts, ideas, needs, beliefs, and wants. Having boundaries creates a whole new set of rules about how people interact with each other. These rules include the following:

- People must ask permission before they can cross over each other's physical and psychological boundary lines.
- "Response-ability" is determined by who owns the problem.
- People do not own, or belong to, each other.

In unhealthy symbiotic families, where there are no personal bound-aries between family members, and where the adults parentize their children through role reversals, separation is especially difficult. In alcoholic homes, where the children may shop, clean, care for younger siblings, and put the drunken parent(s) to bed, the adults often turn to their children for the nur-turing, love, affection, and comfort that parents would ordinarily give rather than receive. This creates an atmosphere in which covert or overt incest or sexual abuse are highly likely, which is why these are prevalent in alcoholic families.

### *Incest and Sexual Abuse*

Fathers who commit incest with their children often experience a high degree of destructive symbiosis. These fathers' lack of bonding and inability to become separate stirs up their buried needs for warmth, closeness, accep-tance, and intimacy. A father who doesn't recognize this is often not able to verbalize these needs at all and is totally unaware of them. He will instead seek out closeness with his children, holding and touching them. His strong fear of abandonment makes filling these needs with an adult woman too risky and scary. The warmth and innocence of a child, however, soothes this fear and creates the safety necessary for the father's unmet developmental needs to surface. In such cases, the man regresses into an infantile state and his unmet needs take over. The false belief that children can't remember any-thing until they are five or six years old supports the formation of a "doll fantasy" relationship. The following poem written by a thirty-year-old woman describes her relationship with her alcoholic father when she was a child.

### THIS DOLL IS A CHILD

Pretty little girl
Dressed in a frilly dress.                                    Hair fixed nice
A doll to play with.

Someone
Combed her hair          Made her clothes           Tied her shoes

Others

Gave her baths
                    Helped her in the bathroom
...and rubbed 'til it hurt                          with perverse explorations.

Wonderful doll she was

Do what she was asked

                                              Help along the way
She'd keep him company on a laundry day,
                              Never making a sound as he would play
                    Then cast her aside until time to play again.
She'd keep him company while Mom was away.
No one ever considered
What he did with his toy doll          Too busy to play other games
          Cast her aside
                    put her on the shelf
                              Until he wanted to play again

He knew she'd be there.

This special doll has feelings
SHE DOES NOT LIKE

Sitting on the shelf        His kind of play        Thrown on the floor
          when through
She fears his anger

Her brilliant eyes shine
From tears                                      Not happiness
                                                  like they should

She becomes more quiet
Realizing she is only a playtoy
          who cannot act on her own

She HURTS

This Doll is a child!
To be
Guided                    Loved                    Nurtured                    Helped

Not for
Sordid pleasure
          To be tossed aside
                    She is not a possession
                    She is not a toy
How will she ever grow up this way?

Destructively symbiotic fathers don't know how to be close and affectionate in nonsexual ways, to be loved unconditionally, or to have an intimate relationship in a nonphysical way. They sexualize most of their relationships. When a destructively symbiotic father turns to his daughter for sex in an unconscious attempt to meet his developmental needs, he is seldom aware of what he actually needs. Most men who commit incest are completely out of touch with their needs and feelings and have no experience in meeting them in healthy ways.

Sexual abuse, whether it is between a mother and child, father and child, brother and sister, or teacher and student, is also anchored in the dominator model. The hierarchical ranking of one individual or group over another sets up inequities of power in which the higher-ranked group has permission to use, persecute, victimize, and dominate another.

From this perspective, incest and sexual abuse can be viewed as problems related both to co-dependency's incomplete developmental processes and to a dysfunctional social structure. This view recognizes the destructively symbiotic, perpetrating parent or other adult as someone who needs to be treated and understood rather than looked upon as a criminal. There *are* adults, however, who are psychopathic, who had almost no bonding or care as infants and who lack a conscience. The circumstances that trigger their incestuous acts are different from those of the destructively symbiotic parent or other adult. The psychopathic parent is not included in this discussion of incest and sexual abuse. If we look at incest and sexual abuse from a developmental and cultural perspective, it becomes clear that society needs to examine them as results of the culture's dominator values.


## A CULTURAL EPIDEMIC

Newspapers, magazines, and books are full of information about the rising incidence of incest and sexual abuse. It's obvious that these problems are not limited to families, as the incidents involve teachers, principals, ministers, priests, coaches, child care professionals, and scout leaders. While unhealthy symbiosis helps to explain the motives behind incest and sexual abuse, does it really explain the epidemic of sexual incidents and attacks being reported?

We don't think so. We believe several other factors are involved. First is the increasing awareness among children that incest or sexual abuse is inappropriate. Many schools and groups, for example, bring in speakers with anatomically correct dolls to discuss boundary issues and appropriate versus inappropriate touching. Such discussions frequently provoke children into revealing that they have been or are currently being abused. As the education of children about sexual abuse has increased dramatically, so has the reporting system.

The second factor is the education of adults. Most adults are horrified about the prevalence of sexual abuse and incest. Many educators and health care professionals now receive training in identifying child abuse, including sexual abuse. In most states, professionals are now legally compelled to report any *suspected* cases of abuse. The penalty clause has convinced many of them to be conscientious in their reporting. This has also increased the reporting.

A third factor is that there is now more support in the legal system for coping with perpetrators and for supporting victims. It's also more common to appoint child advocates for sexual abuse victims and to require mandatory treatment programs for perpetrators. There is a growing awareness that we've seen just the tip of the iceberg. The problem cuts across all ethnic, social, educational, and economic lines. No longer are offenders simply tossed in jail — they need treatment. Most abusers were abused themselves and now find themselves caught in the vicious cycle of cruelty.

The fourth factor is more subtle and is related to the currents of cultural change. History records measurable swings back and forth between dominator and partnership cultures, even though the dominator model has been the prevailing trend for several thousand years. History shows that shifts toward the more feminine values of the partnership model have always been followed by a period of resurging masculine values. The period of rising feminine values during the Elizabethan era in England and the European Renaissance, for example, was characterized by humanitarianism, creativity, social reforms, and greater freedom for women. It was followed by a period of masculine values and renewed attempts to restrict women's sexual roles, by hostility and aggression toward women, and by the persecution of minorities by authoritarian governments.

A more recent conflict between rising feminine values and the prevalent masculine values came during the 1800s, when the feminist movement encountered what is now recognized as *aggravated assault*: severe, bone-breaking domestic beatings; wives set on fire; and wives' eyes put out. This behavior resembles patterns of witch hunting and burning during the 1300s and 1400s and again in the late 1600s and early 1700s.

The rise of the feminine in the 1960s and 1970s through the women's liberation movement, the human rights movement, and the self-help movement has been countered with a rise in Ku Klux Klan activities, fascism, extremist fundamentalist religions, domestic violence, rape, incest, and sexual abuse. Hate incidents and crimes have now become epidemic according to the U.S. Department of Justice.[1]

In 2007, for example, Fairfax, Virginia, recorded a 57 percent annual increase in the number of reported rapes, which follows national trends.[2] Even allowing for the increase in reporting rapes, this still represents an exceptional rise in number. Other contemporary acts of violence against women include public executions in fundamentalist Islamic countries for unbecoming conduct, such as failing to wear the veil or allowing some skin to show in public.

Another facet of the repression of the feminine is the abuse directed at Mother Earth. In the last sixty years, humans have planted missiles and exploded bombs in her body; polluted the air, water, and land with toxic chemicals; stripped her of coal and minerals; and mined and casually consumed her vital elements. These facts clearly demonstrate the disregard for the earth, or Gaia, as a living, feminine being. This disregard is as pervasive as the current disregard for women and feminine perspectives. They must be considered related phenomena.

## THOUGHTS ABOUT BOUNDARIES

Recognizing and creating personal boundaries are major steps in the healing of your co-dependency, for these require restructuring all your relationships. One person often arrives at this awareness before his or her partner or family does, and this frequently creates a relationship crisis. A partner or child who enjoys the symbiotic dynamics and having all his or her personal needs met by others may be upset at this change. He or she may tell you that you are a bad person and play on your guilt.

Creating personal boundaries may cause some relationships to crumble. Choosing to individuate requires clarity and forethought, which will allow you to overcome the resistance you'll meet from those who don't want you to change and who resist change in themselves. Think through the scenarios that may unfold, and prepare to meet them. Once you decide to create personal boundaries and become separate, it's difficult to turn back. You'll also need the support of other trusted friends who recognize your need for boundaries and who will support you when conflict arises.

## TOOLS FOR BUILDING YOUR BOUNDARIES

Building personal boundaries will take a concerted effort. To many people with co-dependent behaviors, boundaries are not important or even necessary. These people must learn to recognize that, paradoxically, without personal boundaries a person can easily become trapped in a relationship and have no way out. Building an individuated self requires that you create boundaries so you know where you end and the other begins.

### Tools for Working on Yourself

Write in your journal each time you're aware that you've experienced being invaded. Include such things as inappropriate touching, having your sentences cut off or completed for you, or people entering private areas such as your bathroom, your desk, or your journal. Also record what you felt and how you responded. Notice the frequency, locations, and patterns and your responses. Make agreements with your family members regarding your boundaries, and give them consequences when they violate them.

## *Tools for Therapy*

List your current unhealthy symbiotic co-dependent relationships, along with reasons for and against separating yourself from them. Discuss these with your therapist. Then role-play with your therapist different things you can do to break unhealthy symbiosis. This is necessary for learning new responses to others' attempts to keep you symbiotically attached.

## *Tools for Support Groups*

- Create a telephone call system and a list of "retreat houses" for your group members, so that everyone in the group can find quick support during a crisis as they are breaking free of their co-dependency traps.

- Develop at least two friends who will remind you during your weak moments exactly how bad your unhealthy symbiotic co-dependent relationship(s) is, so that you can call and ask them for a reality check.

- Seek out groups of people who are living their lives as you'd like to, so you can use them as role models for building an independent self in a supportive environment.

## *Tools for Committed Relationships*

- Both partners can contract with each other to provide feedback about behavior that invades the other person's personal space, such as finishing the other person's sentences, reading his or her personal mail, or rearranging his or her personal belongings.

- Make copies of the following checklist and mark questions you can respond to with yes. Have your partner read a separate copy and answer the questions too. Then share the results.

\_\_\_\_\_ Do you have a sense of being "crazy?"

\_\_\_\_\_ Are you unable to remember periods of your childhood?

\_\_\_\_\_ Are you more than thirty pounds overweight?

\_\_\_\_\_ Have you been sexually abused, or have you abused someone else?

\_\_\_\_\_ Does sex turn you off?

_____ Do you have trouble maintaining an intimate relationship?

_____ Are you ashamed of your body?

_____ Do you sexualize relationships even when you know you shouldn't?

_____ Do you regularly experience migraines, gastrointestinal disturbances, or genitourinary disturbances?

_____ Do you have a feeling of depression that you can't shake?

_____ Do you "freeze" in certain situations, such as when you encounter an authority figure?

_____ Are you afraid of having children or being around them?

_____ Are you accident-prone?

If you answered yes to two or more of these questions, you may have incest hidden in your past. Sometimes memories of incest can be buried for thirty or forty years before they surface.

## CASE EXAMPLE

Joyce seemed like a model client to us. She was forty-one years old, had no major problems, had good self-awareness, was interested in growth, and had a pretty good relationship with her husband. Slowly a different pattern began to emerge. She had no memory of her childhood before age ten, and had a previous history of being battered, being accident-prone, having problems with authority figures, being turned off by sex, and having gastrointestinal problems. We recognized these symptoms as a good indication of sexual abuse during early childhood, possibly incest. While Joyce had no memory of sexual abuse, she also had no memories before age ten.

As we talked with her about her parents, grandparents, siblings, and friends, her memories slowly began to return. She first recalled incidents around age seven that involved an uncle. She couldn't believe that he would do anything hurtful, because her uncle was highly respected by her family. Her father had died in the Vietnam War when she was three, and her uncle (his brother) helped to support the family and saved them from being split up. Her mother was very grateful, because without him Joyce would have gone to an orphanage. For almost a year, she struggled with her faint memories. She began to think the whole thing was just a bad dream. Joyce tried hypnosis, but that didn't really help her achieve memory clarity.

This is a typical pattern for people with repressed memories of early sexual abuse. There is no one to substantiate the faint memory and the generalized feelings of discomfort and anxiety. Friends often discourage making a fuss about something that happened thirty years ago. The truth lay in Joyce's body memory, because her physical symptoms were too obvious.

Joyce's breakthrough came after a series of events — some happening in therapy and some outside it. We asked her to talk to several other adult survivors of incest who remembered the abuse after many years. This was helpful because it validated some of Joyce's feelings and sensations in her body.

The other breakthrough came shortly after that, in a group setting where Joyce reported her conversations with other adult survivors. She talked about associating a vomiting sensation in her stomach with her memories, and as she did this she clutched her midsection. We asked her to draw the sensation on paper. As she drew a red-and-black circular image on the paper, her face became ashen. She said, "Oh my God, I remember him forcing his penis into my mouth. I started choking, and I almost vomited. It was my uncle — I saw his face."

It took Joyce almost two more years to come out on the other side of the problem. She continued working hard in therapy to accept her feelings of guilt and shame. One evening she tearfully recalled how much she needed and enjoyed the attention her uncle always gave her. He took her with him on trips, and when he didn't he always brought her a present. He had money, position, and prestige in her family, so she gained some prestige by being his favorite niece. He threatened several times to send her away to an orphanage if she ever told anyone. She said she eventually got used to his sexual advances and craved his attention.

An important part of Joyce's healing was admitting how much she enjoyed her uncle's attention and affection and acknowledging her desperate need to be loved. This helped her make a big shift. For most adult survivors of incest or sexual abuse, this is the hardest part: admitting and accepting that they enjoyed the bonding part of the relationship even though the sexual part was repulsive. When adult survivors can make this distinction and separate the two parts of the incestuous relationship, it becomes easier to move through the last stage of recovery.

## SUMMARY

Learning to create appropriate personal boundaries is a vital step in freeing yourself from unhealthy symbiotic and co-dependent relationships. Recognize that doing this will take some practice, and be patient with yourself. Celebrate your successes no matter how small or large they may be.

# 17. Forming Bonds of Intimacy

In chapter 4, we discussed bonding and how critical it is for children to experience the safety and security of a deep emotional attunement with their mothers. We also discussed the importance of father-child bonding during the psychological birth and the completion of the essential developmental processes of the counter-dependent stage of development. This chapter focuses on other bonding issues and how to repair them in adulthood.

Much more is now known about healthy bonding, and new information is continually being supplied by a variety of groups studying human behavior and development, including physicians, psychiatrists, clinical psychologists, mental health professionals, pre- and perinatal psychologists, midwives, and parents. All this new information emphasizes the importance of bonding. The lack of a strong infant-mother bond is now recognized as a critical factor in addictions and in attention-deficit/hyperactivity disorder, commonly known as ADHD. Our definition of this condition is "adult deficit disorder." Lack of an infant-mother bond is also the source of the problem in learning disorders, co-dependency, antisocial personality disorders, and feeling disorders. Bonding issues are also factors in other diagnosable mental health disorders, such as borderline personality disorder and bipolar disorder. We see bonding as a factor in dysfunctional family relationships and in larger cultural problems such as global environmental issues. The evidence is overwhelming. Poorly bonded people have difficulty living functional lives.

## THE ELEMENTS OF BONDING

Joseph Chilton Pearce, a child psychologist, recognizes bonding as a central issue of early childhood development and has looked at the circumstances that prevent it as well as at the effects of bonding, or a lack of it, on learning and relating.[1] He has identified five components of strong mother-child bonding during the first few hours, days, and months:

- holding the child and molding it to the mother and the father during skin-to-skin contact
- prolonged and steady eye contact with the child
- smiling happily at the child
- singing and making soothing sounds to the child
- body stimulation, such as stroking and massaging the child

Pearce also identifies eight developmental stages of bonding and human development as a sequence of bonding experiences that hold together the process of life.[2] He describes bonding as an instinct that carries humans toward the full development of their spiritual capacities. His developmental stages are

1. bonding with the mother and father prenatally, at birth, and immediately after;
2. bonding with the father and family immediately after birth;
3. bonding with the earth at about age four;
4. bonding with society at about age seven;
5. bonding with society's body of knowledge around age eleven;
6. bonding with a person of the opposite sex after puberty;
7. bonding with offspring as a parent; and
8. spiritual bonding.

According to Pearce, when you complete the first seven stages, *spiritual* bonding emerges. Once the first seven stages are complete, a person feels connected to the whole world and everything in it.

As with any developmental process, it's possible to return to points where things broke down previously and repair the breaks. The breakdown of early childhood bonding can be healed through committed relationships, therapy, support groups, and individual work. It's also possible to repair the breaks in bonding with the earth, the importance of which is now better understood. Retreats in nature, borrowing practices from Native American traditions, hiking, camping, gardening, and planting trees and flowers are ways that we can heal our relationship with Mother Earth.

Incomplete bonding with society is expressed in the desire for community. According to M. Scott Peck, twelve-step programs such as Alcoholics Anonymous have given many people in this country experiences of true community.[3] In such groups people are able to be their True Selves and find support for healing their bonding and separation wounds. Many religious and spiritual groups, and some people in business, are developing practices within their organizations to help members live more in partnership with each other.

The process of development builds on each of the previous stages. The degree to which the earlier stages are completed determines whether people can complete the following stages. The more bonded children are to their parents as infants, the more likely they will reach the rich, full existence of Pearce's spirituality. Bonding with society's body of knowledge is both an educational issue and a developmental issue, and it's important to recognize that we must examine the effectiveness of our educational system from both perspectives.

The degree to which children have bonded with their mothers, fathers, and families determines the degree to which they can bond with the earth and then with society's body of knowledge — with the ideas about how the world works. As an educational issue, most schools are structured so that they support co-dependency, and they actually prevent the completion of development. This can further traumatize children and solidify patterns of co-dependency.

Healthy bonding in schools requires cooperative activities that recognize individual uniqueness and promote appropriate body contact, such as hugging, making "puppy piles" (where everyone lies huddled together on the floor like puppies in a litter), forming arm-to-arm circles for dancing, and moving students into a tightly coiled spiral shape. Activities like these need to be reinforced with information and dialogues about what constitutes appropriate and inappropriate touching, along with firm support in setting boundaries and individual limits on being touched or having close body contact. Teachers must talk about these things openly and model the kind of respectful, appropriate behavior they desire. This creates a supportive classroom atmosphere, and it helps children learn to discriminate between the characteristics of healthy bonding, which encourages having individual needs and boundaries, and unhealthy symbiosis, which inhibits free choice and carries external expectations that deny personal boundaries.

Bonding with someone of the opposite sex can be difficult, because institutions often discourage appropriate opposite-sex contact, primarily because it activates sexual issues. Instead, schools promote co-dependent patterns of dominance and submission in which gender and sexuality is used as a weapon of intimidation and control to reinforce the dominator model. Male/female competition and ranking, rather than bonding and cooperation, is the norm. If people don't learn male-female bonding skills at home, they certainly won't learn them in institutions.

The lack of effective bonding at all stages is a result of the shortage of effective skills and accurate information for parenting children. Most parents bumble their way through child rearing, doing what they can with what they have. Most fathers have no training at all.

At our current stage of evolution, there is little opportunity for people to reach the spiritual stage of bonding. Some do, of course, but not because the systems inherent in our dominator culture support it. A few courageous people who have a strong inner drive and a vision for something better refuse to let the system hold them back. They strive onward in spite of the cultural restrictions and their own wounds. Such people are sometimes called seekers and "pathfinders."[4]

## BONDING AND LEARNING

In chapter 4 we talked about the fact that poorly bonded children fear the world, particularly change. Their exploration and risk-taking skills are weak, and they need constant reinforcement from the outside. They often become rigid, can't feel, and have addictive and compulsive behaviors. Such behaviors directly interfere with real learning and the use of their sensing, observing, thinking, and feeling functions. Real learning requires children to have self-reflective abilities, have full access to their feelings, have the ability to involve their physical bodies in the learning process, *and* be able to think.

Poorly bonded children can and do adapt to learning structures that use only the thinking function, which our current dominator-based educational system does. Thinking, especially the left-hemispheric thinking that dominates our current educational system, supports co-dependent behaviors in children. Compartmentalization, reductionism, linear thinking, hierarchical ranking, and rationality — all functions of the left hemisphere — dominate Western education.

There are numerous other ways in which educational systems discourage or prevent full bonding and the completion of the developmental processes of the co-dependent stage of development. These ways can, of course, be traced directly to the dominator model. Here are some of the more common ones that educational systems use:

- They rank members hierarchically, with students and their needs at the very bottom.
- By punishing spontaneity and restricting freedom, they teach children to adapt to the system.
- They assume all responsibility for structuring and evaluating the child's educational experience, discouraging feedback from students.
- They reinforce dependence, symbiosis, and isolation.
- They support the dominator model through force or the threat of force, by using compulsory attendance requirements and expulsion (withdrawal of "love"), and by emphasizing the need for degrees and credentials in order to be successful.
- Through the use of a competitive grading system, they teach students to compete rather than cooperate with each other.
- They prohibit feelings, personal issues, and social interaction in the classroom, stressing only information and academics.
- They encourage rigid sex roles.
- They devalue diversity and discovery, and they value conformity and passivity.

You can see that it's difficult to reach the stages of male-female bonding and spirituality. The cultural constraints, unconscious though they may be, make interdependency and the fullness it brings almost impossible.

## BONDING AND PSYCHOPATHS

Studies cite poor bonding between birth and age two as the primary cause of antisocial personality disorder (APD).[5] People with this disorder, estimated to be about 15 percent of this country's adult population, possess a poisonous mix of traits. They are arrogant, shameless, immoral, impulsive, superficial, charming, callous, irresponsible, irreverent, cunning, and deceitful. They readily lie, cheat, and steal and feel no guilt about it. They may even kill. Extreme examples, such as Charles Manson, are found in jails and mental institutions, but others with less severe symptoms can be found in the mainstream of society and in all walks of life. Many of them are now involved in white-collar crime, such as corporate gouging and the exploitation of foreign workers who lack proper residency documents.

Research shows that there are more people with APD in our society than ever before. The increase in unbondedness that helps create APD is attributed to a number of cultural trends:

- the increase in teen pregnancies
- an increase in the number of unprepared teen mothers keeping their babies and parenting them
- rising divorce rates and the breakdown of both families and society
- increases in child abuse
- increases in adoptions
- increases in foster care
- substandard child care
- long periods of infant separation from the mother during the first six months of life

Research also indicates that interruptions in the bonding process, such as hospitalization, parental illness, and too many or too-long absences, significantly disturb children. This is especially critical at birth and during the first six months of life.

Ken Magid and Carol McKelvey identify teenage parenting as the prime cause of the rise of APD in the United States.[6] Teen mothers are children themselves and don't know how to appropriately interact with their infants. The second important factor in the high rate of APD that they point out is substandard care in child care centers. Most providers are poorly paid and minimally trained. The turnover among them is high, and there is often too large a ratio between the adults and the children. Substandard care for children is a reflection of the low value that our dominator culture places on human development.

Treating poorly bonded children who have signs of APD is very difficult. Current treatment practices focus on helping children vent the deepseated rage and sadness they have repressed over their failure to bond. In rage-reduction therapy, for example, children are physically held and encouraged to express their rage and anger. This has proven highly effective with younger children. Once a child reaches the age of sixteen, this treatment doesn't seem to work. These children often end up being "warehoused" in jails and social institutions. This whole phenomenon must be recognized as both a cultural and a developmental issue requiring drastic changes in parenting and new ways of coping with the breakdown of the nuclear family. You may be asking yourself, "Where do we turn to heal all this?"

## BONDING AND COMMITTED RELATIONSHIPS

Many individuals are already making drastic changes inside themselves, especially those who have recognized their addictive patterns. Addiction crises are among the most common sources of "waking up" experiences. Out of the crises that addictions bring, people can enter recovery programs and restructure themselves and their lives. Through twelve-step programs, therapy, and working on themselves, people create new beliefs and new behaviors. Once they admit they have a problem and have broken some of their codependency patterns, they discover the most effective form of therapy available: conscious, committed relationships.

The most effective committed relationships involve "reparenting" contracts. In reparenting, both partners recognize their own unfinished developmental issues with their parents and willingly help each other heal their wounds and complete the bonding and separation processes. When conflict or some other relationship issue triggers old feelings or memories, you can contract with your partner to consciously role-play a parental figure and provide you with what you missed. Reparenting can include bonding support, such as holding, comforting, rocking, feeding you from a baby bottle, singing, and providing touch and nonsexual skin-to-skin contact. Reparenting can also help you develop the skills necessary for separation by encouraging exploration and risk-taking, providing reassurance when necessary, offering positive feedback and affirmative messages when you succeed at separation, and providing mirroring for acts of independence or individuality.

## TOOLS FOR FORMING BONDS OF INTIMACY

Reparenting is easier when you've identified the bonding and separation experiences that you still need. The following exercises will help you identify which experiences you're missing.

### *Tools for Working on Yourself*

- In your journal, record interviews with family members and others who were present during the first year or two of your life. If you can't find anyone to interview, then imagine how each person might have responded, both positively and negatively, about your birth and life in the family. You can also look at photographs taken of you during this period: look at the expressions on your face and the body language of those in the photos. This can give you clues about what was happening during that period of your life.

- Create methods to support your needs for bonding by getting a doll or teddy bear for comfort. Or perhaps "adopt" a bruised and wounded stuffed animal from a thrift store. Buy a rocking chair and rock yourself and the doll or teddy bear when you feel vulnerable and alone. A music box with nursery tunes can also be helpful for comforting your inner child.

### *Tools for Therapy*

- Use information, lists, and charts from previous exercises in this book, and whatever information you can gather from baby pictures, home movies, and talking to your parents, to create a composite picture of your first two years of life, focusing on your bonding and separation experiences. Bring your notes about what you've learned regarding this composite picture with you to discuss in therapy. With your therapist to guide and support you, work to re-create the feelings and experiences of this time period. Search for your deepest feelings and allow them to surface and be released. Deep sadness and rage are two of the most difficult feeling states to access. They almost always require safety and support from therapists who have done their own rage, grief, and sadness work. If anger comes up, have appropriate props such as a vinyl beanbag chair and pillows available to beat on. Use an old tennis racket or plastic baseball bat for hitting them. If sadness surfaces, ask your therapist to hold you or your hand. Or use props such as satin-edged blankets, dolls, and teddy bears to help you express and heal your sadness. If you used to suck your thumb, feel free to do so now if it helps your healing. Often children are shamed to make them stop sucking their thumbs, and then their thumbs are no longer comfort objects.

- Create a reparenting contract with your therapist. Once you become aware of aspects of your early childhood development that were left incomplete, you can ask your therapist to serve as a "contract mother or father" to help you fill in the gaps in your parenting. Contract parents can give nurturing, supportive messages, and correct misinformation by engaging in structured play activities and role-playing with you, reading books to you, and taking part in similar activities that will help you complete your unfinished developmental tasks. You may find that you regress to a young age while engaged in the process of reparenting. You'll need to trust that your contract parent(s) will protect you and comfort you when old feelings such as fear or anger emerge. This kind of deep work is necessary for healing. You can also use a support group to complete both your bonding and your separation processes.

### Tools for Support Groups

Create a reparenting group where people can be contract parents for each other. A support group can also help re-create healthy sibling interactions to replace dysfunctional sibling interactions you might have experienced during childhood.

For this to work most effectively, it requires three- or four-hour segments of time that allow you to temporarily regress to the age you were when you developed issues and to act that age during the time period. It's surprisingly easy to remember how to act the age you want to work on, because the memories are stored in your brain and cells. When you start moving like a two- or three-year-old, your memory of that age returns. The more you can free yourself to behave as you did at that age, and the longer you remain there during your contracted time, the more you'll gain.

The group therapy session begins with each person making an explicit contract by asking for what he or she wants or needs and from whom. Half the group can serve as contract parents for the session while the rest become children. Experience in reparenting therapy and special training is recommended for those acting as contract parents.

### Tools for Committed Relationships

It's possible to complete the unmet needs left from childhood by becoming better bonded and more separate in your current relationship. Remember, the more complete your bond is, the more you'll be able to become psychologically separate and to live interdependently.

The following checklists can help you find the specific things that might be missing from your early childhood experience. You and a partner should go through the lists separately and then share with each other the items you've checked. Then read the list of reparenting activities given in the right-hand column. Select the ones you still need to experience and ask your partner, if it feels appropriate, to provide them for you.

| REPARENTING CHECKLIST: BONDING | |
| --- | --- |
| *Bonding Experiences That You Missed* | *Bonding Experiences That Your Partner Can Provide* |
| ❏ Being touched or stroked | Being given a massage or back rub; taking a warm bath |
| ❏ Being sung to or talked to soothingly | Being held and sung to while listening to soft music |
| ❏ Being given lots of eye contact | Being sung to while your partner looks into your eyes |
| ❏ Being held and rocked | Being rocked in a chair |

| REPARENTING CHECKLIST (*continued*) | |
|---|---|
| *Bonding Experiences That You Missed* | *Bonding Experiences That Your Partner Can Provide* |
| ❑ Being given unconditional positive feedback ("I like being with you.") | Being smiled at and given approving nonverbal signals |
| ❑ Being given compliments on how your body looks | Asking for affirmation of your physical appearance |

| REPARENTING CHECKLIST: SEPARATION | |
|---|---|
| *Separation Experiences That You Missed* | *Separation Experiences That Your Partner Can Provide* |
| ❑ Exploration support | Joining a support group |
| ❑ Mirroring that recognizes your individuality and specialness | Attending couples' workshops |
| ❑ Being able to feel connected with people even when you're away from them | Taking separate vacations |
| ❑ Affirmation of your need to set limits and have boundaries | Developing friends of the same sex |
| ❑ Support for taking the initiative to do things on your own | Signing up for courses or instruction in a new interest<br>Using trust-building exercises such as rappelling, ropes courses, and so on<br>Planning times to be alone<br>Doing a "vision quest" or solo experience in the wilderness<br>Learning a new skill that you always wanted to learn |

## CASE EXAMPLE

Patty was a member of a therapy group that I (Barry) was conducting. One evening she spontaneously reenacted her own birth. At first I didn't know what was happening as she curled up in a fetal position and lay there motionless for a time. Intuitively I covered her with a blanket, and then she started to cry and kick some. I asked the other group members to help me re-create a womb and a birth canal. Slowly over the next half hour or so, Patty relived her birth process. Here's how she described it.

Once I stopped trying to analyze my feelings, I suddenly realized I was back in the womb. I could not deny any longer what was happening to me. I said to Barry, "I'm not born yet!" Now I was more surprised than scared, and support from the group was critical. I knew I did not want to stop. My only awareness was the sound of Barry's voice. He was talking to me about being born, and the sound of his voice was very helpful.

I actually remember not wanting to be born. How could I not want to be born? I was already twenty-six years old. I had my eyes closed, and I saw an image of a large hand about to hit me. My fear of being born turned out to be another important step. I realized I really needed to make a decision to be born. It never occurred to me that I had any choice in the matter. Barry told me that I needed to choose whether or not I was going to be born. I thought about this for a while and then asked Barry, "Are you going to slap me?" When Barry said no, I experienced a deep sense of relief and decided I would be born.

Once again I was crying, but I still had no tears. My cry was like a yell or a fearful, helpless, uncontrolled scream. I wiggled and pushed until I was completely out of breath and out from under the blanket.

To check out whether or not I had completed my "rebirth" process, Barry asked, "How do you know you are alive?" My answer to this was beautiful and simple. I said, "I am breathing, and I really feel good."

Suddenly I felt cold, and Barry wrapped me in a blanket and held me, and I felt content and secure. It seemed as if I was being taken care of for the first time in my life. I then experienced all my senses except taste. I was distracted by colors and textures, and I could feel Barry's voice emitting very calm, comforting feelings as he talked to me. Wow! That is the way to communicate with babies. The whole thing was a truly joyful experience!

Following this experience, Patty and I negotiated a parenting contract. For the next several years, I served as her contract parent, providing her with important bonding messages and, eventually, support for becoming autonomous. When Patty moved to another city, we formally ended our therapeutic relationship. We are still good friends and correspond or visit when she returns to town. Reparenting contracts should have beginnings and endings, so that people recognize that they have completed their developmental stages. This validates their work and acknowledges their growth.

Reparenting contracts can be short- or long-term, depending on the needs involved and the time required to meet them. Not all reparenting activities call for extensive contracts in order to be effective. Sometimes in a friendship or relationship a simple acknowledgment such as "You remind me of my father (or sister, or mother), and I feel close to you because of that" is all that's necessary to show that you're completing unfinished business with other persons.

## SUMMARY

Learning to repair the holes in the bonding process you experienced in infancy requires a deeper understanding of what you should have received and what will now help fill the gap. It's never too late to have a happy childhood — if you're willing to take responsibility for augmenting your early bonding experience. This kind of deep personal growth work can be difficult and scary, but the rewards far outweigh the effort.

# 18. New Forms of Relationship

It seems as if everyone is seeking a new form of relationship — one that's more satisfying and nourishing than what they've had in the past. Often we don't have words to describe this kind of relationship, but we may know what it is *not* — it is not co-dependent.

## INTERDEPENDENCY

A new, interdependent form of relationship emerges after we have recovered from co-dependency. At times, it may look co-dependent, counter-dependent, or independent. When you connect with another person at a deep level, you find a new dance that has many moves, allowing for the free flow of energy between you. When two people become separate, whole, autonomous beings, they no longer need to protect themselves from each other. In an interdependent relationship, you're free to be yourself. You realize that you are loved for who you really are, not for some false image you tried to create.

Partners in this kind of intimate relationship dance weave in and out of deep connection, are not always physically together, and still can fight and argue with each other, but do it fairly and with respect for each other's needs and feelings. What makes this possible is commitment and consciousness.

For this reason, we prefer to call this form of relationship a conscious, committed partnership relationship.

### Characteristics of a Conscious, Committed Partnership Relationship

Here are some common characteristics of this type of relationship:

- Both partners recognize that each brings fear-based behavior patterns and unhealed wounds from childhood into the relationship. They agree that the primary focus of the relationship is to heal these core issues and repattern the behaviors associated with them.
- They are committed to staying with conflicts until personal awareness and resolution occur.
- The relationship has a therapeutic function. The word "therapy" comes from the Greek word *therapea* and means "doing the work of the whole." The relationship itself is a healing *and* a wholing process.
- The relationship has a discovery process. Your intent is to discover, understand, and change yourself and not to try to change your partner.
- The relationship has a basis of self-trust rather than primal trust: rather than believing that the other won't hurt you, you trust yourself more. This means you'll be less hurt by your partner and will feel less responsible for hurting your partner. If you say or do anything that unintentionally hurts your partner, you can trust him or her to be responsible and ask for what he or she wants from you in order to assuage hurt feelings.
- Each partner sees the other as a mirror. This helps you recognize your deepest parts and any parts of yourself you have avoided seeing.
- Each partner focuses on a relationship with himself or herself. Partners agree to cooperate and support the other person's relationship with himself or herself.
- Both partners recognize that children are their greatest teachers. Children can help you become more self-aware and deepen your ability to love yourself and others.
- Conflicts with children are resolved in ways that support their search for personal autonomy. As parents, both partners give up

trying to control their children and instead get to know them and learn from them.

• Both partners recognize that these principles apply to all relationships, including student-teacher, employee-employer, friend-colleague, and nation-nation relationships. The goal is to help humankind learn to live together in peace and love.

## NOURISHING AND TOXIC RELATIONSHIPS

Not everyone is ready for conscious, committed partnership relationships. It's important to assess where you and your partner are in your relationship. There is a spectrum of consciousness and commitment in relationships that extends from highly nourishing to highly toxic. The five levels are as follows:[1]

1.  A highly nourishing relationship is characterized by a high level of both consciousness and commitment. Each partner contributes greatly to the other's growth.
2.  A mildly nourishing relationship has a lower level of consciousness or commitment in some areas. This impairs the contribution each partner can make to the other's life.
3.  A noncontributing relationship entails little consciousness and commitment to growth and learning, and so makes little or no contribution to the partners' personal development.
4.  A mildly toxic relationship incorporates so little consciousness and commitment that each partner feels slightly diminished as a person, and the relationship interferes with the partners' enjoyment of life.
5.  A highly toxic relationship involves no noticeable commitment to growth and, instead, entails excessive demands, intimidation, repression, hostility, and verbal or physical abuse that depletes both partners.

If you're in a relationship that is toxic, or less nourishing than what you want, you must decide what you're willing to try in order to make it more cooperative and supportive. You must also determine your partner's willingness to cooperate with your desire. If this strategy proves to be unsuccessful, then you must find the courage to end this relationship — and any others in which you cannot meet your needs.

## TOOLS FOR CREATING NEW FORMS OF RELATIONSHIP

It's necessary to develop new tools if you want to create a new form of relationship. You will need to understand which co-dependent behaviors you've used in the past that haven't worked and replace them with more effective behaviors.

### Tools for Working on Yourself

Sometimes it's necessary to take a time-out in the middle of a conflict in order to think through your reactions and responses. Try the following activity to gain more clarity:

- Think of three things you don't like about your partner that you want him or her to change. Write them on a piece of paper. Then ask yourself, "How am I like that?" and "When do I do these same things?" Write your answers on the paper. Then ask yourself, "Am I willing to change these things in myself?" If the answer is no, then what right do you have to ask your partner to change these things?

- If you *do* change these undesirable things in yourself, the other person may be encouraged to change as well. This is the only way to change your interactions with others — by first changing yourself. Remember that the ultimate state of stuckness is waiting for someone else to change before you can feel better.

### Tools for Therapy

Relationship or family therapy is actually preferable to individual therapy in the effort to break free of co-dependency. It's possible to do some individual therapy to become more aware of core issues, but partners who want to stay together must learn to cooperate in order to break their patterns. It's also useful for people in a relationship to have a common framework and language that comes with working with a therapist. For individual work, we suggest that you and your partner each have your own therapist to prevent conflict of interest and favoritism issues. If this isn't feasible, then choose a new therapist for couples therapy who doesn't know either of you.

Couples therapy can also provide an excellent setting for working through the conscious completion of your psychological birth. Ask your individual therapists to work as co-therapists who can support you individually. This replicates the joint parenting model and ensures that you each are able to work through the issues that resulted from becoming stuck in both your co-dependent and counter-dependent stages of development.

To succeed in this work, therapists must first build a solid relationship with each partner and provide secure bonding and safety. When the developmental crisis is resolved, everyone can feel okay about himself or herself and each other. Skilled therapists and willing partners are necessary to create the conditions for this completion to occur for both partners.

Commonly, one member in a partnership will "wake up" first and seek therapy without his or her partner. The next task is to get the missing partner to come to relationship therapy. Partners may resist this, so here are a few suggestions on how to persuade them:

- Ask your partner to come to therapy to help you. Most co-dependent partners can't resist this.
- Tell your partner that you're going to talk about him or her in your relationship in therapy, and you want him or her to be there to offer an alternate view of things. Resistant partners may be motivated to come along in order to defend themselves and speak directly about their side of the conflict.
- Ask your partner to join you for a specified number of sessions (one to three sessions) to see how it goes. This is a limited enough request that a resistant partner may agree to it.
- It's not good to issue "or else" ultimatums, but a very resistant partner may need firm limits on what is acceptable to you. If you believe therapy is the only hope for the relationship, then say so and enlist your partner's cooperation. If he or she is unwilling, then you know that this resistance is more important to him or her than taking positive steps toward change.

### Tools for Support Groups

A group of people who want a committed relationship can be an important source of support. It's easy to feel alone and isolated if you're doing this work and most of your friends are not. Meeting occasionally with others on a similar path to breaking their co-dependent patterns can be just what you need.

If partners have studied our developmental framework, or other frameworks for understanding co-dependency, they'll find working together with other people helpful. The interventions, support, and insights of other couples going through the same or a similar process can benefit both those doing the helping and those being helped.

You might also try dividing into gender groups to give the men a chance to talk directly with other men, and the women a chance to talk directly with other women. Sometimes the support of someone of the same gender can be a great help.

## Tools for Committed Relationships

- Knowing how to learn important lessons in your intimate relationships is valuable. Jordan and Margaret Paul, in their book *Do I Have to Give Up Me to Be Loved by You?*, suggest key questions that partners must ask each other at each step of the learning process.[2] Their four-step process, including the key questions, is paraphrased below.

  1. *Explore what's happening.* Will you describe what you believe has been happening to you, to me, to us? What do you think is going to happen next? What would you like to have happen next? What are you doing that is interfering with the resolution of the conflict? What am I doing to interfere?

  2. *Explore your understanding of each other.* Do you feel understood, listened to, and respected by me? If not, what do you need from me to feel more of these qualities?

  3. *Explore your feelings.* How do you feel about our communication? What suggestions do you have to improve it? How do you feel toward me now? What, if anything, do you need from me in order to feel better about me and what we're doing?

  4. *Explore intent.* Are you open to learning more about me? Do you see me as defending a position or as open to learning? Do you believe I want to understand you and your feelings? What can I do to improve in this area?

- One of the most important areas in building a cooperative relationship is making and keeping agreements. The following rules are designed to promote these skills. Take turns reading each rule aloud with your partner. Then put the rule into your own words ("What I think this means is..."), give an example of your own use or misuse of the rule, and ask your partner to comment on the rule. Here are some suggestions for making and keeping agreements:

1.  Make only agreements you're willing and able to keep. Think carefully about the agreement before making it.

2.  Communicate directly any potential broken agreements before they're actually broken. For example, call if you know you're going to be late for an appointment.

3.  Speak with good intent. Do not forecast failure for the agreement. Ask, "Is there anything you can see that might interfere with your keeping this agreement?"

4.  If you do break an agreement, communicate this directly to your partner at the first appropriate opportunity. Avoid unilaterally breaking an agreement.

5.  Tell the truth responsibly and allow others to do the same. For example, "The truth for me is..."

6.  Focus on the problem and the solution. Don't become sidetracked while trying to find reasons or justifications for the problem.

7.  View the other person as being *right* for what he or she is doing instead of trying to show why he or she is wrong. For example, "I notice you weren't able to do the dishes as you had agreed. Can you tell me what happened?"

8.  If the other person is angry at you for breaking an agreement, ask what he or she wants from you in order to repair the damage. Then ask if he or she would be willing to forgive you.

9.  Tell the other person how you see the problem, and give him or her the solution you want; then ask him or her to do the same.

•   Another fun and interesting activity involves making a collage representing your relationship. Both partners can separately construct collages using pictures and headings from old magazines to symbolize how they see the relationship. Then compare the two and look for similarities and differences. A second step is to cocreate a joint collage that represents how both would like the relationship to be. Collages can be displayed at home as reminders of your common vision for the relationship.

## CASE EXAMPLE

Even though they had a conscious, committed partnership relationship, Bob and June came to therapy because they'd hit a wall. We decided to do co-therapy to help them gain some additional skills and information.

Bob said, "I don't know what's going on. We're really getting on each other's nerves." June said, "I love this man very much, but lately he's been doing things that really push my buttons. I'm starting to withdraw from him, and I want to find out why."

It seemed that both were facing new challenges in their lives that were making them more tense. They had also gotten closer in their relationship and let down some of their barriers, so they were more vulnerable to each other. Tension caused both by external factors and their relationship was making them more critical of each other. They were starting to say and do things to each other that were touching previously protected narcissistic wounds.

June was staying at home to care for two small children, ages one and five, and feeling overwhelmed by their demands. She was also feeling overwhelmed by her internal reactions to memories of her own childhood that parenting was bringing up. Bob was less available for June than usual because he was trying to get his business established. They were missing the support they once supplied each other, and they didn't seem to know how to find it under the present conditions.

We worked with them at several levels. First, we helped them find ways to structure more time together and to cooperate with and support each other. However, we knew there were other forces and issues that needed to be addressed. We explored with them the "edges" in their relationship — things they were afraid to say or do with each other.

Through this approach, we identified several areas in their relationship where they were co-dependent and counter-dependent. These included some important things they needed to say to each other about their sexual needs.

Bob was afraid to ask June for sex for fear she would perceive this as pressure or a demand and might withdraw or reject him. Also, there were secrets they had kept from each other about their masturbation habits and sexual fantasies. Being able to talk openly about their sexual needs and habits was frightening to them but also brought them closer together. And it brought up deeper wounds that still remained from early childhood. With our guidance, they were able to partner with each other to heal some of these wounds. They agreed to listen to each other more, to understand where the other was coming from, and to hold and nurture each other when the old feelings surfaced.

After about six sessions, Bob called to cancel their next session by saying they were having more fun together and wanted to take a vacation from therapy for a while. We wholeheartedly supported this idea and said we would welcome them back for a "tune-up" if they needed one.

Bob and June were both eager to have an interdependent relationship and had a clear vision of what it would be like. This vision helped them structure their relationship differently and supported their exploration of what worked and didn't work. Collaborative, cooperative efforts like this one between partners in a relationship are important for working through bonding and separation issues, so that a deeper, more fluid relationship can emerge.

## SUMMARY

The quest for a relationship free of co-dependent behavior patterns requires that you develop new relationship tools. Working with your partner to develop new communication skills can yield rewarding results, but as with any new skills or tools, you'll have to practice with them before you get the most benefit from them.

# 19. Healing the Co-dependent Culture

The idea of trying to change a whole culture, especially one based on domination, is a little intimidating. Where do you begin? Changing institutions would be the most challenging place to start, since they're made up of so many people, and hierarchies and bureaucracies steadfastly resist change until they're at the edge of collapse. So, the best place to start is with yourself.

Once you admit you have co-dependency issues, and that they make your life difficult, if not miserable, you've done the most important thing. From there the path to recovery is clearer, although not always easier. Now you have a vision of something better. A twelve-step program or a support group is important at this stage. Such groups can provide you with allies who have similar visions and can reinforce your vision if it wavers. Remember that it's easy to create co-dependent relationships on your journey to interdependence. The suggestions concerning therapy and how to work on yourself presented in this book will also support you in taking charge of your own healing. This is an important issue.

## DEVELOPMENTAL SYSTEMS THEORY: A NEW PERSPECTIVE ON THE CO-DEPENDENT CULTURE

Even if you clear your own co-dependency issues, such issues will still emerge in other people around you. They show up in work relationships, in friendships, in your children and grandchildren, in media messages, at church, and in politics — they are part of the very fabric of our dominator culture. The same incomplete developmental processes and developmental traumas that caused your personal co-dependent behaviors are also operating in your intimate relationships and in larger human systems — in schools, in churches, and in businesses and government structures. How could it be otherwise? If people have not identified and healed their personal developmental traumas and dysfunctions, of course they will re-create them in all other social structures.

Knowing this, you can be better prepared to encounter the co-dependent culture and the dominator principles that perpetuate co-dependent behavior. We created the Developmental Systems Theory as a way of mapping the co-dependent culture and to provide tools for transforming it. In *The Flight from Intimacy*, our companion book to this one, we discuss the counter-dependent culture and how it's caused by developmental processes left incomplete during the counter-dependent stage of development.[1]

## HEALING THE CO-DEPENDENT CULTURE THROUGH COMMITTED RELATIONSHIPS

In chapter 18, we discussed interdependent relationships and how they can be used to heal old wounds and to complete developmental issues. In interdependent relationships, growth is a primary focus. Committed relationships are different from co-dependent relationships, because one commits not only to the other person but also to oneself. The personal and spiritual growth of each individual is of primary importance.

Interdependent relationships have yet a different focus: partners commit not to the *form* but to the *process*. Commitments stress contracts and agreements that support safety, security, and predictability in the relationship while the partners are working together on healing themselves and each other. The emphasis on partnership supports the move toward cocreation and humanitarian service. The strength and clarity of two united people creates a synergy that can be channeled into projects of great magnitude. As more couples reach this level of evolution, they influence others to do the same, and they create ripples of awareness in society at large. This is not unlike the last step in the twelve-step program for addictions, which calls for people to carry the message to others and practice the principles in all their affairs.

Once a couple has transformed their relationship, they will want something similar at work, at the schools their children attend, in the church they belong to, and in their elected officials. Committed partners who have decided to extend the dimensions of their interdependent relationship out into the community or world are forming new clinics, institutes, businesses, and organizations. Some have become activists who challenge the co-dependent behaviors and assumptions of the institutions they do business with. They know there's a better way, and they're willing to speak out and become models to help others find that way.

## HEALING THE CO-DEPENDENT CULTURE THROUGH COMMUNITY

Even committed relationships are limited in how they can change the whole culture. Individuals are able to help each other in partnerships and provide mirroring, nurturing, support, and healing for each other. The degree to which they can be physically and emotionally present determines how much they can help each other. Your partner may travel, get sick, or have a conflicting schedule, so it isn't always practical to expect his or her constant physical presence.

Also, partners in committed relationships must consider our multifaceted, multidimensional nature. People have so *many* different parts and interests that it's unrealistic to expect another person to share and mirror these exact same parts and interests. We all need committed relationships with many different people who can mirror us, provide feedback, and partner with us in ways that a beloved intimate often can't. A supportive community of friends serves this function.

Your partner may also have his or her own issues surfacing, making it difficult for him or her to always be there to help you with your issues. Again, you may need a support group or network of friends to help you.

*Community* has become a popular term to replace what used to be called *extended family* — the aunts, uncles, cousins, grandparents, and other relatives who lived in close proximity and made up a person's social circle. Community provides the same kind of social and emotional support, except that you have more choice about the membership. In his book *The Different Drum: Community Making and Peace*, M. Scott Peck defines community as a group of people committed to inclusivity, group process, governance by consensus, authenticity and realness, self-reflection, safety for group members, and support for resolving conflicts with wisdom and grace.[2] Peck sees community making as a four-stage developmental process that parallels our four stages of individual development:

1. *Pseudocommunity*, the first stage, is artificial. Relationships at this stage are shallow, and interactions are based on conformity and the pretense that everyone thinks and behaves alike. Conflict, true feelings, and acknowledgment of individual differences are distinctly avoided. This period of pretense, very similar to co-dependency, exists until group members reach their limit on pretending. Then conflict erupts and the group moves into chaos.

2. *Chaos* is characterized by fighting, struggle, and open evidence of individual differences. It parallels the counter-dependency stage. In this stage, the recognized leader of pseudocommunity may be deposed by secondary leaders who try to sabotage the group and throw it back into pseudocommunity. Peck says the only way out of chaos is through emptiness.

3. *Emptiness* is the most critical stage of community. Here members are required to drop their communication barriers and speak honestly. Feelings of pain, sorrow, or sadness often flow freely at this point, as people openly acknowledge their brokenness. They put aside their prejudices, expectations, preconceptions, need to control, ideologies, and need to heal, convert, or fix others. The key to this stage, which parallels the stage of independence in individual development, is the group's ability to embrace not only the positive aspects of life but also the negative aspects. When the group allows the artificiality of pseudocommunity to die, then the group moves into true community.

4. *True community*, the last stage, is a place of interdependence, where members can be their True Selves. True community, especially as modeled in twelve-step programs, supports individuals who want to change their lives, and it does so without judgment.

## HEALING THE CO-DEPENDENT CULTURE
## THROUGH SERVANT LEADERSHIP

The shift from co-dependency to interdependency in business and industry is emerging through the concept of *servant leadership*. This concept comes directly from Jesus and his symbolic act on Holy Thursday of washing the feet of his disciples. This pre–Good Friday event, mentioned previously in chapter 3, created the foundation for servant leadership as an emerging organizational movement.

The central idea of servant leadership is one of mutual participation — participation in decisions, risk taking, management of resources, rewards, problems, and successes. Leadership is a role that can be filled by anyone with the skills appropriate for the task, and it changes as needs and circumstances change. This allows for the more effective utilization of people and their skills. The servant leadership movement is now emerging in a number of different places.

Robert Greenleaf is one noted scholar who has developed this concept. He draws support for servant leadership from a broad spectrum of thought that includes Eastern philosophies and ideas generated by psychology, businesses, nonprofit organizations, churches, education systems, and educational foundations. His analysis of systems is similar to that of Riane Eisler, who developed the partnership/dominator model to describe types of social systems. He refers to the dominator model as "hierarchical" and the partnership model as "primus inter pares"[3] (literally, "first among equals").

Other parts of the servant leadership movement are less visible than those described by Greenleaf. Some other servant leaders are found in middle- or upper-management positions where individuals bring change to their work assignments by means of their own personal paths, such as twelve-step programs, meditation, running and fitness programs, personal growth seminars, or other activities designed to transform people.

## TOOLS FOR HEALING THE CO-DEPENDENT CULTURE

There are many tools that you can use to begin healing the co-dependent culture. One place to start is by diagnosing the level of co-dependency that exists in your work environment and determining how open that environment is to change.

*Tools for Working on Yourself*

• Use the following inventory to determine how open your workplace is to change. Based on the results, decide what changes you want to make there.

## THE OPENNESS TO CHANGE INVENTORY

DIRECTIONS: Place a check mark in the column that best represents your perception.

| Perception | Never | Occasionally | Frequently | Almost always |
|---|---|---|---|---|
| 1. I have direct input into the rules made in this organization. | | | | |
| 2. Many rules in this organization restrict my freedom. | | | | |
| 3. Important decisions are made by top members of the administration. | | | | |
| 4. I'm consulted on decisions that affect me directly. | | | | |
| 5. I have direct access to information and decisions passed down from the top. | | | | |
| 6. When I want an answer to something, I have to ask many people before I find someone who can answer my question. | | | | |
| 7. The goals and purposes of this organization are determined according to input from all those involved in the organization. | | | | |
| 8. I don't have direct input into the goals and purposes of the organization. | | | | |

| Perception | Never | Occasionally | Frequently | Almost always |
|---|---|---|---|---|
| 9. Information and important decisions are shared in face-to-face meetings, where everyone is free to express his or her opinions and feelings. | | | | |
| 10. Important information and decisions are communicated by memos, policy letters, telephone calls, or other indirect means. | | | | |
| 11. I have the power to make the decisions that affect me most directly. | | | | |
| 12. When I have a conflict with a supervisor or administrator, I feel that I lose. | | | | |
| 13. Approved procedures and schedules are rigidly followed in this organization. | | | | |
| 14. I'm free to change what I'm doing in response to the needs of my customers or clients. | | | | |
| 15. Managers, supervisors, and staff seem to be working together toward common goals and objectives. | | | | |
| 16. My job description tells me exactly what I can and can't do as an employee. | | | | |
| 17. I am encouraged to "wear as many hats" as the situation calls for. | | | | |

The scoring system is set up to ensure that you do not unconsciously answer the questions in such a way that you achieve a "desired" score. The value of each of the seventeen items is tabulated according to the tables below. Items 1, 4, 5, 7, 9, 11, 14, 15, and 17 are scored as follows:

1 = Never   2 = Occasionally   3 = Frequently   4 = Almost always

Total score A _____

Items 2, 3, 6, 8, 10, 12, 13, and 16 are scored as follows:

4 = Never   3 = Occasionally   2 = Frequently   1 = Almost always

Total score B _____
Grand total score (A + B) _____

Use the following guidelines to interpret your organization's openness-to-change score. The numbers refer to the grand total.

17–26 Not much change is possible at this time in your organization
27–36 Proceed slowly with caution
37–46 Plan carefully for small changes
47–56 Build a support base first, and be aware of double-talk
57–66 Openness to change is apparent
67+   The sky's the limit

- Review the following list of characteristics that many employers see as essential in employees. See if you can identify which ones encourage co-dependency.
    1. High-level organizational ability
    2. Competence in a wide variety of tasks and the ability to learn additional tasks quickly
    3. Stability and resistance to panic
    4. Skill at diplomacy and emotional manipulation
    5. Resilience, with a high tolerance to pain
    6. High energy, with good resistance to fatigue
    7. Good administrative skills
    8. The ability to defer gratification indefinitely
    9. Crisis intervention skills

10. Strong sense of morality, a strong sense of right and wrong
11. Loyalty and a willingness to put the needs of an important group before his or her own
12. Capacity to never ask "What's in this for me?"
13. The ability to do enormous amounts of work for a minimal payoff
14. High level of nursing and caretaking skills
15. Tendency toward overachievement, leading to the ability to work consistently at 120 percent capacity
16. Tendency to assign low priority to sexual needs and feelings
17. Lack of visible physical conditions that would result in loss of work time
18. Low self-esteem with dependent personality

### Tools for Therapy

Join a therapy group. Ask your therapist if he or she is willing to assume the role of facilitator rather than therapist and facilitate a community-making process as part of your group's structure. Your therapist must be willing to relinquish control during the process if it is to work. Otherwise, the group will likely become stuck in a pseudocommunity.

### Tools for Support Groups

- Join a twelve-step program and observe the components of its structure. See if the structure of the twelve-step group resembles in any way the structure of your family of origin, your primary relationship, or your workplace. If it does, could this be another form of the co-dependent family structure you experienced as a child and young person? If you see any similar patterns, this is a good sign that you are becoming more aware of what a co-dependent trap looks and feels like. You can still use the twelve-step group structure as part of your recovery program, but you can possibly learn how to avoid the co-dependency trap that might be part of that structure.
- Ask members of your support group to create a community-making process using the guidelines given in *A Different Drum*, M. Scott Peck's book on community making.

*Tools for Committed Relationships*

- Examine your intimate relationships for evidence of counter-dependent behavior with regard to community. For instance, do you reach out to others to meet your needs, and avoid meeting them in your intimate relationships? Identify formal and informal groups to which you belong. List which needs each group fulfills. Determine whether your partner could fill some of these needs. Many people who are afraid of the intimacy of a committed relationship will evade it and its challenge by joining pseudocommunity groups. Here they try to get some of their unmet needs fulfilled without risking intimacy, which means they're avoiding dealing with their real issues.

- Examine your primary relationship for evidence of co-dependent behavior with regard to the community. For instance, do you reach out only to your partner to meet your needs and avoid meeting any through the community? Identify personal relationship needs that are regularly not met in your primary relationship. Determine where in your community you might fulfill these needs. Discuss these needs with your partner and make a plan for fulfilling each of your unmet personal needs in a community setting.

## CASE EXAMPLE

Dave's low point in life came one rainy evening in the park near where he used to live before his divorce. He'd lost his job, his wife, his children, and his savings, and he was down to his guitar and a quart of whiskey. He arrived at the park already drunk and planned to spend the evening sipping his bottle and strumming his guitar. As he moved to a sheltered spot to sit, he stumbled in a hole. Over he went. The bottle slipped out of his hand while his guitar flew off to one side and bounced off a large rock nearby. He found himself facedown in the mud, his bottle shattered, his guitar broken, and himself at the end of his rope. He sobbed quietly and beat his fists weakly on the ground saying, "Great Spirit, please help me." Dave, a Native American, had no other place to turn. He decided to return to the teachings of his culture and began to seek a spiritual dimension in his life. He went home, cleaned himself up, and began to ask for guidance from the Great Spirit.

He eventually joined Alcoholics Anonymous and broke his addiction to alcohol. He also returned to his Native American roots and sought the wisdom of his people's ancient teachings. In these two groups, he found surprisingly similar principles based on the partnership model. Through them he found the strength to restore his dignity, and he created a new life for himself and found a new wife and family and a new job.

He felt great peace in his personal life and yearned to bring it into his professional life. He made exploratory inquiries about introducing his personal perspective and experience into his management group, but his supervisors were skeptical. Finally, one day he decided to just do it. He felt sure the principles would work, and that, if he caught flack from people, he would rather ask for forgiveness than ask for permission.

He found the principles to be as effective as he'd anticipated. He first implemented them in his own work group. For example, he got members of the group to commit to helping each other and to asking directly for what they wanted or needed from each other so as not to enable others in the group. Then other company groups heard about his approach, and they tried it. Eventually six of the seven company groups in his plant of almost four thousand employees adopted his partnership-community model of management. Dave recently trained national and international managers from his company's other plants, extending his personal experience out into the world.

Eventually, Dave left corporate life to start his own organization dedicated to carrying these principles into Native American communities. He focused on helping young people in these communities avoid the destructive path of alcohol addiction and taught them how to break their co-dependent behaviors and live healthy, productive lives. He's an example of a man who first did his own personal healing work and then used what he learned to help heal the co-dependent culture. We feel inspired and hopeful because of his success.

## SUMMARY

Our co-dependent culture reinforces co-dependency in individuals, couples, and families, and its influence is economic, social, and psychological. Our culture was not created to trap people in co-dependency, but this is exactly what happens unless people become aware of its effects on themselves and others.

# 20. How We Changed Our Co-dependent Patterns

We struggled with breaking free of the co-dependency trap. We had many challenges to overcome, and we were sometimes not sure that we would succeed. In the following pages, we describe our backgrounds and share how we have worked to change our own co-dependent patterns.

## JANAE'S STORY

I was the first daughter and second of five children born to a farm couple who wanted a girl. Although I had a difficult birth and almost died, my first few months were really good. Then my mother got pregnant again, and she gave birth to my sister when I was eleven months old. During my mother's ten-day hospitalization, I stayed with my grandmother. I remember my mother telling me on several occasions that I refused to have anything to do with her for more than a week after she and my sister came home from the hospital. I was so hurt and angry that I wouldn't even look at her. Three years later a second sister arrived. By this time, my mother had four children under the age of seven and needed help from neighborhood girls to take care of us. I remember my childhood being lonely. My mother was always busy, and we didn't visit much with our extended family. My main source of joy and friendship was my visits to the farm buildings and the many animals and their babies.

During my early childhood, my father struggled to support us by farm-ing. He worked long hours during much of the year. My parents grew most of our food. My mother cooked and baked, strained fresh milk, made butter, froze and canned vegetables, butchered chickens, and sewed all the clothes for herself, my sisters, and me. Somehow she also did laundry, cleaned, and cared for her children. We had a series of mother's helpers during the sum-mers to watch us while she did her farmwife work.

I don't remember feeling much of a connection with my mother. I don't think I ever forgave her for abandoning me at my sister's birth, and I never really bonded with her again. As more and more children arrived, I gave up hope of getting my bonding needs met. I remember feeling closer to my father. He was more available than my mother after my first sister's birth, so I trusted him more. His availability during that period helped me separate from my mother but left me stuck in counter-dependency. I got approval for self-sufficiency and caretaking behaviors, and quickly took on a lot of the parenting and caretaking responsibilities. I became the achiever, or "hero," in the family.

When I was thirteen, my mother killed herself and my five-year-old brother. We found them in the car with the garage full of carbon monox-ide fumes. I was devastated by the loss of my little brother, the one person in the family to whom I felt really close. My mother's family abandoned us in shame after her suicide, isolating us even more. After my mother's death, my next younger sister and I took over the role of "farmwife," doing many of her jobs in addition to our schoolwork. By high school graduation I had pretty well mastered being a manager and caretaker. But during my junior year in high school, my co-dependent needs began to surface. I had a boyfriend and planned to get married right after I graduated from college. In college, I majored in home economics and graduated in three years with honors.

During my senior year in college, I spent a summer at a human devel-opment institute in another state, and a whole new world opened to me. Here I had my first glimpse of another way of life, one with values less rigid than those of my midwestern farm culture. I was exposed to people and ideas that supported openness, exploration, curiosity, and conscious parenting. I returned to college, to my family, and to my boyfriend with a vision of some-thing new and better. Nowhere, however, was there any support for this new vision. My whole family system, steeped in the dominator model, encouraged and rewarded passivity, conformity, and co-dependency. My boyfriend and I eventually broke up. After graduation, I found a job teaching in a small farm town much like the one where I grew up, and the rural patterns of roles and relationships felt familiar. Immediately I began dating Herb, the agriculture teacher in the school, and four months later I married him.

By this time, the strain of maintaining a counter-dependent facade had taken its toll. I quickly surrendered to my co-dependent needs for symbiosis and protection. I turned over my savings to Herb and let him manage it. I got pregnant quickly and quit my teaching job at the end of my first year.

In my marriage, I assumed the very passive role I had seen my mother take in her relationship with my father. I projected my masculine part onto Herb, as we created a traditional relationship with rigid roles. I cooked, sewed, cleaned, and worked at being the perfect wife, while he managed the money, enforced discipline, and made the rules. We had two sons, five years apart. We lived away from both our families much of the time, so I had only my sons and Herb for emotional support. I was lonely, but Herb discouraged me from venturing outside our nuclear family for anything.

With my background in child care and family life, I gave the wife-and-mother role everything I had. I was determined to create the close family I had always wanted. My needs for closeness and protection were so intense that I worked even harder when there were rough patches in the relationship.

After nineteen years of struggle to meet my emotional needs in very unhealthy ways, I found myself physically exhausted and psychologically empty. I felt as though I were dying, and that I had totally lost myself. In a state of crisis, I sought counseling. The therapy helped me validate my emotional needs and gave me support for making changes in myself and my relationship. I joined a therapy group that helped me see how universal my circumstances were and supported me in changing my life. This also revived my vision from my college days of having something for myself. I read dozens of books and enrolled in personal growth seminars and workshops. I found a support system at Overeaters Anonymous (my family's addiction) and in university classes after I decided to go to graduate school. All these experiences helped support my vision of and desire for a better kind of life.

Herb and I went for counseling together a few times. I hoped that we'd be able to transform our relationship into something larger and richer. After two or three sessions, however, it became obvious that my dream would not happen. Herb really wanted me to return to the old form of our relationship. We divorced eventually, and I moved on with my life.

My graduate advisor at the university had suggested that I begin doctoral studies, but I decided to complete a year of graduate work first. During that time I attended a seminar with Jean Houston and then enrolled in her Mystery School training program in New York, where I met Barry. This training focused on the esoteric or hidden teachings of ten major world religious traditions. It required an enormous amount of reading between each monthly weekend session, and the actual training sessions were an immersion experience in the spiritual practices of each tradition.

## BARRY'S STORY

I was the firstborn male in an upwardly mobile working-class family with a large extended family in a small town. According to my mother, I had an easy birth after thirty minutes of labor but bonded with her only tenuously. My mother was just nineteen years old and seemed to be unable to function as a parent after my birth. She was unable to produce milk to breast-feed me, and this apparently was a serious blow to her self-esteem. After trying unsuccessfully for one week, she decided to return to work and turned me over to a teenage babysitter. I failed to thrive, and almost died at six weeks due to a lack of nourishment. At this point, I went to live with my paternal grandmother until I was ten months old. Then I went back to live with my parents and was cared for by a very nurturing nanny.

My father was either absent, injured, or sick during my early childhood. He worked long hours and suffered a work-related accident and chronic respiratory illnesses. He was not there to support me in developing independence from my mother, grandmother, and nanny. I found myself enmeshed in a highly co-dependent extended family.

My later childhood was dominated by "be careful" messages and attempts to please my "mothers." I remember that in grades one through four my grandmother gave me a dime for each A I received in deportment, reinforcing conformist behavior. Her admonition to me was, "Just be a good boy, and don't give your parents any more problems. They have enough problems of their own." I also remember my mother yelling at me occasionally and my father rescuing me later by telling me privately that my mother didn't mean what she said. My grandfather rescued my father from his parenting responsibilities by spending time with me when my father was unavailable.

Adolescence was rocky, but by high school I began to gain some self-confidence. As a sophomore, I was picked for the junior varsity basketball team and ended high school with letters in basketball and baseball. I also joined the Fraternal Order of DeMolay, a Masonic-sponsored, service-oriented organization for young people, in a nearby city where I didn't know anybody, and worked my way up to the highest office in two years.

Fran and I met on a blind date while I was a sophomore in college and she was just finishing high school. After two and a half years of dating, we got married and began re-creating the co-dependent patterns we were both familiar with. We both had problems with intimacy that we managed to avoid by arranging conflicting work and school schedules for the first six years of our marriage.

During my graduate training and the period immediately following graduation, our marriage started falling apart. We had two small children by then, which fulfilled one of Fran's major dreams. I found that I wanted more intimacy than she was comfortable with, but she seemed willing to learn. That phase of our relationship carried us through another eight to ten years. I think neither of us could face the prospect of being alone, so the fear of loneliness kept us together. During that time we tried to build a more cooperative relationship. I learned to cook and take care of myself around the home, and she became more comfortable being out in the world. I also went through outpatient reparenting therapy for about three years, which filled some of the major gaps in my development. This particular type of therapy was done in weekly group meetings and involved having each adult client contract each week to work on a specific issue stemming from his or her early childhood experiences. The therapist served as a "contract mother" for each of the clients in the group, giving each person the nurturing attention and mothering that he or she may have missed while growing up. I developed more basic trust, stopped seeing myself as "special" and therefore different from others, and developed more object constancy. As Fran and I made changes, we began to recognize areas of incompatibility that we had previously not noticed. Our goals and worldviews had become quite different, and our contact with each other didn't nourish us much anymore. We decided to divorce and find our separate ways.

After living alone for several months and dating several women, I began dating my friend Barbara, who had been divorced for about a year. We found we had much in common. Eight months later we eloped to Reno. I felt like I'd met my soul mate. Barbara was my projected idealized feminine part, and I was her projected idealized masculine part. Our co-dependent relationship required us to each live up to the other's projections. Problems occurred when either of us failed to live up to the ideal. I found myself becoming more and more wooden and one-dimensional as the problems between us increased.

Barbara discovered that she had experienced incest as a child, and she suffered from bulimia, an eating disorder. She worked hard to deal with these problems, and I worked hard doing what I was trained to do: take care of her. I became a butler in our relationship, always trying to please her and not get upset with her. I went into therapy again to work my way out of this role and began asserting my independence in our relationship. I also realized that I was still resisting Barbara's problems and was trying to control her and manipulate her into the idealized image I had of her.

Finally, I discovered the key to breaking out of the co-dependency trap I found myself in — surrender. I realized that I had to learn both the masculine and the feminine forms of surrender. The masculine form involved my willingness to take charge of myself and my life without guilt, and the feminine form involved my willingness to receive or accept Barbara and her problems without resistance. Therapy helped me learn the masculine form, and I learned the feminine form in my relationship with Barbara. Together these two concepts helped me break free of some of my co-dependency patterns. Unfortunately, I didn't have much time to enjoy these gains in my relationship with Barbara, because about six weeks after my breakthrough experience with her, she died after a skiing accident. My life was shattered. I was alone, and I wasn't sure I wanted to live. I felt like half a person. This was the real test of my learning. I had to take charge of my life, and I had to reclaim the feminine part I had projected onto Barbara.

One of the hardest parts was to do my grieving while still having to function in the world. I hadn't even been able to say good-bye to Barbara when she died, and this became a major obstacle for me to overcome. Finally, about six months after her death, I asked a friend to lead me on a guided journey to meet with Barbara and say good-bye. He instructed me to imagine someone guiding me to meet Barbara. I imagined a spirit guide in the form of a wise old man who would take me to her. In my mind's eye, he led me into a cave, where we came to a large room filled with mist. Finally, Barbara spoke to me through the mist. She apologized for leaving me so suddenly, and we said our good-byes.

She said she had known for a year that she was going to die, but when she had tried to talk to me about her fears, I'd refused to listen. Instead, I'd tried to talk her out of them (my lack of surrender). Then she chuckled in a characteristic way, and I asked her what was funny.

She said that it gave her great pleasure to tell me that I wouldn't have to be alone for long. She said, "They're sending someone to be with you." My first question was: "Who are 'they'?" She replied, "The members of our soul group." My next question was: "When will this happen?" She said, "I don't know how long it will be, but not very long." Then I asked, "Well, how will I recognize her?" Barbara replied, "You'll know her because her vibration is very similar to mine, only she has evolved further than I had and does not have the same problems I had." My final question was: "How will I find her?" Barbara responded, "You don't have to do anything. She will find you."

We ended our meeting with pledges to meet again somewhere, sometime, in a future lifetime under different circumstances, and then said good-bye. This was an important completion for me and enabled me to begin to fully engage with life again. I set out to find new allies to help me complete the sacred marriage of my inner masculine and feminine selves. Jean Houston taught me how to find my beloved within, and Robert Bly taught me how to find my deep, masculine "wild man." I also enrolled in Jean Houston's year-long Mystery School to get additional support for my integration. I found more than I expected at the Mystery School, because that's where I met Janae.

Later Janae and I would both realize that we had married others because of the unconscious patterns we had learned from our families of origin. When Janae and I decided to marry, we agreed to close the exits and work cooperatively to break free from the remaining co-dependent behaviors we might still be carrying from our childhoods. We believed that if we were willing to stay emotionally engaged and help each other, we could in fact break free.

## OUR STORY

### *How We Met*

JANAE: My time spent training at the Mystery School was a period of great growth for me. Leaving my "mousewife" existence, I dared to drive three hundred miles to Chicago and fly from there to New York. I'd flown just once before in my life, so this was a big leap for me. At the training sessions, I met people from all parts of the country who were in many different professions. The broad range of our studies of spiritual teachings of ancient cultures, combined with the diverse backgrounds of the participants and the spirit of adventure, exploded my horizons. So many possibilities opened to me that I began to feel confused about the next stage of my life.

After my divorce, my sons had both decided to attend school in another state, so I was free, at the age of forty-one, to begin a new life. I felt drawn to Native American teachings and finally decided I would go on a vision quest. I was considering how and where I would do that when Barry and I bumped into each other while dancing at a Mystery School event. During a chat later about the incident, he asked me if I would be coming to Colorado soon. If I were to do so, which was a pretty remote possibility at that time, he wanted me to visit him.

A subsequent letter encouraging me to visit him in Colorado arrived on a day that I received two other messages about going to Colorado. This was a "cosmic three" sign that I should go. A big snow in Colorado, however, prevented me from participating in the planned vision quest. I did attend a weekend class that Barry was teaching, thinking I would be a spectator. Instead, he invited me to *teach* with him! It was like a dream come true, as I had yearned for a partner who shared my interests. The ten days we spent together were some of the most incredible of my life, as we discovered area after area of mutual interest and many common dreams. After having spent so many years in a relationship that wasn't what I wanted, and having so clear a vision of what I did want, it was easy to say yes to life. I made arrangements to move myself to Colorado as soon as possible.

BARRY: I had signed up to attend the Mystery School after completing a week-long training program conducted by Jean Houston in Chicago in November 1983. I was able to do even more completion work at this workshop, which included a healing ceremony that Jean did for those who had lost a spouse, parent, or friend in the past year. I met a woman at this workshop who had lost her husband, and we had time together to talk about our common losses. She told me about the Mystery School and said she was going to sign up. I decided to sign up as well. In February 1984, I began a yearlong program with 120 others, studying and practicing the esoteric traditions of the major religions of the world. Each month I traveled from Colorado to upstate New York to study a different religious tradition.

Although we had both been going to the Mystery School on weekends once a month beginning in February, Janae and I did not actually connect until September. One Friday evening, everyone engaged in free-form dancing before the evening program began, and as I spun around my arm hit Janae in the chest. I apologized and moved on. The next morning I saw Janae and again apologized briefly. We hardly spoke another word to each other all weekend, but somehow I felt her vibration when we were near each other during the weekend, and I recognized that it felt similar to Barbara's. I thought, "Could she be the person that Barbara promised would be sent to me?"

On Sunday afternoon as we were preparing to leave, I decided to give Janae a hug and told her I was attracted to her and wanted to get to know her better. I said, "There doesn't seem to be much time to get to know people during these weekends. Is there any chance you might be coming to Colorado sometime soon?" Her response was guarded.

On the plane back to Colorado, I reflected on my boldness and decided to write her a letter explaining that, since Barbara's death, I was taking uncharacteristic risks by sharing my thoughts and feelings more openly. I received a letter from Janae within a week thanking me for my honesty and vulnerability and announcing that she would be coming to Colorado in the next month to do a vision quest.

Janae had planned to spend ten days visiting Colorado. After four days together, however, we knew we were to marry. The match of our physical, emotional, intellectual, and spiritual bodies was unbelievable and, at the same time, undeniable. We arranged for her to move to Colorado and planned a Thanksgiving wedding. This was the beginning of an incredible journey together. After our legal marriage in Colorado Springs, we asked Jean Houston to perform a spiritual marriage ceremony for us during our trip to Greece and Egypt in January 1985 as part of our "graduation" tour with the Mystery School group.

When we started our trip, we were not sure where this wedding would take place, but we finally settled on the temple at Abydos in Egypt dedicated to Isis and Osiris. It was a powerful spiritual ceremony in which we symbolically reenacted the myth of Isis and Osiris.

### Our Journey to Interdependence

JANAE: Although I'd been separated from Herb for a year, my divorce was final only four months before my marriage to Barry. I'd planned to take time to develop my independence after the divorce. Meeting Barry changed that. I decided I would have to learn independence while in a relationship.

For me, the early days of our marriage were about bonding. The warmth, openness, and deep capacity for feeling that I found in Barry allowed me to reveal the deep wounds from my relationship with Herb. Gradually I found unhealed losses and traumas surfacing from my childhood. With the aid of my therapist and Barry's support, I was able to finally acknowledge my incomplete bonding. Barry held me, stroked me, and provided many hours of nurturing during our first months together. I was able to consciously project my "nurturing parent" onto him in order to heal my bonding wounds.

We worked at creating a partnership and sharing responsibilities such as cooking, driving, and decision making. Within a few months, I began to work on my doctoral degree so that I could function as a full partner. This required me to leap into a whole new world and break free of many old patterns and rigid roles I'd learned. Barry's mentoring supported my buried dreams of achievement, as well as my need to be a separate person. Our intense bonding work, combined with his support for my quest for autonomy, helped me complete much unfinished business from my early childhood.

BARRY: When we got together, I still had much grieving to do over Barbara's death. What helped most was that Janae was willing to listen to me talk openly about my loss, and many an evening she held me as I cried. She didn't rush me through this but encouraged me to take as long as I needed to heal those wounds. Barbara's death had triggered many other issues related to unhealed losses in my childhood, so the healing process also entailed dealing with many early co-dependency issues and patterns.

As we did more healing and bonding, I found it easier to ask for what I wanted from Janae, and I became highly aware of what I projected onto her. I also found that the ability to surrender, which I had learned while with Barbara, had remained with me. When I started resisting something Janae said or did, I would remember and surrender to her.

We've had our share of conflict, but we get through it now very quickly, usually in an hour or less. One of the keys to making our relationship work has been our commitment to making the resolution of all conflicts our first priority. We don't put a conflict aside, even if it comes at an inconvenient time. Our first commitment is to helping each other heal our wounds and complete the unfinished developmental processes we each brought into the relationship. We both agreed that this was the only way we could have an intimate relationship.

We also agreed that we both wanted a partnership that enabled us to integrate our work and our relationship. We frequently spent twenty-four hours a day with each other for as long as two weeks, and then took time to be by ourselves or with others. We did this for about seven years before we began to work more independently. But we've never lost the deep love connection we have with each other. We are free to be co-dependent, counter-dependent, independent, or interdependent with each other. When sometimes we want different things, we are secure enough as individuals to resolve our conflicts and ask for what we want.

### *A New Understanding of Co-dependency*

BARRY: In the context of having an integrated relationship, we decided to start an institute to work together toward world peace. We found the context of conflict resolution and creative leadership broad enough to include all our interests. After a year of preparation, we officially founded the Colorado Institute for Conflict Resolution and Creative Leadership (now the Carolina Institute for Conflict Resolution and Creative Leadership). We began with an eight-day international conference for three hundred people. Our group was composed of about twenty to thirty volunteers and very little money, and we all worked to develop new approaches to conflict resolution. We lost money on our first conference, and we gradually started putting more and more of our own money and time into the institute to help create paying jobs for others who shared our vision but had no money to contribute.

We woke up one day and realized that, without knowing it, we had created a co-dependent organization. Even though we used group decision-making in the institute from the beginning, the unequal contribution of money had created a hierarchy. We noticed that we were making more of the decisions, and others were deferring to us as leaders. We saw that, even though we'd cleared many co-dependent patterns from our relationship, we were not conscious enough to see the same patterns in the organization we'd created. It was a humbling experience, indeed.

Rather than continue to create a dysfunctional organization, we did the only thing we were capable of doing: we stopped what we were doing. The reactions of those who had developed co-dependent relationships with us and the institute were predictable. Some people were angry at us and spent considerable energy making us seem wrong. When we refused to engage their energy, much of it dissipated, and some people then began to look at their own unfinished business and their co-dependent patterns. A few seemed to retreat into counter-dependency as angry victims.

Since that time early in our relationship, we've had numerous encounters with others who wanted to use our relationship to further their development. Because we were used by our parents to help them avoid doing their own work, we recognized that we each had a blind spot. We saw that we were drawing these people and situations from "central casting" to help us get clear of caretaking others. We began to quickly identify this pattern and could extricate ourselves from a situation just as quickly without much damage.

I still have times when I forget that I can ask Janae directly for what I want instead of complaining or just making do and not asking. The other pattern I still struggle with is the tendency to utter self-deprecating statements when I make a mistake.

As I look back on the more than twenty-three years we've spent together, there isn't much I would change. We've both evolved enormously, and while it hasn't been easy at times, it's all been worth it. Very few of the co-dependent patterns I brought with me to this relationship are still there. We will continue to help each other clear away any of those that remain, and maybe someday we'll be totally finished with all our co-dependent and counter-dependent patterns. But this isn't our key focus. The journey is what's important, not the destination.

JANAE: For me, the institute became a child of our union — birthed out of our common vision, nursed during its first fragile months, and supported faithfully with all our resources. Of course, I dug out all my old parenting resources too. I focused on taking care of the needs of other people — creating paying jobs for others while working without pay myself, putting on workshops, organizing conferences, and doing promotional work. All this was for the "good of the institute."

It wasn't until I was nearly exhausted by my own unmet needs that I realized I'd taken on the role of co-dependent "mother." I was astounded at the ease with which I had done this and at the similarity of my behavior while at the institute and while parenting my children. I was also amazed at my earlier inability to see the patterns. Once these patterns penetrated my awareness and I could see the dysfunctionality, it was easy to let go and hope that we could create a new form of partnership at an organizational level.

### *Our Perspective on Relationships*

As you know now from our story, we both came from ordinary circumstances and from typical families in which the parents did the best they could. We acknowledge that our experiences in these families were great teachers, and that these experiences have become resources for helping others. Our experiences helped us recognize our wounds and our desire to create something better that links us to our universal humanness and to the experiences of others.

We acknowledge that this path requires faith, courage, and a higher vision of what's possible. Once your commitment to a higher vision is firm, breaking free of co-dependency is not simply an option. It is inevitable.

# Acknowledgments

We would like to acknowledge the groundbreaking work done by many others and their contributions to the recovery field. Twelve-step self-help groups have helped many people who otherwise would not have had the necessary support to address their addictive behaviors.

John Bradshaw's pioneering work broadened the understanding of millions of people about dysfunctional family structures, particularly his widely acclaimed PBS series, *On the Family*. Riane Eisler, author of *The Chalice and the Blade* and codirector of the Center for Partnership Studies in Pacific Grove, California, helped us better understand the societal roots of the problems of co-dependency. In addition, we greatly appreciate her support of this book and her editorial assistance with the manuscript of our first edition. We feel like partners with her in helping to create a partnership society.

At a more personal level, we would like to acknowledge our parents, Kern and Betty Weinhold and Leland and Milly Branyan, our four children and three grandchildren, our clients, members of CICRCL, and our colleagues who helped us in various ways to formulate our ideas for this book. We have tested the material in this book on ourselves, our clients, and our students and know that it works.

At the production level, we would like to thank our copyeditor, Bonita Hurd, for her helpful suggestions and editing, and Jason Gardner for his continued support while editing and releasing this revised edition of the book.

# Notes

## INTRODUCTION

1. J. Weinhold and B. Weinhold, *The Flight from Intimacy: Healing Your Relationship of Counter-dependency — the Other Side of Co-dependency* (Novato, CA: New World Library, 2008).
2. *Alcoholics Anonymous Big Book* (Alcoholics Anonymous World Services, 2001 edition), 60.
3. E. Larsen, *Stage II Recovery: Life beyond Addiction* (San Francisco: Harper and Row, 1985); R. Subby, "Inside the Chemically Dependent Marriage: Denial Manipulation," in *Co-dependency: An Emerging Issue* (Pompano Beach, FL: Health Communications, 1984); A. W. Schaef, *When Society Becomes an Addict* (New York: Harper and Row, 1987).
4. Larsen, *Stage II Recovery*, 17.
5. J. Weinhold and B. Weinhold, *Healing Developmental Trauma: Processes for Advancing Human Evolution* (Swannanoa, NC: CICRCL Press, 2007).
6. P. Russell, *The Global Brain: Speculations on the Evolutionary Leap to Planetary Consciousness* (Los Angeles: J. P. Tarcher, 1983), 185.

## CHAPTER 1. CO-DEPENDENCY

1. M. Mahler, *On Human Symbiosis and the Vicissitudes of Individuation* (New York: International University Press, 1968).
2. J. Bradshaw, *Bradshaw: On the Family* (Deerfield Beach, FL: Health Communications, 1988); Bradshaw, *Homecoming: Reclaiming and Championing Your Inner Child* (New York: Bantam, 1990); Bradshaw, *Healing the Shame That Binds You* (Deerfield Beach, FL: Health Communications, 1988); Bradshaw, *Family Secrets* (New York: Bantam, 1995).
3. For more information on counter-dependency, see J. Weinhold and B. Weinhold, *The*

*Flight from Intimacy: Healing Your Relationship of Counter-dependency — the Other Side of Co-dependency* (Novato, CA: New World Library, 2008).

## CHAPTER 3. THE CO-DEPENDENT CULTURE

1. J. Weinhold and B. Weinhold, *Healing Developmental Trauma: Processes for Advancing Human Evolution* (Swannanoa, NC: CICRCL Press, 2007).
2. R. Eisler, *The Chalice and the Blade* (San Francisco: Harper and Row, 1987).
3. R. Eisler, *The Power of Partnership* (Novato, CA: New World Library, 2003).
4. Eisler, *The Chalice and the Blade*, 121.
5. E. Pagels, *The Gnostic Gospels* (New York: Random House, 1979).
6. Eisler, *The Chalice and the Blade*.
7. J. Gibbons, "Recent Developments in the Study of the Great European Witch Hunt," *The Pomegranate* 5 (August 1998), available at http://www.pendlewitches.co.uk/content.php?page=myths (accessed October 30, 2007).
8. J. Argüelles, *The Mayan Factor* (Santa Fe: Bear and Company, 1987); J. Argüelles, *Time and the Technosphere: The Law of Time in Human Affairs* (Rochester, VT: Inner Traditions International, 2002).
9. S. Griffin, *Woman and Nature* (New York: Harper and Row, 1978).
10. O. Waters, *The Shift: Revolution in Human Consciousness* (Dover, DE: Infinite Being Publishers, 2006), 12; J. Weinhold and B. Weinhold, "2012: Ascension, Rebirth, and the Dimensional Shift," 2007, available at http://www.weinholds.org/2012_home.asp.
11. J. Houston, *The Possible Human,* 2nd ed. (New York: Tarcher/Putnam, 1997); J. Houston, *A Passion for the Possible: A Guide to Realize Your True Potential* (San Francisco: HarperCollins, 1998), 47.

## CHAPTER 4. A DEVELOPMENTAL APPROACH TO RECOVERY

1. M. Mahler, *On Human Symbiosis and the Vicissitudes of Individuation* (New York: International University Press, 1968).
2. M. Klaus and J. Kennell, *Maternal-Infant Bonding* (St. Louis: C. V. Mosby Company, 1976); M. Klaus, J. Kennell, and P. Klaus, *Bonding: The Foundations of Secure Attachment and Independence* (New York: Perseus Books, 1996); M. Klaus and P. Klaus, *Your Amazing Newborn* (New York: Perseus Books, 1998).
3. Mahler, *On Human Symbiosis and the Vicissitudes of Individuation*.
4. Ibid.
5. J. Weinhold and B. Weinhold, *The Flight from Intimacy: Healing Your Relationship of Counter-dependency — the Other Side of Co-dependency* (Novato, CA: New World Library, 2008).

## CHAPTER 5. THE CAUSES OF CO-DEPENDENCY

1. "Traumatic Birth Syndrome," Chiro-Tips website, n.d., www.chirotips.com/traumatic_birth_syndrome.htm (accessed September 13, 2007).
2. A. Schore, *Affect Dysregulation and Disorders of the Self* (New York: W. W. Norton, 2003), 195.
3. Ibid, 207–8.

4. Ibid.
5. Ibid, 208.
6. A. Cook, M. Blaustein, J. Spinazzola, and B. van der Kolk, "Complex Trauma in Children and Adolescents" (white paper from the National Child Traumatic Stress Network Complex Trauma Task Force, 2003).

## CHAPTER 7. FACING YOUR PROBLEM

1. B. Weinhold, *Breaking Family Patterns* (Swannanoa, NC: CICRCL Press, 2006), 17.
2. A. Miller, *For Your Own Good* (New York: Farrar, Straus, Giroux, 1983).
3. B. Weinhold and J. Weinhold, *Conflict Resolution: The Partnership Way*, 2nd ed. (Denver: Love Publishing, 2008).

## CHAPTER 8. UNDERSTANDING THE CAUSES OF CO-DEPENDENCY

1. M. S. Peck, *The Road Less Traveled* (New York: Simon and Schuster, 1978), 88.
2. B. Weinhold, *Breaking Family Patterns* (Swannanoa, NC: CICRCL Press, 2006).

## CHAPTER 11. ELIMINATING SELF-HATRED

1. H. Clemes and R. Bean, *Self-Esteem: The Key to Your Child's Well-Being* (New York: G. P. Putnam and Sons, 1981).
2. S. Coopersmith, *The Antecedents of Self-Esteem* (San Francisco: W. H. Freeman and Company, 1967).
3. L. Hay, *You Can Heal Your Life* (Carlsbad, CA: Hay House, 2002).

## CHAPTER 12. GIVING UP POWER AND CONTROL GAMES

1. J. Schiff et al., *The Cathexis Reader* (New York: Harper and Row, 1975).
2. R. Bolton, *People Skills* (New York: Simon and Schuster, 1979).
3. B. Weinhold, *Breaking Family Patterns* (Swannanoa, NC: CICRCL Press, 2006).
4. C. Steiner, *Scripts People Live* (New York: Grove Press, 1974).
5. Weinhold, *Breaking Family Patterns*.

## CHAPTER 13. LEARNING TO ASK FOR WHAT YOU WANT

1. V. M. Satir, *Peoplemaking* (Palo Alto, CA: Science and Behavior Books, 1972), 78–79.

## CHAPTER 14. LEARNING TO FEEL AGAIN

1. M. L. von Franz and J. Hillman, *Lectures on Jung's Typology* (Irving, TX: Spring Publications, 1979), 171.
2. P. Zaleski, "A *New Age* Interview: Elisabeth Kübler-Ross," *New Age Journal* (November 1984): 41.

3. A. Miller, *For Your Own Good* (New York: Farrar, Straus, Giroux, 1983).
4. Ibid, 106.

## CHAPTER 16. BUILDING YOUR BOUNDARIES

1. Uniform Crime Reporting Program, U.S. Department of Justice, "FBI Releases Its 2005 Statistics on Hate Crime," October 6, 2005, press release, available at http://www.fbi.gov/ucr/hc2005/pressrelease.htm (accessed October 30, 2007).
2. "Fairfax Reports Decrease in Burglaries, Increase in Rapes," WUSA9 website, August 15, 2007, www.wusa9.com/news/news_article.aspx?storyid=61773 (accessed September 13, 2007).

## CHAPTER 17. FORMING BONDS OF INTIMACY

1. J. C. Pearce, *Magical Child* (New York: E. P. Dutton, 1977); J. C. Pearce, *Magical Child Matures* (New York: E. P. Dutton, 1985), 30–31.
2. Pearce, *Magical Child Matures*, 55–56.
3. M. S. Peck, *The Different Drum: Community Making and Peace* (New York: Simon and Schuster, 1987).
4. G. Sheehy, *Pathfinders* (New York: Bantam, 1981).
5. K. Magid and C. McKelvey, *High Risk: Children without a Conscience* (New York: Bantam, 1988).
6. Ibid.

## CHAPTER 18. NEW FORMS OF RELATIONSHIP

1. R. Bolton, *People Skills* (New York: Simon and Schuster, 1979).
2. J. Paul and M. Paul, *Do I Have to Give Up Me to Be Loved by You?* (Minneapolis: CompCare Publications, 1983); J. Paul and M. Paul, *Do I Have to Give Up Me to Be Loved by You? Workbook* (Center City, MN: Hazelden, 2002).

## CHAPTER 19. HEALING THE CO-DEPENDENT CULTURE

1. J. Weinhold and B. Weinhold, *The Flight from Intimacy: Healing Your Relationship of Counter-dependency — the Other Side of Co-dependency* (Novato, CA: New World Library, 2008).
2. M. S. Peck, *The Different Drum: Community Making and Peace* (New York: Simon and Schuster, 1987), 86–106.
3. R. Greenleaf, *Servant Leadership: A Journey into the Nature of Legitimate Power and Greatness* (New York: Paulist Press, 2002), 75.

# Bibliography

Argüelles, J. *The Mayan Factor.* Santa Fe: Bear and Company, 1987.

———. *Time and the Technosphere: The Law of Time in Human Affairs.* Rochester, VT: Inner Traditions International, 2002.

Beattie, M. *Co-dependent No More.* New York: Harper and Row, 1987.

———. *Playing It By Heart: Taking Care of Yourself No Matter What.* Center City, MN: Hazelden, 1999.

Black, C. *A Hole in the Sideway: The Recovering Person's Guide to Relapse Prevention.* Bainbridge Island, WA: Mac Publishing, 2000.

———. *It Will Never Happen to Me.* Denver: M.A.C. Printing and Publication Division, 1981.

Bolton, R. *People Skills.* New York: Simon and Schuster, 1979.

Bradshaw, J. *Bradshaw: On the Family.* Deerfield Beach, FL: Health Communications, 1988.

———. *Family Secrets.* New York: Bantam, 1995.

———. *Healing the Shame That Binds You.* Deerfield Beach, FL: Health Communications, 1988.

———. *Homecoming: Reclaiming and Championing Your Inner Child.* New York: Bantam, 1990.

Clemes, H., and R. Bean. *Self-Esteem: The Key to Your Child's Well-Being.* New York: G. P. Putnam and Sons, 1981.

Coopersmith, S. *The Antecedents of Self-Esteem.* San Francisco: W. H. Freeman and Company, 1967.

Eisler, R. *The Chalice and the Blade.* San Francisco: Harper and Row, 1987.

———. *The Power of Partnership.* Novato, CA: New World Library, 2003.

Fenell, D., and B. Weinhold. *Counseling Families: An Introduction to Marriage and Family Therapy.* 3rd ed. Denver: Love Publishing, 2003.

Fingarette, H. *Heavy Drinking: The Myth of Alcoholism as a Disease.* Berkeley, CA: University of California Press, 1988.

Gibbons, J. "Recent Developments in the Study of the Great European Witch Hunt." *The Pomegranate* 5 (August 1998*).*

Greenleaf, R. *Servant Leadership: A Journey into the Nature of Legitimate Power and Greatness.* New York: Paulist Press, 2002.

Griffin, S. *Woman and Nature.* New York: Harper and Row, 1978.

Halpern, H. *How to Break Your Addiction to a Person.* New York: McGraw-Hill, 1982.

Hay, L. *You Can Heal Your Life.* Carlsbad, CA: Hay House, 2002.

Houston, J. *A Passion for the Possible: A Guide to Realize Your True Potential.* San Francisco: HarperCollins, 1998.

———. *The Possible Human.* 2nd ed. New York: Tarcher/Putnam, 1997.

Jones, A. *The Jerusalem Bible.* Garden City, NY: Doubleday, 1966.

Kaplan, L. J. *Oneness and Separateness: From Infant to Individual.* New York: Simon and Schuster, 1978.

Karpman, S. "Fairytales and Script Drama Analysis." *Transactional Analysis Bulletin* 7 (1968): 39–43.

Klaus, M., and J. Kennell. *Maternal-Infant Bonding.* St. Louis: C. V. Mosby Company, 1976.

Klaus, M., J. Kennell, and P. Klaus. *Bonding: The Foundations of Secure Attachment and Independence.* New York: Perseus Books, 1996.

Klaus, M., and P. Klaus. *Your Amazing Newborn.* New York: Perseus Books, 1998.

Kübler-Ross, E. *On Death and Dying.* New York: Macmillan, 1969.

Larsen, E. *Stage II Recovery: Life beyond Addiction.* San Francisco: Harper and Row, 1985.

Magid, K., and C. McKelvey. *High Risk: Children without a Conscience.* New York: Bantam, 1988.

Mahler, M. *On Human Symbiosis and the Vicissitudes of Individuation.* New York: International University Press, 1968.

Miller, A. *Banished Knowledge: Facing Childhood Injuries.* New York: Doubleday, 1990.

———. *The Body Never Lies: The Lingering Effects of Hurtful Parenting.* New York: W. W. Norton, 2005.

———. *Breaking Down the Walls of Silence.* New York: Dutton, 1991.

———. *For Your Own Good.* New York: Farrar, Straus, Giroux, 1983.

———. *Thou Shalt Not Be Aware: Society's Betrayal of the Child.* New York: New American Library, 1984.

Mindell, A. *The Deep Democracy of Open Forums: Practical Steps to Conflict Prevention and Resolution for the Family, Workplace, and World.* Charlottesville, VA: Hampton Roads, 2002.

———. *The Dreambody in Relationships.* Boston: Sigo Press, 1987.

———. *The Leader as Martial Artist: An Introduction to Deep Democracy.* San Francisco: HarperSanFrancisco, 1992.

———. *The Quantum Mind and Healing: How to Listen and Respond to Your Body's Symptoms.* Charlottesville, VA: Hampton Roads, 2004.

———. *Working on Yourself Alone: Inner Dreambody Work.* New York: Arkana, 1990.

Pagels, E. *The Gnostic Gospels.* New York: Random House, 1979.

Paul, J., and M. Paul. *Do I Have to Give Up Me to Be Loved by You?* Minneapolis: CompCare Publications, 1983.

———. *Do I Have to Give Up Me to Be Loved by You? Workbook.* Center City, MN: Hazelden, 2002.

Pearce, J. C. *Magical Child*. New York: E. P. Dutton, 1977.

———. *Magical Child Matures*. New York: E. P. Dutton, 1985.

Peck, M. S. *The Different Drum: Community Making and Peace*. New York: Simon and Schuster, 1987.

———. *The Road Less Traveled*. New York: Simon and Schuster, 1978.

Peele, S. *Diseasing of America: How the Addiction Industry Captured Our Soul*. Lexington, MA: Lexington Books, 1989.

Russell, P. *From Science to God: A Physicist's Journey into the Mystery of Consciousness*. Novato, CA: New World Library, 2002.

———. *The Global Brain: Speculations on the Evolutionary Leap to Planetary Consciousness*. Los Angeles: J. P. Tarcher, 1983.

Satir, V. M. *Peoplemaking*. Palo Alto, CA: Science and Behavior Books, 1972.

Schaef, A. W. *Co-dependence Misunderstood — Mistreated*. New York: Harper and Row, 1986.

———. *When Society Becomes an Addict*. New York: Harper and Row, 1987.

———. *Women's Reality*. Minneapolis: Winston Press, 1981.

Schiff, J., et al. *The Cathexis Reader*. New York: Harper and Row, 1975.

Schore, A. *Affect Dysregulation and Disorders of the Self*. New York: W. W. Norton, 2003.

Sheehy, G. *Pathfinders*. New York: Bantam, 1981.

Steiner, C. *Scripts People Live*. New York: Grove Press, 1974.

Subby, R. "Inside the Chemically Dependent Marriage: Denial Manipulation." In *Co-dependency: An Emerging Issue*. Pompano Beach, FL: Health Communications, 1984.

Uniform Crime Reporting Program, U.S. Department of Justice. "FBI Releases Its 2005 Statistics on Hate Crime." October 6, 2005, press release, available at http://www.fbi.gov /ucr/hc2005/pressrelease.htm (accessed October 30, 2007).

von Franz, M. L., and J. Hillman. *Lectures on Jung's Typology*. Irving, TX: Spring Publications, 1979.

Waters, O. *The Shift: The Revolution in Human Consciousness*. Dover, DE: Infinite Being Publishing, 2006.

Weinhold, B. *Breaking Family Patterns*. Swannanoa, NC: CICRCL Press, 2006.

Weinhold, B., and C. G. Hendricks. *Counseling and Psychotherapy: A Transpersonal Approach*. Denver: Love Publishing, 1992.

Weinhold, B., and J. Hillferty. "The Self-Esteem Matrix: A Tool for Elementary Counselors." *Elementary School Guidance and Counseling* 17 (1983): 243–51.

Weinhold, B., and J. Weinhold. *Conflict Resolution: The Partnership Way*. 2nd ed. Denver: Love Publishing, 2008.

Weinhold, J., and B. Weinhold. *The Flight from Intimacy: Healing Your Relationship of Counter-dependency — the Other Side of Co-dependency*. Novato, CA: New World Library, 2008.

———. *Healing Developmental Trauma: Processes for Advancing Human Evolution*. Swannanoa, NC: CICRCL Press, 2007.

———. "2012: Ascension, Rebirth, and the Dimensional Shift," 2007, www.weinholds.org/2012_home.asp.

Whitfield, C. *Healing the Child Within*. Deerfield Beach, FL: Health Communications, 1987.

Zaleski, P. "A *New Age* Interview: Elisabeth Kübler-Ross." *New Age Journal* (November 1984): 39–44.

# Index

# About the Authors

Between them, Doctors Barry and Janae Weinhold have served for over five decades as licensed mental health professionals and have almost sixty years' teaching experience. Barry is licensed as a psychologist, and Janae is a professional counselor. The cofounders of the Carolina Institute for Conflict Resolution and Creative Leadership (CICRCL) near Asheville, North Carolina, they specialize in the areas of developmental psychology, trauma, violence prevention, conflict resolution, cosmologies, and consciousness studies. Barry is professor emeritus and former chair of the counseling and human services program at the University of Colorado at Colorado Springs. He is also the founder and director of the Kindness Campaign, a nationally acclaimed violence prevention program in over six hundred schools and communities. Janae is a consultant in children's mental health and a former adjunct professor at the University of Colorado at Colorado Springs. Both have served as United Nations consultants and are trainers with a sister nonprofit in Kiev, Ukraine. They are the authors or coauthors of thirty-one books. Their website is www.weinholds.org.